# *Philippians*

"That I May Gain Christ"

Titus Chu

Philippians:
"That I May Gain Christ"
by Titus Chu

First Edition, March 2013
PDF & Print on Demand

© 2013 by Titus Chu
ISBN: 1-932020-55-1


Distributed by
The Church in Cleveland Literature Service
3150 Warren Road
Cleveland, Ohio 44111

Available for purchase online.
Printed by CreateSpace,
an Amazon.com company.

Download the PDF version of this book at
www.MinistryMessages.org

Please send correspondence by email to
TheEditors@MinistryMessages.org

Published by
Good Land Publishers
Ann Arbor, Michigan


Unless otherwise noted,
Scripture quotations are from the
New American Standard Bible®,
© 1960, 1995
by The Lockman Foundation.

# Contents

This book is drawn from messages given by Titus Chu from September 2003 to June 2004 to participants in a year-long spiritual labor and time of study that involved churches from around the Great Lakes. The messages were spoken in Toronto, Chicago, Cleveland, and Columbus.

# 1

# Paul's
# Epistles

The book of Philippians is one of the fourteen New Testament epistles written by the apostle Paul. These epistles show us the progression of God's economy, which is His dispensation or administration (Eph. 1:10). Paul's first epistle, Romans, is an introduction to God's economy, and his last epistle, Hebrews, is the conclusion to this economy. We are growing now from Romans all the way to Hebrews.

## Romans: An Introduction
## to God's Economy

Romans is a precious book. Someone once said that if the New Testament is a ring, then Romans is the diamond on that ring. Romans is written from God's point of view concerning the gospel of God (1:1). This book unveils who God is, what He desires, and His plan for accomplishing it. This includes the process of our salvation: first we are condemned (chapters 1–3), then we are justified (chapters 3–5) and sanctified (chapters 5–8), until eventually we are glorified (chapter 8). All of these riches are in Romans.

## First and Second Corinthians and Galatians:
## Problems in the Christian Life

Paul's next three books tell us that after being saved, we will

encounter many problems as we grow in the Christian life—
problems in the local church life (1 Corinthians), problems
between the believers and those who minister to them (2
Corinthians), and problems with religion (Galatians).

As Paul described in 1 Corinthians, after being saved, we
quickly discover how messy the church life is. For example, in
Corinth there were people declaring, "I am of Paul," "I am of
Cephas," and "I am of Apollos" (1:12). We should never belong
to anyone except Christ Himself. We are only for Christ. Paul
was strong in his response—"Has Christ been divided? Paul
was not crucified for you, was he?" (1:13); "All things belong
to you, whether Paul or Apollos or Cephas" (3:21–22). We
don't belong to them; they belong to us. Religious people
want to be of a certain person, but we are not called to follow
a man. We follow Christ. Some may not say that they are
of a certain man but boast of being from a certain church.
People think that if they follow a certain man, or come from
a certain church, they will be "big shots." Paul warned us
to be careful, saying, "You belong to Christ" (3:23). Besides
Christ, we should be of no one and for no one. We belong to
Jesus alone!

The book of 2 Corinthians tells us of another problem. The
believers in Corinth criticized and belittled Paul, who labored
among them, poured himself out for them, and did everything
for their spiritual health. It is possible to say, "I belong to Christ,"
and at the same time criticize those who labor for our growth
in the Lord. We need to be balanced. We don't exalt any of the
Lord's servants by being of them, but we also don't belittle or
despise them.

The book of Galatians shows us the problem of religion,
which is especially typical of those raised in a Christian home.
Because they have absorbed the beliefs and practices of their
parents, they unconsciously become persons under law. This
causes them to lose all their potential to develop and become
useful to the Lord. They think that as long as they know the
terminology, speak the right things, and don't cause trouble,
they are good Christians. Actually, this makes them hopeless

and useless. Religion makes people hopeless. When we fall into religion, we lose our freedom in the spirit and instead focus on doing right things and speaking correct words.

### Ephesians, Philippians, and Colossians: Christ and the Church

The next group of Paul's epistles—Ephesians, Philippians, and Colossians—is very sweet. According to these epistles, once we are saved, we are in the church (Ephesians). Because we are in the church life, we should pursue only Christ (Philippians). When we pursue only Christ, He reveals His headship (Colossians). Here we have three great items: the church, the pursuit of Christ, and Christ's headship.

### First and Second Thessalonians: Waiting for the Lord's Return

After we have Christ's headship, we wait for His return. This is described in the next group of Paul's epistles—1 and 2 Thessalonians.

### First and Second Timothy, Titus, and Philemon: The Administration of the Church

Next we come to 1 and 2 Timothy and Titus, which cover church administration. As we grow in life, we eventually need to handle church affairs. Yet included in this section is a very sweet book—Philemon. After such a substantial portion in 1 and 2 Timothy and Titus regarding elders, deacons, and administrative matters, we need something sweet. The first three books are like a steak, and Philemon is like a sweet dessert. Philemon has only one chapter, but it is rich in life, in brotherly love, and in the operation of the apostle Paul.

## Hebrews: The Conclusion
## of God's Economy

Most Bible scholars attribute the book of Hebrews to the apostle Paul. Hebrews tells us that Christ is everything. Our Christian life as depicted in Paul's epistles begins with Romans and concludes with Hebrews. Romans shows us God's salvation for man and His purpose for man. Hebrews shows us how God's salvation brings us to glory. Paul's fourteen epistles are a matter of growth in life, which consummates in the maturity found in Hebrews.

## Three Characteristics
## of Philippians

The book of Philippians has three positive characteristics: it is pure, focused, and joyful. Every time we come to this book we must remember these three things. First, it is pure. If we have an impure motive when we read this book, it won't be opened to us. It is written only for those who are pure, who have no motive or desire other than Christ Himself. Second, it is focused. Each chapter of Philippians is focused on Christ. This book reminds us that Christ Himself should become the unique focus in our lives. Third, this book is joyful. It is full of rejoicing. If we are pure without any motive and focused only on Christ, we will become very joyful people.

### Pure

Philippians is extremely pure. Paul was not fighting any "isms" in this book, such as Judaism or Gnosticism, which he had to deal with in other books. The only debate he had was whether he should choose to live or die (Phil. 1:21–24). Paul had no hidden motive. There was no impure or problematic background. Only Christ is presented in this book. Paul encouraged us to press on to lay hold of Christ (3:12), gain Christ (3:8), and be found in Him (3:9).

We can be found in many things, but how often can we be found in Christ? Many times, we are found in our occupation, our success, or our money. At other times, we are found in the things we enjoy, such as athletics, the arts, or hobbies. But Philippians tells us to be found in Christ. When people find us, they should find us in Christ.

Purity is the highest virtue. Very few who love the Lord can love Him with purity and say, "The Lord is my first and best love." Many love the Lord but with impure motives. When we deviate from giving the Lord the first place, we lose our purity.

What characterizes the book of Philippians is its purity. The church in Philippi was raised up in a pure way, and the believers were very pure and simple. They just loved the Lord. Why are we so complicated? The Lord said that to follow Him we must be like little children (Matt. 18:3; 19:14). We should not have so many considerations: "If I do this, who will be offended? If I do that, who will be pleased?" Instead we should say, "Lord, I love You and desire only to live unto You. Lord, I am for You forever." This is to be pure.

## Focused

The book of Philippians is very focused. Every person needs to be focused. Suppose a man wants to be a musician. He decides that the guitar is the easiest instrument to learn, so he starts taking lessons. After a few days his fingers hurt, so he gives up. A man who isn't focused will go nowhere. Today he will dream of doing one thing, and tomorrow he will dream of doing another. This shows that he is not focused. No other book of the Bible encourages us to be as focused as Philippians. It tells us that we should only have one focus—the Lord Himself.

If we are pure but not focused, we will go nowhere. We will

keep moving around, but nothing will come of it. If we are focused but not pure, we will become ambitious. Just to be pure or just to be focused is not enough. We need both. Paul said, "I count all things to be loss in view of the surpassing value of knowing Christ Jesus my Lord, for whom I have suffered the loss of all things, and count them but rubbish so that I may gain Christ" (Phil. 3:8). This is to be both pure and focused. Are we this way? Have we counted all things to be loss for Christ? Is gaining Christ our goal? If we can say yes, then we should be very happy. If in our Christian life we can be both pure and focused, then we will have the third characteristic of Philippians, which is being joyful.

## Joyful

Philippians is a book of joyfulness. Joy is the normal result of a life that is pure and focused. If we tell the Lord, "I only want You, and I live only for You," then we will rejoice. Our lives will become very happy. Joy is the source, the initial stage, and rejoicing is the development of joy. When our joy becomes so rich and bountiful that it overflows, that is to rejoice. The Christian life according to Philippians should be so joyful.

Philippians reminds us that as Christians our life should have these three characteristics. Our life should be so pure: "Lord, I love You, and You alone." Then we should be focused, single in goal and purpose: "I give myself to You, Lord. I am not aiming at so many things. I am aiming only at You." Then we will be so joyful, and those around us will be affected. Our lives should be pure, focused, and joyful. This is how Philippians was written, and this is how we as Christians should live.

## The Message of Philippians

Of all Paul's epistles, Philippians is a unique book. It tells us that Christ is our goal, our living, the source of our existence, and the reason we are alive. It shows us that Christ is our Savior and Sustainer. He is everything to us for the sake of our spiritual progress. We should pursue nothing but Christ. As we pursue Christ together, our life becomes full of meaning.

# 2

# Saints
# and Slaves

*Paul and Timothy, bond-servants of Christ Jesus, to all the saints in Christ Jesus who are in Philippi, including the overseers and deacons.*

*—Philippians 1:1*

## A Pure Beginning

The church in Philippi was raised up in a very pure manner. As described in Acts 16:11–40, Paul preached the gospel to a woman named Lydia who sold purple-dyed goods. Lydia believed in the Lord and was baptized, she and her household. She invited Paul to stay at her home.

Satan then took the opportunity to send a demon-possessed woman to follow Paul for many days, declaring that Paul was proclaiming "the way of salvation." Although she spoke the truth, Paul was bothered and cast the evil spirit out of her. Her masters, realizing that they had lost their means of income, had Paul and Silas beaten and put in prison.

Rather than feeling despair after being imprisoned, Paul and Silas stayed up late praying and singing hymns of praise to God. Suddenly a great earthquake freed all the prisoners in the jail. When the jailer saw this, he was ready to kill himself, but Paul stopped him, saying, "Do not harm yourself, for we are all here!" The grateful jailer asked, "Sirs, what must I do to be saved?" Paul's preaching to the jailer was so pure and simple: "Believe in the Lord Jesus, and you will be saved, you and your household" (Acts 16:31).

The entire beginning of the church life in Philippi was pure and without complication. This produced a close relationship between Paul and the believers there. The saints in Philippi cared for Paul and his need (Phil. 4:16). After Paul left them to preach the gospel elsewhere, they sent a brother to minister to his need (Phil. 2:25). This shows how pure the church was and how pure their relationship with the apostle was.

## An Intimate Greeting

Since Paul had this relationship with the Philippians, he began his epistle to them with a very simple introduction. He didn't write to them as "Paul the apostle." He didn't say, "The Lord has committed me with your care, and I am coming to help you." He was not at all formal. Paul was writing a family letter, not an official letter. Since Paul was writing to a local church that he had raised up through his own labor, he wrote in an intimate way.

He began his epistle, "Paul and Timothy, bond-servants of Christ Jesus" (Phil. 1:1). The saints in Philippi understood this. They remembered how Paul came to them, how he was in prison, and how pure his gospel had been. They remembered how the church was raised up. The saints in Philippi knew that Paul was a bond-servant because they had seen how he had no freedom for himself.

## Bond-servants of Christ Jesus

We should not think that as bond-servants Paul and Timothy occupied a very low position, having lost everything. Rather, we should consider how enjoyable it is to be a slave. Actually, people willingly enslave themselves to things. We look for good leadership to provide stability and security in our lives. Very few of us are free. In the religious world, we can become slaves to institutions, principles, or people. In the material world, we can become enslaved to things such as our jobs. We can even come under the slavery of our own selves. Such things prevent us from being true slaves of Christ Jesus.

Paul and Timothy were bond-servants of Christ Jesus. This means they experienced being cared for by the One who rules all things. They were led by the Lord to live a daily life according to Jesus. The One who is over all became their Master. They experienced Christ ruling over them in His heavenly government. They had the living of Jesus under the lordship of Christ.

To serve the Lord, we must give up our freedom and become His bond-servants, His slaves. This is the hardest thing for us to do. It is easy to think, "I want to serve the Lord. I want to give conferences and speak in front of thousands of people. I want to be known and admired." Such thoughts are obviously impure. Paul didn't serve the Lord for his own enjoyment or ambition. Nor did he serve the Lord so that other Christians could enjoy his messages. He served as a slave who did not have any freedom. He served the Lord because he had no choice (1 Cor. 9:16).

## Bond-servant: A Biblical Definition

The Greek word for "bond-servant" is *doulos* (Strong, no. 1401). It comes from the root word *deō* (Strong, no. 1210), which means "to bind." It is the word used for the most common type of slave, those subject to their masters even to the point of death. In Old Testament times, all slaves among the Israelites had certain rights, such as the right to enjoy their own family, have their own possessions, and receive fair treatment. However, they did not have freedom in their activities. They always anticipated their freedom—either the freedom given at the year of Jubilee or sooner (Lev. 25:39–40).

Our concept of a slave is the opposite of what the Bible describes. We think that all slaves live in poverty and are mis-treated and beaten by their masters. Under Mosaic law, however, slaves had the right to their own possessions (Lev. 25:49). They could keep whatever money they earned. Slaves could actually be wealthy and enjoy many material things. If they were mar-ried before becoming slaves, those marriages were honored; their spouses would not be taken from them (Exo. 21:3). This is very different from our concept of slaves being stripped, beaten, and humiliated. The difference between slaves and non-slaves in the Bible is simple—non-slaves could do whatever they wanted, but slaves could only do what their masters told them to do.

The difference between slaves and non-slaves is not a matter of possessions. Those who serve the Lord are not exempt from a normal human living. People in the world have families, houses, and cars; so do the Lord's slaves. However, their whole life is according to Christ. Rather than being oppressed, they are joyful. The Lord's bond-servants can say to people in the world, "What makes us different from you is not what we own but that we have no freedom. You can do what you want, but we cannot. The Lord Himself decides how we live and what we do. We are slaves of Christ, and that is why we are so happy!"

## The Suffering Jesus and the Exalted Christ

Paul wrote that he was a bond-servant of Christ Jesus. "Jesus" implies the suffering One, and "Christ" implies the exalted One. A bond-servant of the Lord experiences the suffering Jesus and follows the exalted Christ. Paul could say, "I am enslaved to a wonderful Master—the ascended, exalted, and enthroned Christ—but in my daily life, I experience the suffering Jesus. He was despised, and I am despised. He gained no respect, and I gain no respect." A bond-servant of the Lord will experience the suffering Jesus (Matt. 10:24–25). People ask, "What are you doing with your life?" The bond-servant replies, "I'm a slave of the Lord." Such slaves walk the same path as the suffering Jesus, but they have a wonderful Master. They can say, "The King of Kings and the Lord of Lords is my Master. He is the One on the throne. However, I also have the experience of the suffering Jesus. I am despised and considered as nothing." This is to be a slave of Christ Jesus.

## Saints: the Holy Ones

Why did Paul write to "all the saints"? Why didn't he write to "the church in Philippi"? The Greek word for "saint" is the same as the word for "holy"—*hagios*. Paul is writing to all the holy ones. God Himself is holy. We, as saints, are also holy and bear God's holy nature (Eph. 1:4; 1 Pet. 1:16).

## Feasting and Celebrating

The word "holy" implies that we, as saints, are not to conform ourselves to the lusts of the world (1 Pet. 1:14–15). In the Old Testament, the children of Israel did this by leaving Egypt and holding a feast unto God (Exo. 5:1). Their feasts were holy convocations (Lev. 23:2). Like Israel, we today, as God's holy people, are to hold a feast or celebration unto Him for His enjoyment (1 Cor. 5:8). We are the very celebration to God, and we are also the celebrating ones, the keepers of the feast, who are enjoying this holy celebration. We, the saved and redeemed ones, have a perfect position before God as a feast to Him.

When the Israelites left Egypt to hold a feast to their God, they experienced a reconstituting work by enjoying all the riches and provisions from Jehovah. This heavenly diet of manna made them a living testimony unto Jehovah and an expression of all His riches. As New Testament saints, we participate in Christ as our feast (1 Cor. 5:7). With this feast, we experience joyfulness and celebration. Thus, through our subjective experience of Him, we become the living testimony of the Lord today and the expression of His unsearchable riches.

In the process of our growth in life, we should often experience a deep touch with the Lord. When we touch Him, we touch holiness. Then something happens—a wonderful joyfulness comes in. We experience a spiritual feasting and celebration. When we take just twenty minutes to abide in Christ through prayer or reading the Bible, we become joyful. We lose ourselves in Christ. This is a celebration. He becomes so precious to us, and we become so precious to Him. God and we enjoy Christ as our mutual feast. We are saints, the holy ones. As such, we are enjoying a feast and a celebration.

## Saints Becoming Slaves

In writing to the Philippians, Paul addressed them as "the saints in Christ Jesus," but he spoke of himself as a bond-servant of Christ Jesus (1:1). We are first saints in Christ Jesus, but by enjoying His holiness, we eventually become slaves of Christ Jesus. The destiny of every saint is to become the Lord's bond-servant (Rev. 22:3). Once we are slaves of Christ Jesus, we have no right to decide our future or manage our own living. Eventually our experience will become like that of the apostle Paul.

To be a Christian is to be in Christ Jesus, but as we grow in the Christian life, we will eventually become those who are of Christ Jesus. "In" is a matter of position, while "of" is a matter of possession. Once we are born again, we have the status and position of being in Christ Jesus. Then, as we grow in life through the process of salvation, we become those who are of Christ Jesus—we belong to the Lord and serve Him practically.

## A Local Church

These saints who were "in Christ Jesus" were also in the physical city of Philippi. They were in a local church. In the process of salvation, we also must be in a local church. The healthy experience of salvation is fully related to being in a local church.

From the introduction of this epistle, it is evident that the church in Philippi enjoyed a sweet fellowship with the apostle Paul. The way he began this epistle is different from most of his other epistles. When he wrote to the Corinthians, who were experiencing problems, he addressed them as "the church of God which is at Corinth" (1 Cor. 1:2; 2 Cor. 1:1). To the Philippians, however, Paul addressed his letter in a very sweet way. He did not call them the church in Philippi, but rather "all the saints in Christ Jesus who are in Philippi, including the overseers and deacons." He addressed them not just as a local church but as organic members of the body of Christ.

Since he addressed them along with their overseers and deacons, it can be seen that Philippi was a church in good order. Paul did not even use the word "elders" when referring to the leaders in Philippi. He referred to them as overseers, indicating that they did not function merely according to position but in life.

In a local church there are overseers who shepherd the church. There are also deacons, administrators who serve the church practically. We must appreciate, respect, and honor our overseers and deacons. The local church in which the Lord has placed us is essential for us to grow in life. It is in our local church that we can grow from being "in Christ Jesus" to being "of Christ Jesus."

# 3

# Grace, Peace, and Thankful Prayer

*Grace to you and peace from God our Father and the Lord Jesus Christ. I thank my God in all my remembrance of you, always offering prayer with joy in my every prayer for you all.*

*—Philippians 1:2–4*

## Grace to You

Paul greeted the Philippians by saying, "Grace to you and peace from God our Father and the Lord Jesus Christ" (v. 2). Paul loved these two words, grace and peace. He used them in almost every letter he wrote. What is grace? Many Christians define grace as unmerited favor or God's material blessing. However, grace is more than favor and goes beyond outward blessings. Grace is a matter of a life relationship with a wonderful person. In that relationship, there is something so soothing, so tender, so satisfying, and so encouraging. When we enjoy Christ, we experience this grace, and this brings us peace. Grace and peace must be our daily experience. When Christ, who is full of grace, reaches us, He brings us into a realm of grace where we experience peace and satisfaction (John 1:14, 16–17).

The best illustration of grace is found in a family. When a father holds his child for the first time, his whole person becomes filled with grace. He has so much love that it is overflowing. In fact, whenever we are with those we are especially close to, we sense love, peace, and rest. This enjoyment is grace on a human level. The highest and truest grace is from our Lord Jesus. Grace means that Christ has come to us.

When you spent time with the Lord this morning, did you experience grace or did you get distracted with all the concerns of the day? Did you touch the living person of Christ by singing a hymn, by opening your heart in prayer, or by enjoying the Bible? Did you experience something so profound that it reached your spirit and touched your heart? If so, you have experienced grace. You forget who and where you are. You feel so satisfied and realize the value of your Christian life. Grace means that Christ comes to you for your enjoyment. This doesn't merely give you a sense of happiness but a deep and profound satisfaction.

We must be brought into the rich enjoyment of a person, Christ Jesus. This brings us a deep satisfaction. The Christian life is so marvelous, because it is the enjoyment of a living person, Christ Himself, as grace.

## Grace Issuing in Peace

Grace and peace are great matters. Throughout our entire Christian life, we will be tested by these. Do we really have the enjoyment of the many rich aspects of the living Christ as grace? If so, the issue will be peace, both inwardly and outwardly. Inwardly, we will have peace related to our stand before the Lord. Outwardly, we will have peace related to our environment.

When we enjoy Christ as grace, something becomes established inwardly, and we find that we are able to stand with the Lord. This brings about an inward peace. In other words, when we experience the Lord meeting our need and becoming our enjoyment in grace, we can cooperate with Him by taking a stand. At such a time, we experience peace inwardly. Many have experienced the peace that comes when we take a firm stand to be one with the Lord's leading in some matter in our lives. As soon as we take this stand with the Lord, we experience peace.

Besides this inward peace, we also experience an outward peace related to our environment as we abide under God's sovereign hand. When we argue and fight with others, it indicates that we are short of the divine life (Gal. 5:13–15). Once a rift occurs, what can restore the peace between arguing Christians or between a husband and wife? It takes more than outward repentance. Even the most sincere repentance may not remove the problem. Only the regular enjoyment of the divine life as grace generates this peace. When we enjoy grace, the Lord comes to us and touches our heart and spirit. He renders us true satisfaction. He becomes so soothing and so comforting. There is something bright and buoyant in our heart. The issue of all this is peace. Having enjoyed the Lord's grace, we are entirely at peace.

Whether we have money or not, whether we have good health or not, whether our situation is easy or difficult, smooth or rough—if we have sufficient grace, we have peace. Money, good health, or a smooth situation cannot bring such peace. We are at peace with our outward environment when we touch the Lord as grace and realize that His hand governs all things in our lives. All our problems, limitations, and weaknesses have been measured to us by God.

When we as believers come together, countless problems and difficulties come with us. Outside of Christ, we may annoy each other and get on one another's nerves. There are many difficulties which could cause angry reactions. It seems we could never have peace. When we look at our church life from a certain angle, we may feel all is hopeless, for the problems seem innumerable. When we pray together, however, we touch grace. Suddenly, our Christian brothers and sisters become so sweet. It seems impossible, but we now love those who once annoyed us. This is because peace issues from grace. We not only have peace with the Lord but also have peace with the believers He has placed us with (1 Cor. 12:18). When we acknowledge His lordship, we experience real peace.

## Paul's Thankful Remembrance

After greeting the Philippians, Paul began to share his heart with them in such a sweet way: "I thank my God in all my remembrance of you, always offering prayer with joy in my every prayer for you all" (Phil. 1:3–4). These two verses are profound. If we were writing to those we care for, we would probably end with, "I thank my God upon every remembrance of you," since we sometimes don't remember them. Paul went further, saying, "Always offering prayer." It seems the Philippian believers occupied his heart all the time. He was always thinking of them and thanking God for them. In Paul's Christian living of union and communion with Christ, the saints in Philippi were always with him.

When we think of other Christians, do we thank God for them? Usually when we pray for others, we do so with the hope of changing them. Instead of thanking God for them, we critique them in our prayers. The Lord might ask us, "What are you saying? Doesn't this brother love Me? Isn't that enough? What more do you want?" Many times when we pray, we are almost working with Satan, because Satan is the accuser of the brethren (Rev. 12:10), and we become accusers too.

Suppose there are three Christian brothers. Brother A prays for Brother B, "Lord, he is too strong. Please help him become more sensitive." Brother B prays for Brother A, "Lord, he is too timid. Please help him become more aggressive." Brother C prays for them both, "Lord, they are too argumentative. Please deal with their strong opinions." Each assumes he knows what the Lord should do. There is very little thankfulness.

The church in Philippi had problems, but Paul didn't talk about them. Instead, he just thanked God all the time for these dear saints. He offered prayer for them with joy.

## Paul Loved the Saints with a Parent's Love

When we become aware of other people's problems, we should try praying as Paul did: "Thank You, Lord, that these dear believers love You." Paul was an effective servant of the Lord because in any situation, he saw something to be appreciated; in every believer, he saw someone to be thankful for. He had discernment to see problems, yet he didn't focus on them. He didn't pray our kind of prayers. If we learn to appreciate even the weakest and most backslidden believers, our service will become much more effective, and many positive things will begin to happen.

Paul's love for the Philippians was like a parent's love. All parents think their children are the best and others' children are not as good. They have so much love for their children that they only see the best in them. They always have hope for their children, even when things are not so encouraging. This was Paul's attitude. He had so much love and care for the Philippian believers that he was constantly joyful in his remembrance of them.

# 4

# The Fellowship
# in the Gospel

*I thank my God in all my remembrance of you, always offering prayer with joy in my every prayer for you all, in view of your participation in the gospel from the first day until now. For I am confident of this very thing, that He who began a good work in you will perfect it until the day of Christ Jesus.*
*—Philippians 1:3-6*

Every time Paul remembered the Philippians, he thanked God joyfully for their "participation in the gospel from the first day until now" (v. 5). The word "participation" can also be translated "fellowship" (see KJV and Darby). This verse brings us to two questions: what is the gospel, and what is the fellowship in the gospel?

## The Gospel

The Greek word for "gospel" (*euaggelion*) is an ancient word used as a royal declaration, the announcing of a new king's birth and later coronation (Kittel, 2:724–725). A new king's reign brought with it a new age, a new era. The entire setting became new. It was accompanied by great celebration and feasting. The true gospel is that the Lord Jesus is reigning as the King of Kings. He has brought in a new age. This gospel is a cause of celebration and feasting. We who have heard the gospel have actually been brought into a fellowship in the gospel. We are no longer in the old creation, but the new creation (Gal. 6:15; 2 Cor. 5:17). We are no longer under the power of darkness, but under Christ (Col. 1:13). We are no longer abused by Satan, but are protected, guarded, and blessed by our new King, the Lord Jesus (Phil. 4:7). Paul was so joyful for the Philippians' fellowship in this wonderful gospel which began from the first day they heard it.

## The Realm of the Gospel

We were once outside the realm of the gospel. We were in the domain of darkness, slaves to sin, living according to the prince of the power of the air (Col. 1:13; Rom. 6:16; Eph. 2:2). One day, by the Lord's mercy, we heard the gospel and came to salvation. We could then say, "Praise the Lord, now I am saved!"

However, for some reason, many Christians stop there. They may become rich in the initial aspects of the gospel, such as the Lord's death and the forgiveness of sins, but that is as far as they go. They can be Christians for years and only think, "One day I will go to heaven." Such people understand neither Christ nor the gospel.

At the center of the gospel there is a King, the Lord Jesus Christ. With the ruling of this King there is a new age and a new realm or sphere. Within the Lord's kingdom there is so much feasting, rejoicing, and celebrating. We should live, labor, and invest our whole person in this realm, proclaiming, "I live unto the King!"

Once we are saved, we begin our fellowship in the gospel. We are conveyed directly to the center of this new kingdom (Col. 1:13). We receive a new life and a new position. We are brought into a new creation and a new kingdom. Everything related to the gospel is new. In this new kingdom there are so many spiritual riches and heavenly provisions to help us advance toward the goal. In the book of Romans, we learn that the gospel of God is not only the forgiveness of sins for our justification, but also many more items, such as sanctification, renewing, transformation, conformation, and glorification. Now that we are saved, our life becomes a "fellowship in the gospel," which will bring us to the final result of glorification.

The end result of the gospel is that we become the same as He is: "Beloved, now we are children of God, and it has not appeared as yet what we will be. We know that when He appears, we will be like Him, because we will see Him just as He is" (1 John 3:2). The gospel is not something for us to do; it is a life for us to live. The gospel is not merely for us to preach; it is a sphere for us to walk in, explore, and enjoy. Our fellowship in the gospel is for us to be more one with the King of Kings. From the first day we were saved, we were put into Christ. Now we abide in Christ, live in Christ, enjoy Christ, and have the outflow of Christ. The gospel is a realm in which Christ Himself is the totality of all the divine work. We have been brought into this realm, and now we are growing in this new kingdom. We are being renewed and transformed by the new life we received at our salvation. Eventually we will be glorified. We will be entirely one with our Lord Jesus and will then enjoy His kingdom for eternity. Until that day, we live and labor in the sphere of this marvelous gospel.

## Paul's Confidence

Paul continued, "For I am confident of this very thing, that He who began a good work in you will perfect it until the day of Christ Jesus" (Phil. 1:6). People are short of trust, especially when they are not pure. But Paul was pure, and the Philippians were pure. Paul required nothing of the Philippians. He simply loved them. The Philippians were the same—they simply loved Paul. Because of the purity in this relationship, genuine confidence could develop. The Greek word for "confident" (peithō) means convinced or persuaded (Rienecker, p. 544). Confidence results in reliance and trust in someone, which leads to commitment. It is not a confidence based on intuition but one built up over time. Paul had the confidence that the Philippians would be perfected and that the work the Lord began in them would one day be complete. He was confident that their love for the Lord would never die.

This confidence in the Philippians came from Paul's years of experience in the Lord. He was able to say, "I know how to get along with humble means, and I also know how to live in prosperity; in any and every circumstance I have learned the secret of being filled and going hungry, both of having abundance and suffering need. I can do all things through Him who strengthens me" (Phil. 4:12–13). Until we have experienced Christ in both good and bad times, we can never share Paul's confidence of Christ's ability to complete His work in us and in others. When we touch the Lord in a sober and solid way and don't merely play church, then we will have confidence in ourselves and others can have confidence in us.

Time will eventually manifest whether our fellowship is in the gospel or we are merely playing religious games. We must be able to honestly say, "I know the Lord is alive. My life is committed to Him." Until He becomes so subjective to us, it will be hard for others to have confidence in us. The work of the Lord Jesus is never in the realm of religion. Paul knew the Philippians had experienced Christ in a real and solid way. He could say, "He who began a good work in you will perfect it until the day of Christ Jesus." We should have confidence in the Lord who has begun a good work in us. We should be able to say, "I know the Lord. He's real to me. Christ is so living! He is so trustworthy!" Thus, we have confidence that the Lord will finish the work He has begun in us. We don't need to be in a religion or a program. We need a living Christ in whom we have confidence. Once He has begun a good work in us, He will finish it.

5

# Enjoying Grace in the Organic Body of Christ

*For it is only right for me to feel this way about you all, because I have you in my heart, since both in my imprisonment and in the defense and confirmation of the gospel, you all are partakers of grace with me.*

*—Philippians 1:7*

### You Have Me in Your Heart

Regarding Philippians 1:7, Kenneth Wuest says, "The expression, 'because I have you in my heart,' could just as properly be, 'because you have me in your heart.' The second way of rendering the Greek is more in accord with the context" (Wuest, 2:33). It is not a small thing to have someone in your heart. The apostle was so thankful and encouraged that the Philippians had him, a servant of the Lord, in their heart. This was the reason he could tell them, "You all are partakers of grace with me." It made no difference that the apostle was in one place and the Philippians were in another. Because they had him in their heart, they enjoyed the same grace he enjoyed. Those who had the apostle in their heart became partakers of all the grace that came from Christ to the apostle.

What this verse describes is very different from our individualistic psychology. We think we should stand alone. We feel that because we have Christ and are in a local church, we can grow, develop, and become effective on our own. We fail to

29

realize that our growth and development depend upon whom we have in our heart. Many of us may never have had such a thought. Then we wonder why we know so many doctrines but have so little experience of the Lord. Paul noted in 1 Corinthians that we have countless tutors but not many fathers (4:15). Tutors may instruct us for a while, but when their job is finished, they are not in our hearts. Fathers, however, care for our growth and labor with us in whatever way is necessary until we are full grown. This produces a sweet life relationship in which they are in our hearts and which insures that we will grow in a healthy manner.

Why are we short of grace? It is all a matter of our heart. What the apostle Paul described is a life union. He and the Philippians were together in Christ Jesus and had each other in their hearts. That became a blessing to the Philippians because it caused them to became fellow-partakers of grace with Paul.

## Partakers with Me of Grace

The church in Philippi was so blessed because they remembered the apostle who had preached the gospel to them, labored among them, watered them, taught them, and given them life. The church in Philippi was healthy because, as they had the apostle Paul in their heart, they became partakers of the grace he experienced.

While in bonds in prison, Paul experienced grace. Paul was in bondage, yet he was open to all for the gospel's sake. Some came to him for help, while others came to challenge him. Some stood with him, while others attacked and defamed him. In such a difficult situation, Paul experienced grace.

As Paul confirmed and defended the gospel, he received so much grace from the throne of Christ Jesus. The Lord became his rich enjoyment, satisfaction, and source of blessing. Real grace only comes from paying a price. If others grow spiritually because we have shed so many tears for them, that is grace. If others love the Lord because we have prayed for them even when it was hopeless, that is grace. Paul knew this kind of grace. The good times and the bad times, the encouragement and the misunderstandings, the appreciation and the slander all brought him grace. The life he imparted and the tears he shed brought him grace. In his bonds and in the defense and confirmation of the gospel, he was in grace.

Seemingly, this grace was given uniquely to Paul in Rome, far away from the Philippians, yet Paul could say to them, "Because you have me in your heart...you all are partakers of grace with me." This is a marvelous picture of the organic body of Christ. There was something mutual between Paul and the Philippians. What Paul experienced became the experience of the Philippians. The grace he received became their grace. The blessing he received became their blessing. This was because the Philippians had the apostle Paul in their heart.

We should make this practical. Many older Christians minister to us. Are they in our heart? Are the church leaders in our heart? Are those who care for our children in our heart? If so, we become fellow partakers of their grace. When those who serve us are in our heart, their grace becomes our grace. The blessing the Lord gives them becomes our enjoyment. We partake of their grace.

Consider the past year. In that time, whom have you prayed for? How much time have you taken to remember and pray for those who serve you? If your heart is filled with yourself, and if your prayers are only limited to your own needs, then you will be lacking in the enjoyment of grace. But if you pray for those who serve you, you will be supplied with the grace that they enjoy.

## The Defense of the Gospel

Paul received grace because he was defending the gospel. He could do this because he believed in and knew the gospel. He was equipped and constituted with the gospel. He defended what mattered deeply to him, what had, in fact, become the meaning of his life. Paul was one with the gospel, so he could defend it.

The Greek word for "defense" is *apologia*, which is from *apo*, "from," and *logos*, "word" (Strong, no. 627). Defending the gospel requires that we be equipped and constituted with the Word. Defending the gospel cannot be based on our opinions or our subjective feelings. We must spend time in the Word of God to be adequately prepared to defend the gospel. If someone says, "Jesus is not the Son of God," we will react strongly to defend the gospel. This reaction won't be based on emotion but on the Word with which we are constituted. If someone says, "You don't need to love the Lord," we will know how to respond, not only because we love the Lord but also because we are equipped with the *logos*. If we are people of the gospel, then we will live for the gospel.

## The Confirmation
## of the Gospel

Paul not only defended the gospel but also confirmed it. The Greek word for "confirmation," *bebaiōsis*, comes from the word *bainō*, "to walk" (Strong, no. 951). The gospel was not only Paul's belief but also his walk. His living matched, upheld, and established the gospel. Confirming the gospel is related to our walk. Many times we try to confirm the gospel by arguing, but the real confirmation is our living. Paul had this confirmation. The Lord was with him. He didn't just preach the gospel; his very walk was the gospel. Because his daily living matched what he said, his gospel preaching was effective. His defense of the gospel was related to the meaning of his life, and his confirmation of the gospel was related to the way he lived his life. People were affected by what they saw in him.

## The Secret of Enjoying Grace

Even while Paul was defending and confirming the gospel from prison, he enjoyed grace. Because the Philippians had him in their heart, they became fellow partakers of Paul's grace. There was such a sweet relationship between the apostle and the Philippians.

Are you enjoying the grace of Christians who care for you? Has their grace become yours? If not, it indicates you don't have them in your heart. Perhaps you have your career, your material possessions, or even spiritual activities in your heart. If you have those caring for you in your heart, then every day their enjoyment of grace will be yours. How precious this is! It is such a beautiful and spiritual life. Because Paul and the Philippians were in the organic body of Christ, the grace he enjoyed could become theirs.

Our hearts might be filled with the pursuit of a career, success, or material wealth, but the Philippians had Paul in their heart. Because of their heart for Paul, the Philippians were in one accord in their care for the apostle. That is why the singular word "heart" is used. Paul and all of his labor possessed the heart of the Philippians.

Praise the Lord for this wonderful secret of enjoying grace! If those who serve us are in our heart, then their grace belongs to us, and this in turn will become a supply to them. This is the secret of enjoying grace in the organic body of Christ.

6

# Treasuring Our
# Spiritual Riches

*For it is only right for me to feel this way about you all, because*
*[you have me in your heart], since both in my imprisonment*
*and in the defense and confirmation of the gospel, you all are*
*partakers of grace with me.*
                    *—Philippians 1:7, with bracketed text from Wuest*

## To Have, To Possess, To Enjoy

When Paul said to the Philippians, "You have me in your heart," he used a very particular word. The Greek word for "to have" in this verse is *echō*, which can also mean to own, to enjoy, to have at one's disposal, and to possess (Kittel, 2:817). For example, suppose you have a Bible. You may merely possess the Bible, or you may *echō* the Bible. If you *echō* it, you really enjoy it—you read it again and again; you underline it, mark it, and highlight it. You are inspired by it and write notes in the margins. It is not just a book that sits on your table or bookshelf. It is something you hold so dearly. You enjoy it every day. Because you *echō* the Bible, it is alive to you.

You may have many things, but only some of them really mean something to you. For example, suppose you own a basketball. To you, it may be a small and insignificant possession. It doesn't mean anything to you. You may play with it once in a while, but it's not that important, and you don't give it much thought. To a professional basketball player, however, that basketball is extremely significant. He reacts to the ball very differently than you would. The basketball player *echoes* the basketball. The basketball is a part of him. To others it is nothing, but to him it is important and meaningful. It is his life. It is something that his whole person responds to.

If you *echō* something, you have a deep and personal reaction to it. You don't merely possess it; you respond to it. You get so much enjoyment out of it. In Greek, this is what it means to have something—you feel so alive because of it. Again, if you have the Bible in such a way, then you will pick it up all the time. It is not a mere possession. It becomes a part of you, something for your constant enjoyment. The Bible is alive to you, and you read it again and again. This means that you *echō* the Bible.

## Our Possession and Enjoyment

Unfortunately, not many of us treasure what we have. Because the saints in Philippi were healthy, they treasured the apostle and his ministry to the extent that he did not just belong to them, but he was in their heart. This caused them to be fellow partakers of grace with the apostle. Unfortunately, when we say that we have Christ or an apostle, it doesn't have much impact or meaning. What value do we truly give the things of the Lord? What value do we give those who serve us? Do we really possess them, or do we just have them? If we possess them, if we *echō* them, that means we treasure them. We are excited and made alive by them. There are all sorts of positive reactions within us. If we truly treasure the Lord, we will live for Him. Our life won't have any meaning without Him. The apostle Paul could say to the Philippians, "You have me in your heart. You *echō* me and all my spiritual riches." This is so precious, but it is lacking today.

We should treasure our spiritual possessions. The problem is that we may not know what we possess. God's gift to every believer includes the Lord Himself, the Bible, the believers, the church life, and the serving ones, including the apostles.

## The Lord

We possess the Lord: "He who has the Son has the life" (1 John 5:12). As Christians, we should make it our practice to enjoy and treasure this One we possess. We can pray, "Lord, I know I have You, but I want to appreciate and treasure You. I want to love and experience You in the deepest way." As we call on the Lord, we know the riches of His salvation subjectively (Rom. 10:12–13). We can call upon Him throughout the day. As we are walking, driving, or even working at a busy job, we can remember the Lord and take some time to gaze on Him (Heb. 12:2). We can enjoy His sweet and precious name. That will help us *echō* the Lord. We will have Him not merely as a possession; we will treasure Him in our heart.

## The Bible

We also possess the Bible with all of its "precious and magnificent promises" (2 Pet. 1:4). Yet we may never take the time to *echō* the Bible. For some reason it is more difficult to pick up the Bible than a novel or a magazine. However, once we pick up the Bible it becomes so easy to read. Spontaneously we are energized and enlivened (John 6:63). The living word operates within us (Heb. 4:12) and fills us with life and joy.

## Fellow Believers

God has also given us fellow believers. If we are honest, we must admit there are times we don't want to see them. Sometimes when we are relaxing at home and the doorbell rings, we groan within. We would rather just be left alone. However, if that visitor is a fellow believer and we sit down and have fellowship, our old feeling disappears. We become joyful and sense the flow of life. Sometimes we don't even talk about spiritual things, yet we are revived. The presence of the Lord is with us. We are in Christ, and our time together is so sweet. Through experiences like this, we learn to love and treasure our fellow believers (1 Thess. 4:9).

## The Church Life

Why do we enjoy gathering together with other Christians who in many ways may be quite different from us? We treasure the fellowship we have together because, like the Philippians, we have one another in our heart. As the apostle John wrote, "We know that we have passed out of death into life, because we love the brethren" (1 John 3:14). As we are enjoying fellowship together, we realize, "I love these people. I love the church life. The Lord is so real when I am here with them." We feel so happy and satisfied. The church life becomes a precious treasure to us.

## The Serving Ones

In principle, those who serve us are our possession, just as the apostles are ours (1 Cor. 3:21–22). We should *echō* those who serve us and care for our spiritual growth. We should have them in our heart, just as the Philippians had Paul in their heart.

Serving the Lord is not easy. Taking care of so many people can be draining. It is a good practice to encourage those who care for us and to stand with them. Then we will be fellow-partakers with them of grace. If we practice this, our church will be different. If we develop the habit of thanking those who care for us and telling them, "We have you in our heart," our church will be made alive.

The churches Paul raised up all had problems. The problems in Corinth alone were enough to give Paul headaches. But one church, the church in Philippi, became the apostle's joy. He called them "my beloved brethren whom I long to see, my joy and crown" (Phil. 4:1). Paul knew that the Philippians *echoed* him. They didn't merely possess him; they treasured him. This became a supply and strong encouragement to Paul.

Suppose someone asked the Philippians, "Why do you follow Paul? Do you follow a man?" How should they have responded? On one hand they could have said, "No, we don't follow a man. We follow Christ. He is our Lord." On the other hand they could have said, "We do love Paul. We love his spiritual riches, and we even fellowship with him in the gospel. We can't deny that he has made Christ so real and living to us. We truly have him in our heart. In a sense, he belongs to us. We come back to his riches all the time because we are made alive by them. We love and honor our brother, because he has helped us to follow Christ. We *echō* our dear brother. What this brother enjoyed has also become our enjoyment." They had Christ, and they also had the apostle Paul.

## What Do We Treasure?

What we have in our heart decides the vitality of our Christian life. Some may think, "Some day I'll get a professional degree. Then I can be promoted and have a better salary." If this is what they treasure, it means nothing. It may be necessary to get a professional degree, but we shouldn't treasure it. We may possess an education and career, but these should not be our treasures. They should not fill our thoughts. Instead, we should be able say, "I have a professional degree, but it doesn't occupy me. I have a good job, but I don't treasure it. These things are necessary, but they are not my life. What I really treasure is Christ, the Bible, the believers, the church life, and the Lord's servants with all their spiritual riches! This is what is in my heart."

We may be overloaded with spiritual riches yet not treasure them. Our bookshelves may be filled with spiritual books, yet we may never *echō* them. Instead, we treasure material possessions, leaving little room in our heart for the real things. We should love and treasure all that God has given us.

The Philippians *echoed* Paul in their heart. They gave an

"Amen" to whatever he did. They responded positively to whatever he spoke. This is what we should learn from the book of Philippians. May we all learn to *echō* the things that truly matter.

# 7

# Caring for People in the Inward Parts of Christ Jesus

*For God is my witness, how I long for you all with the affection of Christ Jesus.*

*—Philippians 1:8*

## The Affection of Christ Jesus

In Philippians 1:8, the Greek word for "affection," *splagchnon*, denotes "the inward parts...the seat of feeling and is the strongest word in Greek for the feeling of compassion" (Rienecker, p. 545). It also signifies inward affection, tender mercy, and sympathy (Strong, no. 4698). The Lord loves us with inward affection, which includes tender mercy. If the Lord loved us without mercy, we would probably be consumed by fire. Because the Lord is merciful and sympathetic, however, He can tell us, "I understand you. I know what you are going through."

Because the Lord never sinned, loved the world, or lived according to the flesh, we might wonder if He could ever fully understand us. However, the Lord does understand because He is full of tender mercy and sympathy. For this reason we can always come to Him. When we want to call on the Lord but dare not because we feel so unqualified and shameful, the Lord has tremendous mercy and sympathy. His inward parts are filled with affection. He loves us and knows what we are going through. His mercy is according to our need, so we don't have to be afraid of Him. We can always come to Him for grace.

Paul's relationship with the Philippians was not one of natural affection but was according to the innermost being of Christ Jesus, which is most tender toward the believers. When we love others according to our natural affection, our love is affected by who they are or what they have done. Our loving care toward one another should be according to the tender inward parts of the Lord. Paul longed after the Philippians in the very longing with which the Lord longed after them, for he was abiding in the inward parts of Jesus Christ. We should never abide in our natural affection for one another. Rather, let us seek to abide in the Lord and to love one another out from His deep and tender parts.

## Paul's Longing for the Philippians

When Paul touched the Lord in His inward parts, he realized how much the Lord longed after the believers in Philippi. This caused him to long after them also. In verse 8, the Greek word for "long for," *epipotheō*, also means "to yearn after....The idea implied is eagerness" (Rienecker, p. 545). We should ask, what does the Lord Himself long for? He primarily cares for the church (Eph. 5:25), which is expressed in local churches, such as the church in Philippi. The local churches are His testimony on the earth today. They are His expression and are therefore precious to the Lord. When Paul prayed to the Lord and entered into His deepest, most intimate parts, he touched the Lord's longing. Paul's own inward parts were touched by the Lord, so he longed for the Philippians. This longing developed within Paul as he remembered and petitioned for them (Phil. 1:3–4).

## Caring for People according to the Lord's Inward Parts

Our care for people should not be according to demands but according to the inward parts of Christ Jesus. The way Paul longed after the Philippians in the inward parts of Christ Jesus should be a pattern to us. Sometimes we get frustrated with those we serve because we want them to change but they don't. Our view for them may be right, but our heart is wrong. Our heart needs to go through the inward parts of Christ Jesus.

Paul learned a great secret in the Christian life. It is possible to do spiritual things without the heart of Christ. This is especially true of our care for people. We become so demanding when we want those we serve to be different than they are. We have so many expectations for them, and we do our best to bring them up to our standard. Even if we are right, we are wrong. If we do not enter into the Lord's heart for them, there will be something wrong. If we would come to the inward parts of Jesus Christ, we would find sympathy and tender mercy for those we serve. It is only in this mercy and sympathy that we can exercise the Lord's care for them.

The Lord's inward parts are filled with love, mercy, tenderness, and sympathy. He is much broader than we realize. We should never serve others with the attitude, "Shape up or ship out!" If there is no mercy or tenderness in our care for others, we have not gone through the inward parts of Christ Jesus. How do we respond if a Christian brother tells us, "I feel so dry. The Lord is not real to me"? Do we respond, "Did you read your Bible and pray this morning? You didn't? No wonder you're dry! It's your fault!" Yes, it is true he should have some time with the Lord in the morning. Yes, he bears some responsibility if he is spiritually dry. But does our response come from the Lord's heart? Our desire that he be made alive is right, but our attitude is so wrong. Our heart has not gone through the inward parts of Christ Jesus.

The Bible doesn't condemn us for not doing this or that. Instead, it conveys the tender love, mercy, and sympathy of our dear Lord Jesus Christ. It tells us again and again to come to the Lord Jesus. He will restore, forgive, and heal us. He is a merciful and sympathetic High Priest who intercedes for us (Heb. 4:14–16; 7:25). Whatever we need, He will supply. He loves us, shepherds us, and cares for us. In the Lord's heart, there is so much affection. When we enter into His heart, deep into His inward parts, we become the same as He is. We become tender, merciful, and sympathetic toward others. May we all become like the apostle Paul, loving and caring for others in the inward parts of Christ Jesus.

# 8 | Loving People in Full Knowledge and All Discernment

*And this I pray, that your love may abound still more and more in real knowledge and all discernment.*

*—Philippians 1:9*

Paul was wise. He knew that the church in Philippi was very pure, focused, and joyful, but something had happened. They had begun to hear a lot of confusing things. In many other churches, elements of Judaism had crept in, robbing them of their simple and pure love for Christ (Gal. 1:6–7). Such elements were intermingled with the things of Christ, and it was hard to reject them. Paul realized that the Philippians were in danger of being influenced by these things, so he prayed that their "love may abound still more and more in real knowledge and all discernment."

## That Your Love May Abound

As Paul entered into the Lord's inward parts on behalf of the Philippians, he entered into Christ's concern for them (Phil. 1:8). This concern was that their "love may abound still more and more" (v. 9). It is interesting that Paul would tell the Philippians that their love needed to abound, since they were already filled with love. There were others who lacked love, such as the Corinthians; to them Paul wrote an entire chapter

45

on the meaning of love (1 Cor. 13). The Philippians were not like that. They loved Christ, they loved Paul as the Lord's servant, and they loved one another. Even so, their love needed to abound more and more; it had to advance and become so much higher.

In verse 9, the Greek word for "to abound," *perisseuō*, means to cause to superabound or excel, to exceed, or to have more abundance (Strong, no. 4052). It implies becoming considerably more than what is expected. If I were to invite you for dinner, you would expect to be fed a decent meal, but if I were to provide enough for you to take a few meals home as well, that would be something superabounding. Paul desired that the saints would exercise their love in such a way. The Philippians were already rich and genuine with pure love. Paul used this word to admonish them to continue, to develop, and to attain to a higher level of love.

For love to abound means that it is elevated, having a high view and expectation. For example, all parents love their children, but not all have love that abounds. Some parents have a view for their children that is very high. This is not just an emotional love but a love that desires what is best for their children. This means that their love abounds. Others love their children but have no view for their future. We can't say they don't love their children, but it is not an elevated love. Parents whose love abounds have high expectations for their children.

The Lord loves us with an elevated love which always seeks to bring us higher. He wants our lives to be high and heavenly. He wants us to have this same elevated love with high expectation, a love that abounds more and more. We don't want to be common people but to go higher, even becoming heavenly in our love. Paul was like this. He did not just love with natural affection. He was one with the Lord's love for the Philippians and sought to bring them into an elevated state. He wanted them to be one with the Lord and live according to the Lord's desire. This is why Paul wrote, "That your love may abound still more and more."

## In Full Knowledge

The Greek word used here for "knowledge," *epígnōsis*, denotes "exact or full knowledge, discernment, recognition, and is a strengthened form of [*gnōsis*], expressing a fuller or a full knowledge, a greater participation by the knower in the object known, thus more powerfully influencing him" (Vine, 2:301). It is not a knowledge based merely on intuition but a knowledge of divine revelation according to the living Word. The fullness of this knowledge brings us into participation with who God is, what He desires, how He operates, and the consummation of His work. Full knowledge not only encourages, regulates, and leads us but also becomes the base of our walk and service, especially pertaining to God's interest and the church's benefit.

This full knowledge becomes ours as we are constituted with the Bible and all its riches, because full knowledge is related to the living Word. To have this knowledge, we must spend time in the Bible and be constituted with its riches. If our knowledge has such a broad scope, including who God is, what He desires, how He operates, and the consummation of His work, it will be a solid base for our Christian life and church life.

Knowledge regulates us, equips us, and protects us. This is why we need to be in the truth, in the Bible, and in spiritual writings. We need this as our base. We need to be equipped and constituted with spiritual knowledge so that we can stand against anything that isn't healthy. With such knowledge we can stand against everything that would distract us from a pure love for Christ. For example, if someone suggests that Christ is not the Son of God, we will know how to react. Knowledge protects us and enables us to follow the Lord properly.

Lack of knowledge can cause us to do peculiar things. For example, if we don't know who God really is, we may pray in a peculiar way. A student may pray, "Lord, even though I didn't study for this test, please give me a good grade. If You give me an 'A,' I promise I will read the Bible more." How can the Lord respond to such a strange prayer? We put the Lord on the spot. Either He doesn't answer us, so we say that He is not real, or He does answer us, and we think He is a magician. The problem is a lack of knowledge. Anyone who prays this way doesn't really know God.

Sometimes Christians are naive about spiritual things because of a lack of knowledge. For example, we might pray, "Lord, lead me," but the Lord can only lead us according to the knowledge we have. As knowledge matures, it becomes full knowledge, *epignōsis*, and then the Lord's leading becomes crystal clear. This knowledge becomes the base of our Christian walk and service. We know who God is and what He cares about. We know how God works and how this work will consummate. Then we can refrain from anything that is not of Him or His desire. We know how to live our lives and how to invest ourselves. We should pray, "Lord, equip me with the rich knowledge concerning You and Your desire. As I labor in Your Word, may the knowledge I gain eventually mature into full knowledge. Then I will be able to live and serve for Your interest and the profit of Your church."

## In All Discernment

In verse 9, the Greek word for "discernment," *aisthēsis*, also means "insight, perception" (Rienecker, p. 545). God desires that we who love the Lord not only have full knowledge for the advancement of His interest but to also have the capacity to perceive things clearly and understand their true nature. A person with discernment can see through falsehood and impurities.

When we begin to love the Lord, we can easily become zealous and lose our discernment. Those with spiritual knowledge are also in danger of losing their discernment, for they are most apt to be overtaken by zeal. Our tendency is to respond to situations naturally rather than responding in Christ. We are prone to be caught up by movements and stirred up. It is easy to jump on bandwagons, but spiritual things need time to be tested. Some things are of Christ, and others are not. Discernment is needed in addition to knowledge.

Although the apostle Paul realized that the Philippians were pure, he also realized that they could be negatively influenced by others. For example, a visitor from Jerusalem, where the believers were zealous for the law (Acts 21:20), might say to the Philippians, "What Paul teaches is good, and I enjoy what he shares, but it just needs a little adjustment. We should remember to keep the Sabbath. Did you know that we all keep the Sabbath in Jerusalem?" The Philippians first needed knowledge for their protection, and then they needed discernment to see past the motives of those who were not so pure (Phil. 1:15).

There are few things more important than discernment. If we lack discernment, we will not be able to follow the Lord through to the end. There are just too many persons and things that will come along to divert us from Christ. Discernment is the most difficult virtue for a Christian to acquire and to exercise. Often what seems to be true on the face of something is very different from what is going on beneath the surface.

If we are to carry out what the Lord has revealed to us as the full knowledge, we must also be able to exercise all discernment. Knowledge gives us our view and goal, but it is discernment that gives us the ability to see the real situation as we go forward. Full knowledge allows us to know God and His interest; discernment allows us to protect and preserve that interest. That is why the Bible says the spiritual discern all things (1 Cor. 2:15, Darby). They can see the real nature of things.

This discerning ability will also bring us to see the Spirit's moving and leading (1 Cor. 2:10–12). How the Spirit moves and leads has everything to do with the discerning ability. The more we are in the Lord and enjoying Him, the more this ability of discernment will be developed. We will know what is profitable to the Lord and what is offensive to Him. We will know what is conducive to His interest and what is contrary to it.

Paul surely loved the Philippians. He prayed for them joyfully (Phil. 1:4). Because the Philippians had Paul in their heart, as Paul enjoyed the Lord's grace, they became partakers with him of the same grace (v. 7). Paul was in the Lord's inward parts and joined in His longing for the Philippians (v. 8). He prayed that their love would abound, becoming so high and elevated. For this they needed full knowledge to protect them. They also needed all discernment, because sometimes impurities can grow in the hearts of fellow believers. Loving more abundantly with full knowledge and all discernment would protect them—both the pure and the impure. They needed to love even those who were impure, loving them according to the knowledge of God's purpose while discerning their real condition and considering what is best for their growth.

May we all learn from Paul's concern for the Philippians. May our love abound still more and more in full knowledge and all discernment.

# 9

# Approving by Testing and Purified by Light

*So that you may approve the things that are excellent, in order to be sincere and blameless until the day of Christ; having been filled with the fruit of righteousness which comes through Jesus Christ, to the glory and praise of God.*

*—Philippians 1:10–11*

There are two sides to the opening verses in Philippians. Firstly, there is God's side. Philippians 1:6 says, "For I am confident of this very thing, that He who began a good work in you will perfect it until the day of Christ Jesus." God had begun a work in the Philippians, and He was responsible for fulfilling it. Secondly, there is the side of human responsibility. Philippians 1:10 says, "So that you may approve the things that are excellent, in order to be sincere and blameless until the day of Christ." This shows that there was something very practical that the Philippians had to do. Both of these verses point to the day of Christ's return. When we believed in the Lord Jesus, God "began a good work" in us, and He "will perfect it until the day of Christ Jesus," but for us to be "sincere and blameless until the day of Christ," we need to "approve the things that are excellent."

## Approving the Things That Are Excellent

In verse 10, the Greek word for "approve," *dokimazō*, means "to test, examine, prove, scrutinize (to see whether a thing be genuine or not), as metals....To recognize as genuine after examination, to approve, deem worthy" (Thayer, p. 154). In other words, an item is tested, and afterward its genuineness and worthiness are acknowledged. This has spiritual significance, because genuineness comes from God Himself. God is the most genuine One. He has no hypocrisy or impure motive. This is eternally true. Furthermore, everything that is from God, of God, unto God, produced by God, and that leads us to God is worthy and has high value.

Paul wrote to the Philippians that they needed to "approve the things that are excellent." They needed to test whether certain things were truly genuine and worthy. This is a lesson we all need to learn. For example, some Christian preachers have the ability to stir up hundreds of people to love the Lord and give their lives to Him. We should appreciate this, yet we should also recognize that it is not sufficient. It is not enough for people to be stirred up. They need to learn how to test things and discern whether they are genuine. It is easy to be stirred up without being led to what is genuine and valuable in the Christian life. We should be sober about spiritual things. As we are listening to a Christian preacher, we have to consider: are we only being stirred in our emotions, or are we being brought to God? When we attempt to lay hold of spiritual things, we must discern their genuineness and worthiness.

The church life in Philippi must have been wonderful, because the believers were so lovely, simple, and pure. However, it seems their sincerity caused them to lose the ability to test things and discern whether they were genuine. This is why Paul told them to "approve the things that are excellent." We must be careful. We should not allow our simplicity and purity to cause us to become naive and lose our discernment (Matt. 10:16). For instance, there are many Christian groups with young people who love the Lord and are consecrated to Him. If these young believers seek direction from their pastor, he may tell them, "Since you love the Lord, you should go to Bible college and seminary." What such young people really need to hear is, "Learn to love the Lord even more. Exercise to have the Lord in your daily life, interacting with Him all the time. He will lead you and show you how best to follow Him." Instead, young people who love the Lord are quickly directed to an institution rather than to the Lord Himself. Because these young people are simple and pure, they follow that path. This is why it is so important to approve things by testing. It is too easy to be misdirected and lose the ability to discern what is excellent.

## Not Common but Excellent

Paul admonished the Philippians to "approve the things that are excellent." These excellent things are the things that are not common, that bear the nature of Christ, and that cause us to grow and to be built up. For example, on the shelves of Christian bookstores there are so many expositions of the Bible. If we read one of these books and find that it does not lead us to the Lord Himself, then that book is just common. However, if a book does lead us to the Lord, then it is one of "the things that are excellent." These are the things that allow Christ to operate in us to produce His testimony.

The local churches are included in "the things that are excellent." No local church should be common. Every local church should build up the body of Christ (Eph. 2:22). Some churches are happy places; others are filled with frustrations. We should appreciate that the Lord uses each of them to produce His testimony.

To live a true church life is not common but excellent. It is something fully approved by Christ, because it accomplishes His purpose. We should all aspire to bear the testimony of Jesus Christ. Our attitude should be to always live Christ (Phil. 1:21) and be found in Him (3:9). We pursue Him together (2 Tim. 2:22). We build one another up (Eph. 4:16). We are not common but bear the nature of Christ. We live for the purpose of God. Our living is one with God's desire, and our life together is for the Lord's testimony. With us, there is something uncommon, something excellent. We live for the building up of the body of Christ in our local church.

## That You May Be Sincere

Paul desired that the Philippians would be "sincere and blameless until the day of Christ." A sincere person is pure, single, and without hidden motives. The Greek word for "sincere" here is *eilikrinēs*. This word is from "*heilē* (the sun's ray) and [*krinō*, properly to distinguish, i.e., decide (mentally or judicially)]; judged by sunlight, i.e., tested as genuine (figurative):—pure, sincere" (Strong, no. 1506). A pure person is one who is judged by the light. The Greek word *heilē* refers to the rays of the sun's light, implying an intense and piercing light. This implies that to be pure means we live under the rays of the sunlight. Our inward being is constantly examined and judged by this light. Such an intense light exposes and kills the negative things, and it dispenses and transfuses the positive things.

When we are young, we want to do things for the Lord. As we grow older, our desire is increasingly to be one with the Lord. When we are young, our desire is to carry out a great work; when we are old, our desire is simply to live out Christ. This is because as we grow older, the shining of the light penetrates further, and we realize who and what we are. We come to know even our tears of repentance are not completely genuine. The more we are exposed, the more we realize the need for this exposing light to terminate who we are. Light exposes what we do outwardly, but the rays expose our inward being. As we encounter this light, we increasingly realize that it is not what we do that is the problem; it is our inward being that is the problem.

## Purified by the Lord's Ray

Sincerity refers to our purity and simplicity. Our initial purity, which we have when we first believe in the Lord, needs to be maintained and also needs to grow (1 Pet. 1:22). For our purity to grow, we need the rays of the divine sunlight. Purity does not come by our natural effort. We cannot force ourselves to be pure. Rather, purity comes by the judging ray of our Lord, which frees us from falsehood. The Lord Jesus Christ Himself is the reality of purity. When the Lord operates as the sun and diffuses His light as a ray into our being, it generates in us the ability to discern what is excellent. Our purity is the result of the shining of the Lord's ray.

We need such a shining to touch our person. This will make us pure and keep us from falsehood. Purity does not result from receiving light in a general way. It results when a ray—a light with a high degree of intensity—penetrates deep within our being. Watchman Nee appreciated this ray, writing, "Thou healing sun! Thou hope of man! I really love Thy ray" (Martin, no. 514, v. 7). This hymn says to the Lord, "I really love Thy ray," not, "I really love Thy light." Light exposes, but a ray of light penetrates. After we have been under a ray of light that penetrates our being, we shall be purified. We should even love such a ray, because it frees us from what is negative and infuses us with what is positive. The ray helps us to be simple, sincere, and genuine. The ray allows us to have a richer and fuller enjoyment of the Lord.

## The Ray's Freeing, Killing, and Supplying

When the ray of the Lord's light shines, it exposes everything in our inner being (Eph. 5:13). Whatever is negative is killed by the light, and whatever is positive is supplied. Suppose I love movies too much. One day as I am watching a movie, something within me says, "What are you doing this for?" I begin to struggle inwardly, and I can't get over a deep realization that I have become enslaved to movies. After this experience, I will debate whether I should watch movies anymore. The good news is that this same ray of light that exposed my enslavement also frees me (cf. John 8:32–36). If I say, "Lord, I love You, and I love Your ray," I begin to lose interest in movies. This doesn't necessarily mean I will never watch another movie, but

I am no longer enslaved to them. The Lord's ray has killed my bondage to movies.

Until the ray comes, it is likely that we are enslaved to something. We need the ray of the Lord's light to judge us and to keep us pure. This doesn't mean that we will only do "spiritual" things. It means we are delivered from being enslaved to movies, sports, hobbies, or any distraction from Christ. After the ray comes, we may still do those things, but in an entirely different way. We are enabled to use the things that once enslaved us. Rather than being enslaved to a sport or hobby, we use it.

The examining ray not only frees us from what enslaves us but also kills anything improper. Instead of struggling to give up things we should not be involved with, we become joyful and lose our interest in them. If someone asks us, "Why don't you do such-and-such anymore?" we can't explain. All we can say is, "Praise the Lord! I don't know why, but I'm not interested in that anymore. I just love Jesus." Because we are under the Lord's ray, we become simple. We recognize when the Lord is bothered by something in our lives. The ray kills what is impure or improper, enabling us to live in the Lord's presence in a very human way.

The ray of the Lord's light purifies us by freeing us from enslavement and by killing what is unhealthy. This is like the treatment of cancer by radiation. When radiation keeps hitting and burning a particular group of cells, eventually the cancer is killed. However, the divine, spiritual ray is much better than radiation treatment, for it not only kills what is unhealthy but nourishes us and infuses Christ as life into us also (John 8:12). The Lord doesn't expect us to grit our teeth and try so hard to be pure. There is not one genuine spiritual victory that comes through our self-determination. Instead, the Lord delivers us by killing whatever is in the way of our spiritual growth and replacing it with Himself. When the ray comes, it examines and exposes us; it kills the unhealthy things; it also infuses us with spiritual nourishment. The ray dispenses all that Christ is into us. Eventually this process produces a pure, sincere person.

## Guarding Our Purity

Purity is relative. How pure is pure? For example, are we pure toward the Lord? It's difficult to say no, but it's also difficult to say yes. The fact that we are interested in spiritual things indicates that we are at least somewhat pure. However, this does not prove that we are completely pure or that our purity will last. That is why we must pay attention to our initial purity, the purity we received when we first believed in the Lord Jesus (2 Cor. 11:2–3). When we first began to love the Lord, that was His mercy. No one can say, "I love the Lord," or, "I give myself to the Lord," without the Lord's mercy (Rom. 9:16). That initial purity needs to be kept, and it needs to grow (2 Tim. 2:22). Otherwise it can easily be lost over time.

We first believed in the Lord because He had mercy on us and attracted us. We realized how marvelous and lovely the Lord was. We consecrated ourselves to Him, saying, "Lord, I belong to You. Lord, I love You. I want to serve You all my life." This was all by the Lord's mercy. This was our initial purity. Following this, we grow in different ways through the years. For example, we grow in life, in truth, and in our service for the Lord. At the same time, we grow in complications. After many experiences, difficulties, and frustrations, it is easy to lose our purity and become overly complicated, losing our simplicity toward Christ and toward one another. We still need the Lord's mercy so our purity can grow beyond the initial stage. We need to pray, "Lord, as I grow, I still need Your mercy. Please keep me from complications. Help me retain my simplicity. Make me just as pure as I was when I first loved You. May my purity grow and mature."

In our life of loving the Lord, purity is a crucial element. As we grow in the positive things, there is always the potential for negative things to develop simultaneously. If we love and pursue the Lord with others, we are sure to grow and mature in life, truth, and service—these are the excellent things. At the same time, complications will grow. Our natural human abilities will grow. Our capacity to maneuver and play politics will grow. These negative things can grow to the point where we trust in our own abilities rather than the Lord Himself and in our own arrangements instead of the Lord's leading. We need to guard our purity so that it will not be overcome by the growth of these negative things. We have to be very careful, always beseeching the Lord to keep us pure: "Lord, I open to Your ray. Expose any complications in my reasoning that are a frustration to You. Expose any impure motives, and any impure things I do, that would lead me astray. Expose anything that will eventually damage me or damage others. What You expose, Lord, I pray You will also put to death. Kill anything that takes away my simplicity toward You, complicates my relationship with You, or distracts me from loving You. Whatever You put to death, replace with Yourself, nourishing me and infusing me with all Your spiritual riches."

## Being Kept from Religious Falsehood

Every local church should be a divine community, but we may have learned to live in this community without Christ, behaving and talking in acceptable ways. We may use certain terminology, yet lack the reality of the Lord's divine work. This is religious falsehood. We need the ray of the Lord's light to deliver us from false spirituality. Without the Lord's judging ray, we will be in religion, learning to say certain things, practicing certain rituals, and behaving certain ways. In the religious world, those who do these things are accepted, and those who do not do them are rejected. For this reason, religion leads to exclusiveness.

The Lord Jesus Himself is very inclusive, but religion makes us exclusive. It causes us to condemn other people, but the Lord wants to receive these people to Himself. Look at how pure the Lord was in the Gospels. He did not interact with people to develop His work or to gain success. Christ responded to each situation in such a pure way, only caring for God's interest. However, the more we are in religion, the more we condemn. If we are in religion, we always judge who is right and who is wrong, what is approved and what is not. If we are pure, we don't care for these things. Instead, we trust the Lord, who is everything to us. Our purity can never come through our natural effort. It is the Lord Himself who is the reality of purity. As we allow His ray to work in us, we become like Him. This frees us from religion. By His judging ray, we are kept pure from religious falsehood. We care only for His interest, and we receive all whom He receives.

As the Lord shines His purifying ray into our being, we will experience His judging, and we will be strengthened to stand with His terminating work in us. So many things of self will be burned away. This ray also heals us and supplies us. As the Lord shines into us, He generates in us the discerning ability that is so vital in the church life. We will know the things that are excellent. Through this process, we will become healthy before the Lord, and we will know what it is to be "filled with the fruit of righteousness which comes through Jesus Christ, to the glory and praise of God" (Phil. 1:11).

# 10

## Living according to a Divine Commitment

*Now I want you to know, brethren, that my circumstances have turned out for the greater progress of the gospel, so that my imprisonment in the cause of Christ has become well known throughout the whole praetorian guard and to everyone else, and that most of the brethren, trusting in the Lord because of my imprisonment, have far more courage to speak the word of God without fear. Some, to be sure, are preaching Christ even from envy and strife, but some also from good will; the latter do it out of love, knowing that I am appointed for the defense of the gospel; the former proclaim Christ out of selfish ambition rather than from pure motives, thinking to cause me distress in my imprisonment. What then? Only that in every way, whether in pretense or in truth, Christ is proclaimed; and in this I rejoice. Yes, and I will rejoice.*

*—Philippians 1:12–18*

In the first eleven verses of Philippians, Paul laid the groundwork. In verse 11 he wrote, "Having been filled with the fruit of righteousness which comes through Jesus Christ, to the glory and praise of God." We almost expect Paul to conclude his letter at this point, adding only, "Please pray for me in my imprisonment." Yet, although he was confined and in a very poor situation, he announced that his confinement had "turned out for the greater progress of the gospel" (v. 12). Two things had happened. First, his chains were manifested as

61

being in Christ "throughout the whole praetorian guard and to everyone else" (v. 13). Second, others, trusting in the Lord because of Paul's imprisonment, were emboldened to speak for Christ (v. 14). Because of Paul's bonds, Christ was being preached. Since Paul was regulated by a divine commitment, whatever situation he was in resulted in the greater progress of the gospel.

## Paul's Impact on the Unbelievers

Paul had already thanked the Lord for the Philippian believers' "participation in the gospel" (v. 5). Now he wanted to let them know that, even in his bonds, he was still pioneering in the gospel among the praetorian guard who watched over him. These elite soldiers were responsible for guarding the palace and those who, like Paul, were awaiting Caesar's judgment.

Paul claimed in verse 13 that his "imprisonment in the cause of Christ" had "become well known throughout the whole praetorian guard, and to everyone else." The Greek word for "well known" is *phaneros*, which is from the root, *phainō*, meaning "to shine, to light up" (Kittel, p. 1244). The result of this shining is that something is manifested, made known, evident, and clearly seen. Paul was saying that his bonds were being manifest clearly as being in Christ and that this testimony was evident to the whole praetorian guard and everyone else. He realized that the effect he had on his guards would in due time have an impact on the entire group. Through this one captive, the gospel of Christ was advancing out from the very heart of the Roman Empire. Eventually his ministry would have an impact on the entire earth.

We should have this view as we labor. For example, if we go to a university to preach the gospel, we should have the confidence that the whole campus will be stirred up by us. Perhaps we only preach in a small corner of the campus, but we have faith that in due time our preaching will impact the entire campus.

## Paul's Impact on the Believers

Paul's bonds not only manifested something of Christ among his captors; they also caused most of the believers to have increased confidence in the Lord (v. 14). This emboldened them to speak for Christ. Paul's pattern caused the believers to become bold to proclaim the gospel without fear.

They became confident in the Lord when they saw that Paul's testimony to them was borne out in his bonds. This gave them the boldness to preach the same gospel Paul preached. Some may have received the gospel without the full assurance of its worth. However, after seeing Paul's boldness in his captivity, they became more confident in what they had believed. As a result, they had "far more courage to speak the word of God without fear" (v. 14).

## A Grand Heart

Paul's grandness is displayed in what follows. Some were preaching Christ out of envy and strife, not sincerely but out of selfish ambition, supposing to cause Paul distress in his imprisonment (vv. 15, 17). Others did so from goodwill, out of love for the apostle, knowing that he was appointed for the defense of the gospel (vv. 15–16). Paul's appraisal of all this was only that Christ was being proclaimed (v. 18). This was his commitment, what he focused on, the very thing that gave his life meaning. Even if others' speaking was calculated to do him harm, as long as Christ was being proclaimed, he was joyful.

To our thought, such impure gospel preaching would surely bring forth nothing good. Doesn't the tree determine the fruit (Matt. 7:17–18)? In fact, we might assume that the Lord would withhold His blessing from those who preached out of envy. However, God honors the name of Christ for the sake of those who hear, even though He may not honor those who proclaim it. Therefore, we may sometimes hear that a certain group has a very large turnout or response to their work. Whether or not they are purely for Christ is for God to judge. Eventually He will say to those who preach impurely, "I never knew you; depart from Me, you who practice lawlessness!" (Matt. 7:22–23). However, the Lord does not withhold His blessing when the name of Christ is proclaimed.

Paul recognized that even those who preached Christ from envy were his brothers. He was against any teaching that distracted from Christ, but he always tried to avoid confrontation that might result in division. For instance, he never forced anyone to choose between himself and other ministers of the Lord (1 Cor. 1:10–13). While others preached Christ impurely, adding other things, Paul simply stayed focused on his commitment, rejoicing that Christ was being proclaimed. Such grandness marks a true servant of the Lord. How great his heart was, and what a pattern this is to us!

## Christ Plus Something Else

God only wants Christ, but religion always adds something else. When a church begins to receive something in addition to Christ, that church loses Christ as its center, and starts to institutionalize. Those who preach Christ plus someone or something else think Christ Himself is not enough—in addition to Christ, something else is required. Such reasoning changes our whole Christian experience.

Some make certain persons an issue, as the Corinthians did (1 Cor. 1:11–13). It is true that we should honor those who have led us in Christ. As they follow Christ, they become our example (1 Cor. 11:1). We should closely follow their "teaching, conduct, purpose, faith, patience, love, perseverance, persecutions, and sufferings" (2 Tim. 3:10–11). Such persons, however, cannot replace Christ Himself.

Teachings are another thing that can replace Christ as our center. No church can survive without teachings to justify its existence. However, such teachings can become the "plus" in our Christian experience. Paul's gospel was only Christ. The

Judaizers added affliction to Paul's chains by preaching Christ plus the law, which included practices such as circumcision, dietary regulations, and the observance of the Sabbath. They promoted their teachings using the name of Christ while actually drawing people away from Christ.

Practices can replace Christ as well. Actually, practices can cause even more damage than a person or a teaching, for practices are easy to grasp. It is easy to do what others are doing rather than look to the Lord. Our practice, however, should be a matter of the Lord's leading. Otherwise, what is of Christ will eventually be swallowed up by outward movements.

## The Corrupting Power of Envy

The word translated "envy" in verse 15, *phthonos*, is closely related to the verb *phtheirō*, which means to corrupt, defile, or even destroy (Strong, nos. 5355 and 5351). Paul only cared for the advancement of the gospel, while others preached Christ out of envy and strife (Phil. 1:15). When the self-life develops this way, it seeks to destroy the person it envies. If this is our case, we will feel relief at the downfall of the one we envy instead of feeling a genuine concern for that person. We should fight for what the Lord has committed to us, and this includes all those with whom He has placed us. When we are caught by envy, however, we no longer struggle on that person's behalf. Envy can even drive people to use the basest tactics to smear or discredit those they view as a threat to their own person, teaching, practice, or ministry. When we hold only to Christ, however, such things have no ground within us. Since envy and jealousy are with every one of us, we need the Lord's mercy and grace that we would not allow these to develop into something that damages His body.

Envy and jealousy eventually issue in strife. Because Lucifer was envious of God's position, he became Satan (Isa. 14:12–15). It is because of envy that the entire world system arose. Envy, if fostered, causes people to seek to destroy those who are its target. The religious leaders who sought the Lord's death did so out of envy (Mark 15:10). In the same way, some Christians undermine other Christians because of envy. We should not forget that the religious world is a part of the satanic system, which is born of envy and conducive to it.

### Differing Motives in Preaching Christ

Some preached Christ from good will and out of love (Phil. 1:15–16). The Greek word for "love" here is *agapē*, which is the highest love. Such love swallows up all our feelings of envy. It allows us to focus on Christ and pursue Him as Paul did.

Those opposing Paul preached Christ "out of selfish ambition, rather than from pure motives" (v. 17). To preach without sincerity is to preach with no holy motive. Their goal was to add affliction to Paul's chains. I believe those associated with James were in a position to intervene on Paul's behalf before he was taken to Rome but chose to do nothing. This is tragic, but such things do happen when people get caught by religion rather than Christ. In contrast, Paul acted out of love, even encouraging the collection of money for the believers in Jerusalem by the churches he had raised up (1 Cor. 16:1–3).

### Rejoicing in Grace

Whoever does the genuine work of the Lord, as Paul did, will become a target. Paul could have responded by attacking others but didn't. As others sought to destroy him, he rejoiced that, whether in pretense or in truth, Christ was being proclaimed (v. 18).

Paul's rejoicing was not merely happiness; it was an enjoyment of grace. The Greek word for "rejoice" in verse 18, *chairō*, is the root of the Greek word for grace, *charis* (Strong, nos. 5463 and 5485). Rejoicing in such an environment and under such circumstances requires grace. To endure is one thing, but to truly rejoice is another. Paul could rejoice because he was one with Christ. He could say, "If Christ is being proclaimed, I rejoice, regardless of the motive. I am enjoying grace, which no man can take from me."

## Governed by a
## Divine Commitment

Those who live without a commitment live an empty life. Those who live according to the divine commitment live a life full of meaning and will see the gospel advance wherever they go. They will be able to rejoice regardless of what others may do because they only care for the working out of the divine commitment. From my youth, I have been clear that I must serve the Lord according to what He has revealed to me. Therefore, whether I was a student, a librarian, or a full-time Christian worker, my life has been full of meaning.

A person of commitment is one whose life has meaning, regardless of circumstances. Paul was able to have such a grand heart because he was governed by what the Lord had committed to him. Whether he worked with his hands, journeyed to raise up churches, or was imprisoned in chains, his life always had purpose. I hope we all could be governed by such a divine commitment.

# 11

# The Assurance of Further Salvation

*What then? Only that in every way, whether in pretense or in truth, Christ is proclaimed; and in this I rejoice. Yes, and I will rejoice, for I know that this will turn out for my deliverance through your prayers and the provision of the Spirit of Jesus Christ.*
*—Philippians 1:18–19*

## Paul's Rejoicing

From verse 12 of this chapter onward, Paul made his stand clear. He was absolutely for that which God had committed to him. He did not waver from this divine commitment, even in the most extreme circumstances. He was able to rejoice, even if Christ was being preached by some "evil workers" who intended to cause him distress in his imprisonment (Phil. 1:16, 18; 3:2). In spite of their efforts, Paul never left his stand. He could not be drawn off to retaliate. Even though he had a reason to, he could not be brought to attack those who were mistreating him.

We may think that he should have done more to expose them. The Judaizers dogged his footsteps from city to city, teaching Christ plus ordinances and troubling every church that Paul had raised up. In their envy, they preached Christ from selfish ambition, not purely, and perverted the gospel of Christ (Phil. 1:15, 17; Gal. 1:7). While Paul was in prison, he may have received reports that one church was having a conference concerning the

Sabbath and another was being counseled to be circumcised. Through this speaking, the Judaizers were trying to tear down all of Paul's labor in the gospel. Their desire was to make the gospel of grace of none effect (cf. Mark 7:13). In spite of all this, however, Paul could say, "What then? Only that in every way, whether in pretense or in truth, Christ is proclaimed; and in this I rejoice. Yes, and I will rejoice" (Phil. 1:18). To him, as long as Christ was being proclaimed, God's commitment was still being carried out.

Such grandness is the mark of a genuine servant of the Lord. His grandness, however, did not mean he was willing to sacrifice the churches or the truth in the name of being tolerant. Rather, it simply indicated that he was happy to see the Spirit working, regardless of the means. In the process, however, he surely suffered, for he longed to see the fulfillment of what God had committed to him, and the preaching of the Judaizers was frustrating this.

The ability to rejoice is a high virtue of the Christian life. It is not psychological, emotional, or of the will. Nor is rejoicing merely the ability to endure things. True rejoicing only comes with the enjoyment of God's grace. When grace comes to us, we become one with the Lord and enjoy His sweetness and tranquility. Rejoicing is the spontaneous result. Alarming and even drastic situations may arise, or things may happen that are encouraging and pleasant, but we stand firm with the Lord in His commitment, enjoying His grace. Paul stood firm. He enjoyed Christ, and Christ was being preached, so he was happy. This was how he chose to live.

## Subjective Knowing

In verse 19, Paul said, "For I know that this will turn out for my deliverance." Paul had the assurance to say, "I know" based upon his subjective experience and spiritual sense or intuition. One person's subjective knowledge can be deeper than another's, based upon their levels of experience. For instance, young believers who are late for work may pray, "Lord, hold the bus for me." Then they may feel peace as though their prayer was answered, and sure enough, the bus is still there. Even though such an experience is not very advanced, it is still a genuine experience of the Lord and causes us to know Him. Such knowing of the Lord should underlie everything in our Christian life. If we do not progress in this kind of knowing and do not have much experience of Christ in our daily life, we will be frustrated in our Christian life and church life. Our experience of knowing must continually advance.

To speak lightly about others indicates a lack of regulation by a rich inward knowing. Our speech and behavior should be governed by the inner knowledge that comes from the Spirit's anointing (1 John 2:20, 27), the inner constitution of the divine life (John 10:10; 8:12), and the equipping of the divine truth (1 John 2:21; 2 John 4). This inner sense, or knowing, should regulate and lead us in our daily life. Without it, we may find ourselves speaking nonsense. If we only have outward knowledge without ever having developed the inner ability to walk in oneness with Christ, we may feel free to do or say whatever we please. Having this experience of "I know" is crucial.

## The Church's Prayer and the Spirit's Supply

When Paul wrote Philippians, he was not in an easy situation. He was imprisoned, waiting to appear before Caesar. While he was being held in Rome, others were preaching a perverted gospel among the churches that he had raised up. A leader of one of these churches might have written, "Paul, you told us to focus on Christ. Now we are being told we will be in trouble if we don't also keep the law. Dear brother, what should we do?" Paul must have been troubled by this. He wouldn't simply say, "It doesn't matter. It is in the Lord's hands." He surely had a lot of feeling. I believe he shed many tears. Yet in spite of this, he was rejoicing (Phil. 1:18), for he had an expectation. Within him there was a knowing that this would neither defeat nor destroy him but would turn out for his deliverance.

The Greek word for "deliverance" in verse 19, *sōtēria*, indicates more than merely being delivered from prison; it also means "salvation" (Strong, no. 4991). Paul indicated that two things would turn the situation for his salvation: the prayer of the Philippians and the supply of the Spirit of Jesus Christ. We should know how to intercede for those who are serving the Lord. No matter how spiritual they are, they need our petition. We should not just leave them to labor on the front lines without our prayer.

The Greek word for "provision," *epichorēgia*, is from the root word *chorēgeō*, which means "'to lead a stage chorus or dance'...then, 'to defray the expenses of a chorus;' hence, later, metaphorically, 'to supply,'" (Vine, 4:94). In ancient times, troupes of actors would travel from city to city and perform works of drama and theater. Such a group was called a chorus and was sponsored by a wealthy patron, called a choragus, who would provide whatever was needed to make the performance a success. Paul's choice of words indicated that he was putting Christ on display in Rome. The choragus who was richly supplying him for this display was the Spirit of Jesus Christ Himself. For his magnification of Christ, Paul was inwardly being supplied with all the riches of the Spirit of Jesus Christ. Paul needed both this supply and the prayer of the church to elevate his experience of salvation to another level that he might display Christ to every person who saw him in any situation at any time.


## Paul's Desire to Advance

Paul was a spiritual man. He experienced being caught up to the third heaven and to Paradise where he heard "inexpressible words, which a man is not permitted to speak" (2 Cor. 12:4). He received revelation upon revelation of Christ, and he was given to "fully carry out the preaching of the word of God" (Col. 1:25). How, then, could Paul say that he still needed salvation?

Paul wanted to press on (Phil. 3:12–14). He desired more transformation, increased revelation, and a higher experience of this marvelous salvation. I believe that by this time, Paul had been saved about twenty-five years. He had attained a high degree of spiritual maturity. Even so, his desire was to experience something further of Christ's salvation in his spirit, his soul, his body, and his environment. In all of our lives, we need the Lord's saving work in these four areas.

Paul had the assurance that he would experience the Lord's further salvation because he had the prayers of the church and the rich supply of the Spirit of Jesus Christ.

# 12

# Magnifying Christ and Living for Others

*According to my earnest expectation and hope, that I will not be put to shame in anything, but that with all boldness, Christ will even now, as always, be exalted in my body, whether by life or by death. For to me, to live is Christ and to die is gain. But if I am to live on in the flesh, this will mean fruitful labor for me; and I do not know which to choose. But I am hard-pressed from both directions, having the desire to depart and be with Christ, for that is very much better; yet to remain on in the flesh is more necessary for your sake. Convinced of this, I know that I will remain and continue with you all for your progress and joy in the faith, so that your proud confidence in me may abound in Christ Jesus through my coming to you again.*

*—Philippians 1:20–26*

## Paul's Expectation and Hope

Paul was on display twenty-four hours a day while a prisoner in Rome, for he was always under the watchful eye of his guards. It was his earnest expectation and hope that in this environment he would not be put to shame, that is, he would not display something other than Christ, such as despair, vexation, or murmuring. Some were trying to cause him distress in his imprisonment (Phil. 1:17), but his divine commission was to magnify Christ. He had brought Christ to Rome, and he was confident that he would enter, through the Philippians' prayer and the ever-sufficient supply of the Spirit, into a higher realm of salvation than he had ever known (v. 19).

Expectation and hope are closely related, but not identical. For instance, as Christians, our hope is Christ's coming again, but we don't all live as though we are expecting Him. If someone were to say, "Christ is coming back tonight!" we would all stop whatever we were doing and run off to repent. We all hope the Lord will come, but most of us would ask Him to wait, for we lack an earnest expectation and do not feel prepared. If we all earnestly expected the Lord's return, perhaps He would have arrived by now, for His bride would have made herself ready (Rev. 19:7), matching her hope with a fervent desire. Hope is our stand; expectation produces our readiness. Paul's expectation and hope were to magnify Christ as he was on display in Rome.

## Boldness to Magnify Christ

As Paul was being led about in chains, it would have appeared that he was a common criminal. In that shameful situation, however, he could boldly say, "I will not be put to shame in anything, but that with all boldness, Christ will even now, as always, be exalted in my body" (v. 20). The Greek word for "exalt" in this verse is *megalunō*, which means "enlarge, magnify, show large" (Strong, no. 3170). Though Paul was imprisoned, he still expected Christ to be magnified in his body. The Greek word for "all boldness" is *parrhēsia* (Strong, no. 3954), from *pas* (Strong, no. 3956), which means "all" and *rheō* (Strong, no. 4483), which means "to pour forth, to utter." There was something so full in Paul that it poured forth, even in his bonds, to make Christ manifest to all who saw him. The Spirit was filling him and constituting him. The divine riches were overflowing from within him. He was rich in life, in truth, in revelation, and in experience. He never gave the feeling that there was some lack or deficiency with him or that he blamed anyone for his circumstance. Instead, wherever he went, the riches of Christ gushed out.

He was very bold. No confinement could frustrate him from magnifying Christ.

When Paul stood on trial before King Agrippa, before being sent on to Rome, he said, "I would wish to God that whether in a short or long time, not only you, but also all who hear me this day, might become such as I am, except for these chains" (Acts 26:29). How bold he was in that threatening atmosphere! Christ was magnified in his boldness. His buoyancy exalted Christ and brought honor to Him.

When the fragrance of the Spirit in our lives causes others to respect and honor Christ, He is magnified. It is more than a mere verbal declaration. We all must enjoy the Spirit to the extent that something of Christ is pouring forth from us, causing Christ to be magnified.

## To Live or to Die

Paul told the Philippians, "For to me, to live is Christ and to die is gain" (Phil. 1:21). I know of no other person in history who said such a thing and who meant it the way Paul did. On the one hand, he desired to break loose from all that held him back from fully enjoying Christ. He was not simply waiting to die a martyr's death. He was contemplating something wonderful. Paul had known and experienced the Lord for many years, yet a barrier still prevented him from knowing and experiencing his Lord in full. The only way for him to be one hundred percent with Jesus was to be loosed from the limitation of his physical existence. Even such a spiritual brother as Paul had to admit that he only knew in part (1 Cor. 13:9). Therefore he savored the possibility of being one with the Lord in eternity. To him, this was far better than living in the flesh, seeing the Lord only dimly in a mirror (1 Cor. 13:12). Today we suffer some degree of distance from the Lord, and we often sin and must come to the Lord to confess our repeated failures. However, one day we will enjoy His presence in full, face to face. In that nobler existence we shall enjoy a fellowship with the Lord that is completely unhindered.

Paul was constrained, however, by another consideration—the Philippians and their need. When he considered the believers in Philippi and how he and they had each other in their hearts, he realized that his remaining in the flesh was more needful to them. For their sake he would remain and continue with them for their progress and joy in the faith.

If Paul did not remain with the Philippians, he feared that their progress would stop; if he did remain, he could continue to lead them forward. Apparently it was up to Caesar Nero to determine whether Paul would live or die, but Nero was merely under the Lord's hand. Paul was confident that the Lord would work according to his desire to remain with the churches. This man was so spiritually mature that his logic matched God's desire. He had the option before the Lord to live or to die, and he chose to continue his earthly labors, for he realized that this was best for the Philippians.

The only things that held Paul to this earth were the believers and the local churches. May the Lord give us all the same heart and help us to be the same kind of person! May we live for Christ and also for the believers who are with us!

## Becoming a Cause
## for Rejoicing

Paul concluded this section by saying that he would come to the Philippians again that their confidence in him might abound in Christ Jesus (Phil. 1:26). No doubt, the experiences Paul passed through since he had last seen the Philippians had changed him. He had conveyed a monetary offering from the Gentile churches to the believers in Jerusalem with the hope of keeping the oneness and fellowship between the Jewish and Gentile churches (Rom. 15:25–31). His desire was nearly defeated by the religious atmosphere in Jerusalem (Acts 21:20). In his attempt to maintain the oneness with the Jewish believers, he joined them in keeping the law (Acts 21:21–26) and as a result, was imprisoned. Perhaps the Philippians wondered what had happened to him. But he could say, "When I come to see you again, it is so that your confidence in me might abound in Christ Jesus. You have seen a zealous Paul, an aggressive Paul, a struggling Paul, a preaching Paul, and a firm Paul. But when you see me again, you will see a spiritual Paul. I now realize there is no need to try to please anyone other than Christ. In Jerusalem I woke up, and in my imprisonment I have seen even more. I tried my best to keep the oneness in the body, but now I realize this oneness only comes through Christ." Paul had progressed, and through this progress, the rejoicing of the Philippians in Jesus Christ would be more abundant.

It should be the same with every one of us. We should not be the same as we were two years ago. We all need to grow. Then others will have reason to rejoice because of us in Jesus Christ.

## 13

# A Conduct Worthy of the Gospel of Christ

*Only conduct yourselves in a manner worthy of the gospel of Christ, so that whether I come and see you or remain absent, I will hear of you that you are standing firm in one spirit, with one mind striving together for the faith of the gospel; in no way alarmed by your opponents—which is a sign of destruction for them, but of saalvation for you, and that too, from God. For to you it has been granted for Christ's sake, not only to believe in Him, but also to suffer for His sake, experiencing the same conflict which you saw in me, and now hear to be in me.*
—*Philippians 1:27–30*

### Conduct according to Citizenship

Paul charged the Philippians to conduct themselves in a manner worthy of the gospel of Christ. The Greek word for "conduct" is *politeuomai* (Strong, no. 4176), which means "to behave as a citizen." It suggests a behavior consistent with whatever culture or kingdom one belongs to. High school boys tend to walk in a certain way, thinking that it is attractive to girls. Graduates of a famous university may carry themselves differently than those from another college. Residents of a major cosmopolitan center may act differently than those from a small town. Our conduct is based upon our realization of what kingdom we belong to. This is why Paul wrote, "Conduct yourselves in a manner worthy of the gospel of Christ" (Phil. 1:27). It is not a matter of behaving according to some code of morality. We are in the divine kingdom that displays God's testimony on the earth. Our behavior should match our heavenly citizenship (3:20).

## A Worthy Conduct

In verse 27, the Greek word translated "worthy" is *axiōs*, the root of which means "weighing, having weight, having the weight of another thing of like value, worth as much" (Thayer, p. 52). This implies that we should conduct ourselves by weighing what is appropriate for the greater progress of the gospel of Christ. The gospel of Christ should be the element that leads us and by which we measure our living. The conduct of a healthy believer is weighed and deemed appropriate in light of the gospel of Christ. When we make a decision, the gospel of Christ should be the factor by which we weigh things. When our living matches the gospel of Christ, our decision is right.

When I came to the United States forty years ago, the gospel of Christ was the element that governed my decision. Therefore, my conduct was worthy of the gospel. I was seeking to live the life that, according to God's kingdom, was best. All of us should weigh our conduct by what is best for the gospel of Christ. Our existence should be measured according to the gospel of Christ. If we live in this kingdom, every decision we make will be worthy of it. We will choose whatever furthers this gospel. The gospel will be the living element that animates all our manner of life.

## Four Matters for a Worthy Conduct

In describing a conduct worthy of the gospel of Christ, Paul presented four matters. First, we should stand "firm in one spirit, with one mind striving together for the faith of the gospel" (Phil.

1:27). We should struggle together alongside other believers who share our same commitment. Second, we should in no way be alarmed by our opponents (v. 28). We will confront opposition. This opposition does not necessarily come from without. It may come from religious zealots who turn people away from Christ as the rightful center of the church. Third, to us "it has been granted for Christ's sake...to suffer for His sake" (v. 29). We must remember that Christ suffered first. And fourth, we have the same conflict as those who, like the apostle Paul, are struggling to uphold us before the Lord (v. 30).

## In One Spirit, with One Soul

The first item needed for a conduct worthy of the gospel of Christ is to "stand firm in one spirit, with one mind striving together for the faith of the gospel" (Phil. 1:27). The word "mind" here can also be translated "soul" (Kittel, p. 1342). To stand fast in one spirit is to be in the organic oneness of the divine life; to strive together with one soul is to take the gospel of Christ as our focus. Our standing fast in one spirit spontaneously results from the divine life shared by all believers. The moment we touch this life, we become one spirit organically with all other believers. To be one soul with others, however, is not as easy as being one spirit with them. Think of all the different kinds of souls among Christians. Some are quiet and reserved; others are outgoing and even wild. How can we be one soul? The secret is to humble ourselves, as the Lord did (2:8). With humility of mind toward one another (2:3), we must focus on Christ and His gospel.

Any time our soul is distracted from Christ, we become opinionated and are no longer one soul with those who are simply for the gospel of Christ. Even debating about biblical truths can cause us to lose the experience of being one soul. When our soul is unto the gospel of Christ, however, we are able to strive together with one soul. To be one soul requires that we share the same unique focus—the gospel of Christ.

## Striving Together

When we become focused upon the gospel of Christ, we begin to experience something called "striving." In verse 27, the Greek word for "striving together" is *sunathleō* (Strong, no. 4866), which comes from the root word *athleō* (Strong, no. 118), meaning "to contend in the competitive games." As we strive together, there is a prize in view, so we dare not slow down or become distracted. If we together have such a heart and exercise, we will be able to run with endurance, for our whole being will be occupied with winning the prize (Heb. 12:1; 1 Cor. 9:24–25). When we are focused on the gospel of Christ, we enjoy an organic relatedness as members of His body, and spontaneously we desire to run together so that the gospel of Christ may achieve its goal.

## Striving for the Faith
## of the Gospel

Paul told the Philippians to strive together "for the faith of the gospel" (1:27). What was it that caused us to begin running this race, and why are we still running it? What keeps drawing us on?

When Paul reached the end of his journey, he appeared to have nothing left. The churches in Asia had turned away from him (2 Tim. 1:15), and many of his coworkers had deserted him (2 Tim. 4:10). He had no vast work to look upon for encouragement. He had just a few brothers who were still faithful. He had nearly nothing to show for his life-long labor. Yet he was happy and could say, "I have fought the good fight, I have finished the course, I have kept the faith; in the future there is laid up for me the crown of righteousness" (2 Tim. 4:7–8). His whole life was for Christ and His gospel. He was able to say that he had kept the faith. When the church becomes messy and nothing around us is encouraging, Christ Himself operates more and more to be our true encouragement to continue striving together for the faith of the gospel.

I began pursuing the Lord in 1954. You may ask, "How have you been able to continue striving for the faith of the gospel for so many years?" It is not because of me. I know I am here because the Lord has been faithfully operating; I just kept responding. I don't know how it happened—I just became a Jesus lover. It is the Lord who has been attracting and drawing me, and He has called me on. I could have had a comfortable life and a successful career. I gave that all up to serve the Lord, and today, by His mercy, I am still focused on the faith of the gospel.

## Not Alarmed by Our Opponents

The second item needed for a conduct worthy of the gospel of Christ is to in no way be alarmed by our opponents. As we are standing fast in one spirit, with one soul striving together for the faith of the gospel, we shall encounter opposition. A healthy local church will always confront religious "dogs" (Phil. 3:2). So many have been hurt by the biting of these dogs, who talk of things other than Christ. After such "fellowship," they end up wounded and bleeding, yet often do not know why. As a result, they begin to withdraw from full participation in the church life.

It would seem that Paul should have said, "Kick all such dogs out of the church. Excommunicate them!" However, he never did this. It is inevitable that when believers begin to strive together for the faith of the gospel, there will be some who raise questions and plant doubts. Often when Christians begin to lose their love for the Lord and their church, it is because of this. If we were to question them, we would find that their withdrawing began right after receiving "fellowship" from a particular person. In Paul's day, religious zealots from Jerusalem sought to bring the believers of all the churches into law-keeping, such as circumcision, the Sabbath, and dietary regulations (Acts 15:1). This raised questions and doubts concerning the gospel Paul preached. Paul realized that after a church is established, such dogs will certainly come to oppose the pure gospel of Christ and replace it with a mixture of Christ plus something else.

As we stand fast in one spirit, with one soul, we strive together to bring the faith of the gospel to those around us. In this way, God's goal can be accomplished. When the church life is like this, it is wonderful! When this takes place, be assured that some will come in and draw people away from the experience of the faith of the gospel. However, Paul's word indicates that their works will come to nothing, for they will experience destruction (Phil. 1:28; 3:19). We do not need to deal directly with those who oppose. The Lord will take care of them. The gospel that Paul and his coworkers preached eventually prevailed. Even to this day, the faith of the gospel of Christ still prevails as we strive together in one spirit and with one soul.

## Suffering for Christ's Sake

The third item needed for a conduct worthy of the gospel is that we suffer for the sake of Christ. When we look at the situation of so many believers today, we should be brought to tears. So many have been hurt and drawn away from this gospel by religious zealots promoting something other than Christ. This causes a real suffering for those who have a heart for the building up of Christ's body. Christ has suffered the most. Our sufferings reveal that we are one with Him. It has been graciously granted to us "for Christ's sake, not only to believe in Him, but also to suffer for His sake" (1:29). His sufferings produced the church, yet today the church as His bride still is not ready for Him (Rev. 19:7). Since Christ's bride is produced out of Christ Himself, our focus in the churches must be upon Christ alone. We must pursue Christ, gain Christ, grow in Christ, and be built up in Christ. For this to occur, there is no way but to suffer.

Therefore, let others have the benefits, the comforts, the recognition, the power, and the wealth. The disciples might have felt very hopeful when the Lord said, "All authority has been given to Me in heaven and on earth" (Matt. 28:18), but His work was to go to the cross. The Lord's sufferings for the church must become ours. Since we are one with Him, we share in His work and in the sufferings that are necessary for the building up of the church. Our suffering with Him is a great honor that the Lord has graciously bestowed upon us. We are not only His believers; we are His co-sufferers, not for the accomplishment of redemption, which only He could do, but as His co-laborers for His present work of building up His body (Col. 1:24).

If you are determined to stand firm in one spirit, with one mind striving together for the sake of the gospel, you must be prepared to suffer. Much of the suffering we experience is the result of religious dogs drawing believers away from the gospel of Christ. The dear ones who are affected by the dogs lose their joy and resolve. Some fall away from the church life; others remain, but no longer trust the church leaders. What a suffering! Yet we have to learn to trust all such things to the Lord. We should not seek to root out those who cause such suffering. Instead, we must continue to struggle forward so that the Lord may gain what He is after. Let us leave everything to the Lord. He has a way to deal with every situation. We need His mercy that we ourselves would not oppose Him by promoting something other than Christ and His gospel.

## Experiencing the Same Conflict

The fourth and last item needed for a conduct worthy of the gospel is that we have the same conflict as those who, like the apostle Paul, are struggling to uphold us before the Lord. Thank the Lord for those who serve Him for His gospel and who share our struggle. They want to hear of our affairs, that we are standing firm in one spirit, with one mind striving together for the faith of the gospel (Phil. 1:27).

When Paul said, "Experiencing the same conflict which you saw in me" (v. 30), many of the Philippians would have had a lot of feeling. Paul was referring to the days when he first arrived in

Philippi to bring the gospel to that city (Acts 16). The Philippians witnessed his struggle at that time. Paul and Silas were put in prison. They could have had many reasons to think that they had made a big mistake. Paul could have wondered, "Why did I ever believe that dream of the Macedonian man? Now everything is finished." They could have looked at each other and wept. Instead, they joyfully sang hymns, even though they had no idea that the Lord would release them. How could they do that? It was because this faith within them caused them to struggle forward even as they were shackled in that discouraging cell. As they enjoyed and magnified Christ, singing hymns together, an earthquake miraculously opened the prison doors and loosed the prisoners' chains. The jailer received the Lord, and his entire family was saved and baptized.

Now, as Paul wrote to them, he was once again imprisoned, and he wanted the Philippians to know that his struggle still remained the same—to enjoy and magnify Christ. Even those who had a hand in Paul's imprisonment could not cause him to fall away from this stand. In Philippi he had continued steadfast, even though everything seemed to be going in favor of those who opposed him, and now in Rome he knew even more clearly that his struggle was not in vain. He encouraged the Philippians with these words.


## Our Stand

The Judaizers had their arguments as to why the Philippians should keep the Law of Moses after believing in Christ. However, Paul told the Philippians to stand fast and strive together for the faith of the gospel. He encouraged them to conduct themselves in a manner worthy of the gospel, behaving as citizens of the Lord's kingdom. They had witnessed Paul's struggle among them for the gospel, and now they were entering into this same struggle.

Likewise, we are not standing upon a certain teaching or practice. Our stand is for Christ alone. In nothing should we be frightened by the zealots who promote things other than Christ. Instead, we should be willing to suffer so that the body of Christ may be built up among us. We have received the same gospel Paul preached. Now we need to stand firm in what we have received and strive together for the faith of the gospel.

# 14

# Encouragement, Consolation, Fellowship, Affection, and Compassion

*Therefore if there is any encouragement in Christ, if there is any consolation of love, if there is any fellowship of the Spirit, if any affection and compassion.*

—*Philippians 2:1*

Philippians 2 begins with "therefore." By this simple word, Paul indicated that, based on the previously stated facts of conducting ourselves in a manner worthy of the gospel (1:27–30)—being proper among ourselves, toward the Lord, toward those who oppose, and toward the apostles—there should be encouragement in Christ, consolation of love, fellowship of the Spirit, and affection and compassion. All of these virtues become the basis of our fellowship with one another.

### Encouragement in Christ

The Greek word for "encouragement" in this verse is *paraklēsis*, which is composed from two Greek root words. The first is *para*, which means "beside" (Kittel, p. 771). When we properly encourage others, we do not merely encourage them to go on. Rather, something of us goes with them for their going on. In our encouragement, we walk beside them. The second Greek root word is *klēsis*, which means "calling" (Kittel, p. 394). The thought is one of purposeful support, that is, we walk alongside others to strengthen them to conduct themselves in a manner worthy of the gospel of Christ (Phil. 1:27).

This is an "encouragement in Christ"—that is, it is carried out in Christ. We stand by one another in Christ. It is very different from much of the encouragement we usually offer one another. If someone is discouraged, we may say, "Cheer up. Tomorrow will be better. Look unto Jesus!" However, the encouragement that Paul spoke of is in Christ, based on all that He is and all that He has accomplished. When we begin to see, understand, and experience the purpose for which the Lord called us, we experience true encouragement. Such encouragement only comes from being one with the divine calling. It elevates us to a higher plane. The more we are captured by divine revelation, the more we experience this encouragement.

## Consolation of Love

The Greek word for "consolation" here also begins with the prefix pará. This indicates that consolation, like encouragement, is not merely a matter of words. Consolation requires that we invest our person in what we speak. Only when our person and our words are one will the consolation we supply be genuine and effective. We have all experienced two kinds of consolation. Some people try to console merely with words, while others have their person invested. They do not come to us just to carry out the job of consoling. Their heart is with us and remains with us even after they leave.

The consolation that Paul was seeking in 2:1 is "consolation of love." The Greek word for "love" here is *agapē*. The verb form of this word means "to love out of an intelligent estimate of the object of love"; it "contemplates the attributes and character" of what is loved (Vincent, 4:167). In other words, it is a love that treasures its object. It is often said that *agapē* love is God's love. This is true, but more accurately, *agapē* is the love of what is esteemed to be of high value. In the Septuagint, the word *agapē* is used when speaking of parents' love for their children, because parents prize and value their children above all else and seek what is best for them.

When we are caring for our fellow believers, do we value them in this way? If not, then what we offer them is not true consolation. This is why some abandon the church even after receiving our care. We may protest, saying, "We visited them and even brought them gifts." The fact is, however, that we did not love them with this kind of love, for we felt we could afford to lose them. No parents would have such a heart toward their children. If we want to console others, we must value them as if they were our own children.

When we treasure others with this kind of love, we no longer react merely to human need. Before the Lord, we consider their situation from every angle and take precautions on their behalf, seeking what is best for them. We essentially give up our own rights so that they may grow in Christ. If we possess this kind of love, we will be able to offer genuine consolation to others.

When we console others, we should do so out of the high value we ascribe to them, being willing to pay any price. Furthermore, we should console others according to Christ and the experience of Christ (2 Cor. 1:3–4). As we experience Christ and as we are with others, we bring them this experiential Christ for their consolation. When we are so one with Christ, we can truly console others in love.

Sometimes instead of being rich in encouragement and consolation, we are rich in personal preferences. If we can only love those who share our views and practices, our *agapē* love has disappeared, for we no longer value others according to Christ. For a healthy church life, there is much need of encouragement in Christ and consolation of love. We cannot console others, however, unless we value them above our own views and practices. Otherwise we are struggling to win others over to our preferences instead of seeking what is best for them in Christ.

## Fellowship of the Spirit

In verse 1, Paul also spoke of the "fellowship of the Spirit."

Encouragement and consolation come from being like-souled with our fellow believers, but fellowship of the Spirit comes from being one with the Spirit. In some Bible translations, Spirit is capitalized, indicating the divine Spirit. Other translations use the lowercase, indicating our human spirit. Our fellowship both with the Lord and with one another is a spiritual exercise.

## Affection and Compassion

Encouragement, consolation, and fellowship are accompanied by affection and compassion. Affection is within and is expressed through compassion. An affectionate person will do compassionate deeds.

How do we help those in a troubled situation? We should console them in Christ. We should console and treasure them in love, unveiling to them the God who gives perseverance and encouragement (Rom. 15:5). We should fellowship with them in spirit. In all this, however, we cannot have a superior attitude. We must come with humility of mind, following the Lord's example (Phil. 2:5–8).

When I was visiting a certain country to minister there, I was told that my meal at the restaurant cost what would be, for a local worker, many days' wages. I offered to pay, but the local believers insisted that they would provide for me. I allowed this once, but I decided not to eat there again, for I was happy to eat what they served in their homes. Then I heard of another who had come to minister there. After eating at that same restaurant, he informed his host that he would eat nowhere else. What a lack of feeling for the local believers! We have to be with others according to who they are. If they are poor, we should be happy to eat with them just as they eat. This is affection. Those whom we are with should sense that we are one with them. Without such a heart, there is no way to minister encouragement or consolation.

Suppose the Lord gives us a Christian brother to care for who is suffering under a heavy load. Others might try to get him to study the Bible with them. Due to his situation, however, he may not be able to receive such help, not having a heart to study at this time. This is where compassion comes in. When he says, "Things are so hard right now," we should say, "I know what you mean. Let's pray together." Our prayer with him may even be with sighing and tears.

Through encouragement, consolation, and fellowship, we bring God to others in a human way. When Moses came down from the mountain after being with the Lord for forty days and forty nights, the skin of his face was shining. Rather than subduing everyone with his countenance, he covered his face with a veil for the sake of the people (Exo. 34:28–35). Often we go to people's homes looking like Moses with his face uncovered: "Here I come. I have just been praying three hours for you!" However, those whom we visit may not be ready for a visit from God at that moment; they may instead need a visit from one who is a man like them. Moses came into the people's presence in a lowly manner. All of his glorious experience was hidden. Instead of displaying his profound enjoyment of God, he came as a common one among them. He seemed to cover up all that had been transmitted to him.

I have seen many Christian workers who refuse to cover themselves in this way. Instead, they declare their revelations and visions in the name of wanting to be used by God. Few realize that if we really want to serve others, we need a proper humanity. Many feel so able to reveal Christ and His purpose, yet they lack the humanity that makes them accessible to others. They feel like heroes in their visitations, yet what others really need, they lack. If we are without affection and compassion, we will only be able to give others doctrines and teachings. We need to learn to come to others as their fellows, in lowliness and meekness, as our Lord Jesus did.

# 15

# Being of
# the Same Mind

*Make my joy complete by being of the same mind, maintaining the same love, united in spirit, intent on one purpose. Do nothing from selfishness or empty conceit, but with humility of mind regard one another as more important than yourselves; do not merely look out for your own personal interests, but also for the interests of others.*

*—Philippians 2:2–4*

## Focusing on Christ

Paul desired that the Philippians would fulfill his joy "by being of the same mind, maintaining the same love, united in spirit, intent on one purpose" (2:2). The way for us to be of the same mind is to have the mind of Christ and to be according to Him (Phil. 2:5, Rom. 15:5). If our focus is on practices and teachings, there will always be differences. Our focus must be on Christ alone if we are going to be "united in spirit, intent on one purpose."

Every Christian has the freedom to follow the Lord's leading. Suppose some feel everyone should listen to the ministry of a certain preacher. Is this right or wrong? It may be right for some, but it is normal for the Lord to lead others differently. It is good to encourage others with what has helped us, but once we begin to insist on something, we are no longer being of the same mind or united in spirit. We should insist on nothing but Christ. If we are all focused on Him, even though we may not all be doing the same things outwardly, we are of the same mind, for we are all following the Lord. Why do some have one practice and others have a different practice? It is because of Christ and how He leads each one. We should all be focused on Christ. If our mind is occupied with Christ and His believers, we are healthy.

For instance, Paul encourages us to pray (1 Tim. 2:8, 1 Thess. 5:17), but this can take different forms. How loudly should we pray? Should everybody participate at the same time? Should we stand, sit, or kneel as we pray? What is the right way? The right way is to focus on Christ, follow His lead, and allow others to do the same.

## Doing Nothing from Selfishness or Empty Conceit

In verse 2, the phrase "united in spirit" is a translation of the Greek word *sumpsuchos*, which has also been translated "joined in soul" (Darby) and "of one accord" (NKJV). Paul tied this with "being of the same mind" and being "intent on one purpose." To Paul, being of one accord is very much related to the mind, for our mind determines who we are. In verse 3, he went deeper and stresses that we must have humility of mind.

Paul contrasted humility of mind to selfishness and empty conceit. The Greek word for "selfishness" in this verse is *eritheia*, which means "ambition, self-seeking, rivalry, self-will being an underlying idea in the word" (Vine, 2:68). It implies seeking after position and glory. Once someone has even a little manifestation or spiritual understanding, ambition can rise up. It often takes the guise of seeking to become more useful or fruitful. Such motives could be pure, but they could also be for the advancement of self. It is right for us to develop, grow, and learn to be effective in service. However, it doesn't take much to cross over into self-ambition, because appreciation and recognition from others feeds the self.

Throughout the years, I have noticed that selfish ambition is one of the most difficult matters that a Christian worker confronts. For some reason, it is difficult for us to be happy simply with pleasing the Lord. We should be careful of our motive in expanding our Christian work. For over fifty years, I have served the Lord according to the principle that if He opens a door, I enter; if He paves three feet of road, I walk three feet. We should fully utilize whatever the Lord measures to us and develop it for His interest (2 Cor. 10:13). We should not desire anything for ourselves.

Some attach themselves to those who are more influential just to have the opportunity to air their views. Even if we gain indirect influence in this way, it is not a profit to the Lord's body. Selfish ambition leads many to struggle to have the final word or the greatest prestige, even to the point that they would undermine others. They maneuver themselves into a position of authority because of selfish ambition. I have seen this happen over and over again during my years of serving the Lord.

Conceit, in contrast, is not as damaging as ambition and self-seeking, but it is something meaningless that can cheat the one controlled by it. Sometimes we boast in an experience which we have had and others have not. We think such stories will add something to our stature in the eyes of others. Such things must not possess us. The Lord is with us—isn't this enough? When the Lord returns, He will not ask about our unique experiences; He will ask, "Were you of the same mind with others in following Me?" Be careful about what occupies your mind, for your mind is your person.

## Regarding Others as More Important Than Ourselves

I consider the clause, "with humility of mind regard one another as more important than yourselves" (v. 3), to be one of the best expressions concerning the body of Christ. When our mind has the quality of humility, we are able to regard one another as more important than ourselves. Paul does not present this as an ethical teaching, as something we should do. Such a teaching could never be obeyed. We are all at the center of our own thoughts. None of us would choose to be looked down upon or treated as nothing. Would we regard others as more important than ourselves? This is not possible unless we possess humility of mind, and it is only when we discover our own inadequacy that humility of mind is generated within us.

When a new president takes office, he sails in on his victory. He has overcome many obstacles to reach that office. Once the reality of his new responsibilities sets in, however, his attitude changes, his relationship with others changes, and the way he carries his commitment changes. This is because he has come to understand his inadequacy. It is not an easy lesson.

All people like to feel they are valuable. No one is naturally humble. Even though I may not be a good cook, I still comfort myself with the knowledge that I can chop onions. My English may not be that good, but I can point to some ability in math. I can find something that bolsters my pride. In the body of Christ, however, we eventually discover that, regardless of how capable we may be, each of us is still only one member. Once we see the body of Christ, our understanding changes. We have the sense that we need the other members, and we begin to be able to regard others as more important than ourselves (1 Cor. 12:12–26).

The clause "regard one another as more important than yourselves" means to consider others "to be above, be superior in rank, authority, power" (Thayer, p. 641). This can by no means be achieved by human effort. It comes to us through the realization that we need others and that anything we may have is absolutely due to the Lord's mercy and grace.

Paul recommended Apollos to the Corinthians even though Apollos had been helped by Priscilla and Aquila, Paul's spiritual children (1 Cor. 16:12; Acts 18:24–26, 1–3). Though Apollos was Paul's spiritual grandson, Paul could say, "I planted, Apollos watered" (1 Cor. 3:6). He recognized that God worked through all the gifted members. He realized that no one person was able to carry out all of God's work. His appreciation of

Apollos's labor indicated that Paul was truly a spiritual man. He appreciated others and esteemed them better than himself in some respects, recognizing that they could do what he could not. To see the body is not a small thing.

The first mark of those who regard others as more important than themselves is the realization, "I am inadequate. Because of this, I cannot have any selfish ambition." When we are young, we feel that we are ready for anything. As we grow older, however, we begin to realize that whatever we can accomplish is totally a matter of the Lord's blessing. The move of the Spirit is a totality of His operation through so many believers.

## Looking Out for Others' Interests

The more we are able to regard others as more important than ourselves, the more we will be able to "look out...for the interests of others" (Phil. 2:4), or as Darby's New Translation reads, "regarding not each his own qualities, but each those of others also." We no longer consider only what we are able to do, but now we also begin to appreciate what others are able do. When we look at the nearby churches, we value the work of all those who are serving. When we look at our own church, we see how those with us are serving according to their God-given portion. Do we have something of value ourselves? We certainly do, yet now we are also able to value the qualities that others possess.

When we consider the believers around us one by one, we should thank the Lord for each one's portion, growth, and manifestation. The Lord is working in each of them. One may be energetic and able to lead, and another may be so sweet. They are each members of the body of Christ. As we value each member, our experience of the body is enriched. This should be such a reality in our daily living. It is not a matter of doing the same thing that others are doing. The reality of the body is high and heavenly, and it is not easily grasped. Whoever has the reality of these verses has seen the body and entered into the experience of it.

## A Mind for the Body Life

Paul's desire for the believers in Philippi was that they would be "of the same mind, maintaining the same love, united in spirit, intent on one purpose" (Phil. 2:2). When we are focused upon Christ, we think the same thing. Paul also stressed that we, in humility of mind, should regard one another as more important than ourselves (v. 3). In all these matters the mind is emphasized, for our mind is our person. Although Paul never referred to the body of Christ here, this portion is one of the most helpful with regard to the practice of the body life. The secret of living the body life is to focus only on Christ. When anything else is being exalted, whether a person, a practice, or a teaching, the reality of the body of Christ disappears. Even when we make the oneness of the body our focus, we are in danger of losing this oneness by making it an issue.

To think of others as being more important than ourselves is not something we can do naturally. We are inclined to neglect others and to lift ourselves above them, boasting in what is good about ourselves. This kind of mind, however, is not good for the body life. The mind that is good for the body life is a mind that is of one accord and is humble, regarding others as being more important. If we have such a mind, we will regard not only our own qualities, but the qualities of others also (Phil. 2:4, Darby). This kind of mind is necessary for the body life God desires.

# 16

# Having the
# Mind of Christ (1)

*Have this attitude in yourselves which was also in Christ Jesus,
who, although He existed in the form of God, did not regard
equality with God a thing to be grasped, but emptied Himself,
taking the form of a bond-servant, and being made in the likeness
of men.*

*—Philippians 2:5–7*

## The Experience of Christ

In Philippians 2:5–11, Paul presented a profound view of
the experience of Christ for the sake of accomplishing God's
eternal plan. No other verses in the entire Bible portray this
matter so clearly. In this portion, Paul carefully chose every
word as he unveiled the mystery of Christ's incarnation and
crucifixion.

The background of this portrayal of Christ is Paul's
concern for the Philippians. Unlike the Galatians, they did
not have a problem regarding matters of truth. Paul's concern
for the Philippians was their lack in the experience of Jesus'
humanity. This is why he charged them to be "of the same
mind, maintaining the same love, united in spirit, intent on
one purpose" (v. 2) and to "do nothing from selfishness or
empty conceit, but with humility of mind regard one another
as more important than yourselves" (v. 3). In our church life,
we should be the kind of person Jesus Christ is. If we are

rich not only in truth but also in the experience of Christ's humanity, if the affection and compassion Paul spoke of in verse 1 are expressed among us, then both our serving and our church life will be full of vitality.

### The Mind of Christ

The clause "have this attitude in yourselves" in verse 5 is translated "let this mind be in you" in the King James Version and in Darby's New Translation. So Paul began this section by describing the mind of Christ. Who is this Christ? He is the One "who, although He existed in the form of God, did not regard equality with God a thing to be grasped" (v. 6). Oh, what a great statement concerning Christ! Christ's existence equaled God's existence. From eternity past, His form was that of God. Intrinsically, essentially, and substantially, He was God. Our Savior existed in the form of God from eternity past. Who was God? Christ. Who was Christ? God. Where is God? In Christ. Where is Christ? In God. He and God are one. Paul's marvelous statement portrays how rich Christ's eternal preexistence was. All the deity, divinity, divine attributes, intrinsic elements, and essential virtues of God Himself dwell in this person, Christ (Col. 2:9).

The context of these verses is that Paul was dealing with the need of the believers. He presented Christ as the unique pattern. Often we hold onto our own interests at the expense of others' interests. Christ, however, possessed the unique treasure of being in the form of God. Although Christ, as God, was eternal, rich, and unlimited, He did not regard equality with God a thing to be grasped, "a thing to be seized upon or to be held fast, retained" (Thayer, p. 74). Instead, He "emptied Himself, taking the form of a bond-servant" (v. 7) for the sake of the church. This is the mind of Christ.

We should be impressed by this. Jesus did not raise His voice in the streets to proclaim who He was (Isa. 42:2). He was the very God, yet He did not count this as a thing to be held fast.

Most of us do not have this mind. When we experience God even a little, we broadcast it to the world. In our fallen condition, we grasp at things all day long. The temptation to do this will be with us our entire lives. I have seen many who have held fast to something in the church in order to become successful, but they have not become spiritual. How can we come out of such impulsive grasping at things? It is by laying hold of Christ. He provides us with another mind. We must spend time to allow Him to work His mind, His person, into us.

Many feel they deserve more than they have received, so they are not satisfied. When they see an opening to improve their lot, they try to grasp it. This is not according to the mind of Christ but of Satan, who as Lucifer initiated this kind of grasping in the universe.

## The Mind of Christ versus the Mind of Satan

There is a clear contrast between what Christ did and what Satan did as Lucifer. Christ was equal with God, yet did not hold fast to this equality; Lucifer was not equal with God but sought to seize this equality by force. Lucifer was "the anointed cherub who covers" (Ezek. 28:14). He possessed the highest position in the universe, next to God (vv. 13–15). He desired to establish his throne on the same level as God's throne; his intention was to be like God (Isa. 14:12–14). He wanted to share in God's glory. God had placed Lucifer directly under Himself, but this was not good enough for him. He was not attempting to overthrow God—no one could do that—but he wanted what God had. Because of this, he became Satan, the Adversary (Thayer, pp. 571–572).

In Christ's body, there is an organic order. This order is something sweet; it is not rigid or oppressive. We should not demand that others submit in a certain way. We should, however, recognize that God cares for us according to this organic arrangement.

In Lucifer's effort to seize equality with God, he said, "I will ascend to heaven; I will raise my throne above the stars of God....I will make myself like the Most High" (Isa. 14:13–14). He wanted to be able to say, "No!" when God said, "Yes!" and to say, "Yes!" when God said, "No!" This is what brought in God's judgment. Fallen humanity now has this same kind of mind. It can be seen in human society and even in the church life—the mind to seize equality. This is offensive to God. In His body, there is an organic order. In this order, everyone is necessary, although each is placed differently (1 Cor. 12:18). Every member is precious, and we must appreciate and value what others have.

If we love the Lord, we must let the mind of Christ be in us (Phil. 2:5). His mind was such that He let all things go, even His status as the One through whom all things were made (John 1:3). We can choose between two minds. One is that of Satan, which leads to endless grasping. The other is that of Christ, which leads to acceptance of God's arrangement. If we do not have the mind that is willing to drop all for the sake of accomplishing God's will, we will be like Satan, grasping at things that have not even been measured to us. We must have the mind of Christ if we want to satisfy God.

## Emptying Himself

Not only did the Lord "not regard equality with God a thing to be grasped" (v. 6); He also "emptied Himself" (v. 7). This is somewhat like a father who lets go of all sense of dignity as he gives his young daughter a ride on his shoulders. He happily lifts her up and allows her to steer him around the house by pulling his hair. In this way he empties himself. If that father demanded respect and honor because of all he did for his family and continually pointed out how they owed everything to his hard labor, that family would experience no real love or joy. To empty ourselves is to drop whatever status, position, or claim we may have.

## Taking the Form of a Bond-servant

When Christ emptied Himself, He did not drop His deity. Inwardly, He was God. Outwardly, however, He was not in the form of God. He took the lowest place when He became a man, not taking the form of a king but of a bond-servant. When He took this form, He emptied Himself of all the rights and enjoyments that He possessed as One who existed in the form of God.

When people become bond-servants, someone else determines what they must do, when they will eat or sleep, what money they may hold, and whom they will marry. Their future and fate lie in their masters' hands. When the Lord became a man, He took the form of a bond-servant. He became a man totally under God's hand. Inwardly He was still God, but in form He went from the highest place to the lowest.

## Being Made in the Likeness of Men

Christ's "being made in the likeness of men" (Phil. 2:7) implies that He went through a process. He only cared for what God desired. In Him there was nothing that resisted God's will. He voluntarily gave up the form of God so that He might enter into this process and accomplish the universal salvation that we partake of today. Regardless of the magnitude of the sacrifice, He went through every step of this process to fully accomplish what was in the heart of God.

If we want to live the church life, if we really want to be profitable to the body of Christ, we must let this mind be in us. When we have this mind, we place God's interests above everything else. The mind of Christ points us to the One who is carrying out God's purpose. Whatever God desires, Christ desires. Because His mind was set upon God's desire, He emptied Himself; He took the form of a bond-servant; He was made in the likeness of men. He chose to embrace God's will, emptying Himself of every other possibility. How marvelous our Christ is!

**17**

# Having the Mind of Christ (2)

*Being found in appearance as a man, He humbled Himself by becoming obedient to the point of death, even death on a cross. For this reason also, God highly exalted Him, and bestowed on Him the name which is above every name, so that at the name of Jesus every knee will bow, of those who are in heaven and on earth and under the earth, and that every tongue will confess that Jesus Christ is Lord, to the glory of God the Father.*
*—Philippians 2:8–11*

## Found in Appearance as a Man

While the Lord Jesus was on the earth, He was "found in appearance as a man" (v. 8). He was restricted and confined, needing to eat, sleep, and labor, just as we do. He grew up as a typical boy. I doubt that as a child He said to Joseph, "Do you know who I am? I am Almighty God. Make sure you behave around Me." Instead, Jesus grew just as any boy would and gradually, as His understanding grew, so also did His knowledge of who He was (Luke 2:40, 48–49). As a man, He labored as a carpenter until He was about thirty (Mark 6:3; Luke 3:23).

If it were me, I might have been tempted to reveal who I was to my brother James or my cousin John. Jesus, however, never did this. He would not be found in appearance as being different from other men. He certainly had the ability, as Satan said, to turn stones into bread, but He never did such things for His own sake. While He was among the despised Galileans, He lived as they lived. If Jesus were to be found in appearance as a man among us today, He would follow the prevailing conventions of our time. He would wear clothes similar to ours, use a computer, and probably even carry a cell phone. This is what it means to be "found in appearance as a man."

Many people don't have this attitude. They want to stand out and be noticed by others. Rather than conforming to the current fashion, they put their own stamp on things. Paul, however, was not like this. He only desired to be found in Christ (Phil. 3:9), who was in appearance as a man. If we also desire to be found in Christ, we will have this mind. We will not struggle to stand out from those around us. Instead, we will be found in appearance as those for whom we are burdened (1 Cor. 9:19–23).

## Obedient to the Point of Death

Christ, "being found in appearance as a man...humbled Himself by becoming obedient to the point of death, even death on a cross" (Phil. 2:8). Christ's obedience involved not only His actions, but also His attitude. The Greek word for "humble" here is *tapeinoō*, which can also mean "abase, bring low" (Strong, no. 5013). Christ took a submissive attitude toward God in all things. His whole being was geared to the Father as the One with authority. He was attentive to whatever God had to say, becoming obedient even to the point of death.

Jesus maintained His lowly position and waited obediently on His Father. Our situation is often the opposite. We may do things in the Lord's name without waiting for His leading. Unlike us, Christ never behaved in a rash manner because He was continually attentive to the Father. His will was surrendered to His God, and His obedience was unto death. There can be no greater obedience. This is what the Father demanded.

The death that the Lord bore was beyond all other experiences of death. The death the Father ordained for Him required Him to die as a criminal in the company of criminals. He died naked, lonely, and forsaken by those closest to Him. Besides all this, God required that He die with the weight of all the sin and sorrow of the human race upon Him (Isa. 53:4–5). He died as One forsaken by God Himself. This was the most extreme experience in which He "humbled Himself by becoming obedient to the point of death, even death of a cross" (Phil. 2:8). He died forsaken, alone, and bearing all the weight of the world's sin and rebellion against God, until even God had to give Him up as though He were the source of all that was wrong, as though He were the unique perpetrator of every sin ever committed against God (1 Pet. 2:24). He declared, "My God, My God, why have You forsaken Me?" (Matt. 27:46). This was the death unto which the Lord was obedient.

Our Lord died on a cross like a common criminal. We cannot fathom why He went through all this for our sakes. Why would He suffer so on our behalf? Doesn't this act drive us to love Him? This is the mind we must have in the church life.

## Highly Exalted

Because Christ humbled Himself to the uttermost, God exalted Him to the uttermost. The word "exalt" already indicates being placed on high, so for God to highly exalt Jesus means God super-exalted Him. God has led Him to the highest place and "bestowed on Him the name which is above every name, so that at the name of Jesus every knee will bow, of those who are in heaven and on earth and under the earth, and that every tongue will confess that Jesus Christ is Lord, to the glory of God the Father" (Phil. 2:9–11).

## Bestowed on Him a Name
## above Every Name

In verse 9, the Greek word for "bestowed" is *charizomai* (Strong, no. 5483), which is a form of the Greek word for "grace" (*charis*). The Father graced Jesus with a name that is to be honored above all others. Since Christ never sinned but paid the price for sin, why should it be a gracious matter that God gave this name to Him? Hadn't He earned such a name? It might seem so to us, but to the Lord it was not so. His heart was only focused on one thing: to do the will of God.

Our name represents our person with all our attainments. For instance, the name "George Washington" includes all that he did for the founding of the United States of America. When you say "Jesus," God and man are both included. All that He accomplished—His incarnation, crucifixion, resurrection, ascension, and enthronement—is included. In the name of Jesus is the fulfillment of everything on God's heart. There is no other such name!

All who have ever lived—whether angels, demons, or men—must bow to this name, and every tongue must confess, recognizing He is Lord. Hallelujah! This One is on the throne! Yet even Christ being confessed as Lord is to the Father's glory, not to His own. We say, "Jesus is Lord!" and this glorifies God. From beginning to end, everything that Christ has passed through has been to accomplish God's desire. This is the mind of Christ, the mind we must have in our church life.

Paul told the Philippians, "With humility of mind regard one another as more important than yourselves" (Phil. 2:3), and "Have this attitude in yourselves which was also in Christ Jesus" (v. 5). He pointed them to our Lord, who humbled Himself and took the form of a slave, becoming obedient to the point that He submitted to the most humiliating death: that of the cross (vv. 5–8). How is it possible for us to be "of the same mind, maintaining the same love, united in spirit, intent on one purpose" (v. 2)? It is by letting this mind be in us.

# 18

## Working Out
## Our Salvation

*So then, my beloved, just as you have always obeyed, not as in my*
*presence only, but now much more in my absence, work out your*
*salvation with fear and trembling; for it is God who is at work in*
*you, both to will and to work for His good pleasure.*

*—Philippians 2:12–13*

The church in Philippi had a very sweet relationship with
the apostle Paul. They stood with him for the furtherance of
the gospel and cared for him financially (Phil. 1:5; 4:15). They
loved the Lord, the gospel, and the apostle who served them.
Paul, however, realized that they were confronting a problem.
Since Philippi was a garrison city for the Roman army, many
of the believers there were probably soldiers who tended to be
competitive. Paul warned them, "Do nothing from selfishness
or empty conceit, but with humility of mind regard one another
as more important than yourselves" (2:3). Because they loved
the Lord, they desired to distinguish themselves in His service.
Their self-life, with its competitive nature, may have caused
them to jostle with one another, contending to be more effective
than others. Because of this, Paul realized he could not yet allow
himself to be martyred, for such a dear church was in need of
his labor for their further salvation (1:24–25).

Paul helped the Philippians by encouraging them to be of
the same mind and united in spirit (Phil. 2:2). This was only
possible by their letting the mind of Christ be in them (v. 5). Paul

described the mind of Christ as being humble (v. 8). No one likes to become lower than others. Everyone likes to be noticed and respected by others. For this reason, Paul stressed the matter of being humble. His stress was not on Christ's accomplishment of redemption; rather, he portrayed Christ's humbling of Himself in accomplishing that redemption for us. How low Christ became! Christ's pattern shows us that the way to become a blessing to the church is to become very, very low. This is the secret of spiritual growth and of gaining Christ (Phil. 3:8).

## Work Out Your Salvation

Paul called the Philippians "my beloved," saying, "So then, my beloved, just as you have always obeyed, not as in my presence only, but now much more in my absence" (v. 12). This indicates how much he appreciated them, for he did not use this term when writing to every church. Paul also recognized they had always obeyed him. Their obedience to the Lord was also their obedience to the apostle.

What follows, however, is one of the most difficult portions to understand in this book: "Work out your salvation with fear and trembling" (v. 12). Oh, how we might wish Paul had followed this by saying, "Sorry for my mistake. I meant to say, 'We are all saved by grace!'" Who can work out their salvation? Doesn't this indicate some effort on our part? How can a salvation we work out be totally of God's grace?

The Greek word translated "work out" here is *katergazomai* (Strong, no. 2716). This word means "to carry out to the goal, to carry to its ultimate conclusion" (Wuest, 2:73). This working out will continue all our life. Day by day, we are in this salvation. We will never grow out of our need for it.

What did the Philippians need to be saved from? They needed to be saved from the most dangerous thing confronting anyone who loves the Lord: the self-life. Regardless how much spiritual experience and maturity we gain, our self-life can never be allowed to boast. The Lord is jealous. This salvation reminds us that, besides Christ Himself, there is not one thing we can rely upon or boast in. For our entire Christian life, we will be doing this one thing: working out our own salvation. Yet everything is in the principle of salvation. It is totally of the Lord.

## So Great a Salvation

The book of Hebrews gives us a very good picture of salvation, even calling it "so great a salvation" (2:3). It tells us that Christ has become "to all those who obey Him the source of eternal salvation" (5:9). Salvation comes from Christ. He is the author of our salvation (2:10), and we are those who will inherit salvation (1:14). As we draw near to God through Christ and He continually intercedes for us, we experience this salvation (7:25). God arranges everything in our environment just for this salvation. Today, we eagerly await Christ, who "will appear a second time for salvation" (9:28). How can we work out anything of our own salvation? We must understand this to mean the completion of the work of salvation already begun. Based upon the picture portrayed in Hebrews, this salvation begins with Christ as the author; it is worked out during our entire life; and its full manifestation will not be until the coming of Christ. This salvation is "so great"! It is the totality of our Christian experience.

To "work out" does not imply that we produce our own salvation. It means we must complete it. The Lord has already redeemed us and regenerated us. Now He is providing us the environment necessary for the working out of our salvation. He even tells us we should eagerly await His second coming "for salvation" (Heb. 9:28). At the same time, however, He warns us: Be careful! Do not neglect this salvation! (2:3).

Most of the time we don't realize we need salvation. In the things we can do well or easily, we simply do not seek it. This is why we often come short in working it out. We don't realize that when we buy a shirt, we need to experience salvation. When we have our hair cut, we need to apply this salvation. As we carry out our daily chores, are we experiencing this salvation? Many times, we reject this salvation because we do not realize how much we need to lay hold of it.

## Fear and Trembling

Paul told the Philippians, therefore, to "work out your salvation with fear and trembling" (Phil. 2:12). Fear is experienced within, while trembling is exhibited without. We should fear that we are not completing the salvation we have been given. The fear of not partaking of this salvation will drive us to work it out. How great a salvation we need just to be saved in the way we style our hair! We need to be saved in the way we love others and in the way we serve the Lord. The working out of this salvation is to be experienced in every aspect of our lives, yet we exclude the Lord in so many areas. This is what we must fear.

Instead of going all the way with the Lord, we usually stop after taking a step or two. The Lord wants to take us higher, but we like to stay in our comfort zone. I was a librarian when the Lord called me to serve Him full time. I could have lived a comfortable life if I remained a librarian. My wife and I both had good incomes. I would have still loved the Lord and served Him in some fashion, but I feared missing "so great a salvation." The Lord had called me, and I had to follow. To stop short would have been to neglect this great salvation.

Only those in fear and trembling work out this salvation. Without this fear, we reject His salvation too easily. Like those in the Lord's parable of the great supper, we use the necessities of our daily life to excuse ourselves from answering the Lord's call (Luke 14:18–20).We do not realize what we are rejecting. We do not see that in all matters we need to be saved. How we need to work out our salvation with fear and trembling!

Those in fear and trembling are very much before the Lord and seek fellowship from others. They are not lifted up in their own eyes, but are very low. They are fearful of acting independently and learn to depend upon other members of the body of Christ. If we could see how great this salvation is and how easily we could neglect it, we would certainly experience a healthy fear.

## Salvation from Our Self-Life

We do not always feel the need for salvation, for we think we are competent. Everyone's self-life is capable in some area. If we are good in music, we may not seek to experience the Lord's salvation as we sing or play an instrument. If we are good with young people, we may not seek to know the Lord's salvation as we are with them. We must experience salvation in everything. If the Lord gives us a revelation, that revelation requires our salvation. If I have some gift, that gift requires that I experience more salvation. Our self-life too easily appropriates for our own use the things the Lord has given us for our salvation. How we need to be saved from our self-life! We need salvation so that nothing replaces Christ as our boast and source of confidence (Gal. 6:14; Eph. 3:12).

Once, after watching my interactions with different people and noticing how I handled various situations, a businessman told me, "If you were not serving the Lord full time, you would be a successful multimillionaire." To my realization, however, this is not true. If I have any wisdom or ability, it has all come from this salvation. In business, such a salvation is not required, yet it is this very salvation which has produced who I am today. I have grown in Christ for over fifty years. This growth has come from laying hold of this salvation out of fear and trembling. I have nothing that I can boast in or lay claim to. It is all the Lord's mercy. Anything I have or do apart from Christ and His body is nothing and accomplishes nothing in the working out of this salvation.

To be saved from our self-life, we have no other recourse but to abandon ourselves to God and cry out, "O Lord, save me!" We need to be saved from all things we think we can do apart from God, and especially the things we do for God. In fact, we can do nothing apart from Christ (John 15:5). Oh, how low we need to become! The self cannot be allowed to gain credit for anything; the scope of God's salvation must encompass everything in our lives. In everything, everyday, we must tell the Lord, "I need You to save me today" (2 Cor. 6:2).

## God Working in Us

Paul continued, "For it is God who is at work in you, both to will and to work for His good pleasure" (Phil. 2:13). Even the realization that we need such a salvation, the fear that causes us to desperately lay hold of it, and the trembling as we seek to do His good pleasure are all from God. He encourages us, helps us, and enables us to partake of this salvation.

One Christian brother has testified, "I received my doctorate from a prestigious university. So did my colleague. I became a professor in a university, and so did he. I published papers, and so did he. One day I came to myself and asked the question, 'What is the difference between me, one who loves the Lord, and this other person who does not?' Then I realized only a foolish person would be such a professor. A wise person would serve the Lord!" He thus felt led to drop his professorship and serve the Lord full time. This is an example of God working in someone both the willing and the working for His good pleasure.

## A Wonderful Salvation

We should be in fear lest we miss this marvelous salvation, which is totally wrapped up in Christ. Today we must faithfully bring to completion this salvation that the Lord is working out in us. When He appears a second time, it will be "for salvation" (Heb. 9:28), that is, for the completion of this great salvation. What a wonderful salvation! We should be in fear that we might neglect it (Heb. 2:3), for it is God Himself who is working in us both the willing and the working for His good pleasure (Phil. 2:13). What a mercy that we can participate in such a complete salvation! How awful if we neglect it, yet how awesome if we gain it!

# 19

## Appearing as Lights
## in the World

*Do all things without grumbling or disputing; so that you will
prove yourselves to be blameless and innocent, children of God
above reproach in the midst of a crooked and perverse generation,
among whom you appear as lights in the world.*

*—Philippians 2:14–15*

### Do All Things without
### Grumbling or Disputing

Paul related the salvation he spoke of in Philippians 2:12–13
to something very practical. He said, "Do all things without
grumbling or disputing" (v. 14). The Philippians seemed to
be doing very well spiritually. They loved the apostle Paul
and strove together alongside him in the gospel. In what
matters did they need to experience salvation? Since they were
such spiritually successful believers, seeking to distinguish
themselves in the Lord's service, they were in danger of falling
into the religious world.

Grumbling comes from our emotions. Disputing involves
the logical exercise of our mind. Paul said emphatically that
we should do all things without grumbling or disputing. This
seems impossible, especially for those given to serving their
church. Since they are so faithful, they will be pressed, for
there is so much to do. It then becomes very easy to grumble
and dispute, and with good reason.

121

In the church life, our grumbling and disputing is directed at three targets: God, those leading the church, and the conditions and situations in our environment. We complain to God, saying, "Why me?" He might answer, "Why not you?" As for the church leaders, we are often critical of their decisions and even their personalities. We may feel they are not giving us the recognition or responsibility we deserve. Much of our grumbling and disputing, however, is directed at the various situations we encounter. When we begin to complain and dispute, eventually contentions arise among us.

If we did not feel that we had a case, we would not grumble or dispute. Many of our complaints appear to be justified. The two million Israelites in the wilderness with Moses seemed to have good cause to murmur and complain. Even after water had gushed forth from the rock (Exo. 17; Num. 20), it was not comparable to the Nile. Their arrival at Elim sounds quite pleasant, but what could seventy palm trees mean to two million people (Exo. 15:27)? At least in Egypt, they could have taken a bath and eaten a variety of tasty foods. Now they were in a dusty place, eating the same food day after day (Num. 11:6). Wouldn't it seem reasonable to complain? I doubt that I would have been able to last for one month in the wilderness. Probably many of us would have soon headed back to Egypt.

While Exodus is famous for its complaints, the book of Job is famous for its disputes. Satan was allowed to do many cruel things to Job. Eventually, after having lost everything, including his children, Job was reduced to scraping his flesh with shards of pottery to relieve his itching boils (Job 2:7–8). Even his wife added to his suffering, suggesting that he curse God and die (2:9). Then three of his friends came to reason with him, and Elihu, a comparatively young man, had some things to say that seemed reasonable. Eventually, God Himself appeared to Job and charged him to gird himself up and answer to Him (38:3). However, upon seeing God, Job said, "I have heard of You by the hearing of the ear; but now my eye sees You; therefore I retract, and I repent in dust and ashes" (42:5–6). All our disputes vaporize when we truly see God. In fact, our disputing and complaining indicate that, at that moment, we are not before the Lord and we do not see Him.

It is God who places us together in the body just as He desires (1 Cor. 12:18), yet as we begin to strive to carry out something for the Lord, we may do so without any fear and trembling that we might grumble or dispute. Instead, we may be very confident in our disputing and do things according to what we feel is profitable. As a result, the sweetness in the church life disappears, and the supply of life between us dries up.

## Thorough and Open Fellowship

When we grumble, we deny the headship of Christ, and when we dispute, we deny His wisdom. We unconsciously assume that we, rather than God, know what is best. This is why grumbling and disputing are so offensive to the Lord. Those who grumble and dispute display a lack of trust in Christ their Lord. Practically speaking, Christ is not their Lord.

Satan is always working to provide reasons for us to grumble and dispute. He knows how easily these destabilize a healthy church. Rather than grumble and dispute, we should fellowship with one another thoroughly and openly. True fellowship means we refuse to live a life that bypasses God or bypasses others; we recognize and submit to God's arrangement and Christ's headship. This will save us from our grumbling and disputing.

## Becoming Blameless and Pure

Those who know how to stand with what the Lord is doing in the church life and in their environment become "blameless and innocent, children of God above reproach" (Phil. 2:15). The Greek word for "innocent" here is *akeraios*, meaning unmixed, unadulterated, pure, and sincere

(Rienecker, p. 552). To be innocent is to be pure, which is deeper than being blameless. We may be comparatively pure when we are twenty, but by the time we are thirty, other motives will likely have grown up in our hearts. In principle, the older we become, the more difficult it is to remain pure, for we tend to become more and more complicated. While we may still appear blameless, we may no longer be pure. We should not be naive lest we be taken advantage of. Being pure and being naive are not the same thing. Those who are pure are filled with understanding, for they have been enlightened to see what is not of Christ within themselves. Even Bible knowledge can lead to impurity when used to puff up the self (1 Cor. 8:1). Blamelessness has to do with our outward living, while purity has to do with our inward condition. Being blameless can be something of religion (cf. Phil 3:6), but purity can never be of religion. A pure person is one focused on Christ and Him alone.

## Without Blemish

In verse 15, the Greek word for "above reproach" is *amōmos*, meaning without spot or without blemish (Rienecker, p. 552). It is the same Greek word used in Ephesians 1:4 and 5:27. The Lord is building His church with precious stones (1 Cor. 3:12). A single blemish in a precious stone mars its clarity and causes it to lose much of its value. This describes us. Often we start out in a pure way, wanting to be a useful servant of the Lord. Then, as our service to the Lord is appreciated by others, a blemish of pride grows and spots of self-appreciation accumulate. Eventually, instead of being transparent, we become opaque. We must guard against such spots. It is so easy for impurity to come in. When we were first saved, this was not our case. We should be in fear and trembling, for it is too easy to lose our focus on Jesus only and begin to live for self-gain. Are we able to declare, "Lord Jesus, I am Yours, and I live for Your satisfaction alone"? This must be our stand.

## A Crooked and Perverse Generation

Paul admonished the Philippians to become "children of God above reproach in the midst of a crooked and perverse generation" (2:15). Whatever generation of the world we are in, we must recognize that Satan is its ruler (John 12:31). In every generation, he works to make people crooked and perverse to prevent them from developing into what God desires. We all once walked according to the course of this world, making us fit only for God's wrath and judgment (Eph. 2:1–3). Satan uses the world to frustrate and divert mankind away from God.

The Greek word for "crooked" here is *skolios*, which also means "curved" (Thayer, p. 579). This is related to a person's growth and development. Being crooked implies the loss of a proper conscience, as when someone is unprincipled. Each generation stresses something that will damage a person's humanity. For instance, a trend of this age is to endorse homosexuality. Certain Christian denominations even promote the idea of homosexual marriage. This crookedness frustrates people from discovering what God intends for them as human beings.

The Greek word for "perverse" here is *diastrephō*, which means "to turn aside from the right path, to pervert, corrupt" (Thayer, p. 142). Why is it that so many believers cannot grow well spiritually? It is because they are under the influence of this generation, which causes them to become crooked and perverse. They are unable to live as children of God above reproach, for they themselves have been caught in the means used by Satan to bend and turn aside the people of this generation.

God has given every believer talents that are of use to Him. These talents are meant for us to use unto His glory. However, Satan utilizes each generation of the world to cause the believers to become bent and crooked. Under the influence of each generation, people end up far from where God intended, wasting their God-given talents on things that yield nothing to God. Satan makes them feel that this is in their interest, but actually it is in Satan's interest. Therefore, we should be moved when we read the phrase "crooked and perverse generation." Look at all mankind today. So many precious individuals have been thwarted from reaching God's goal and have become ruined in relation to the purpose God had for them. When we set our heart on something other than God or seek something other than what God is seeking, we inevitably become a part of this perverse generation. What a frustration this is to God's plan for man! Instead of being distracted from Christ and conformed to this age, let us run the race set before us to win the crown (1 Cor. 9:24–25; Rev. 2:10).

## The World's Development

The apostle John wrote, "Do not love the world nor the things in the world....For all that is in the world, the lust of the flesh and the lust of the eyes and the boastful pride of life, is not from Father, but is from the world" (1 John 2:15–16). The world began its development with three brothers who were the descendants of Cain (see Gen. 4:20–22). Jabal was the father of all who "dwell in tents and have livestock," which relates to making a living. Jubal was the father of all who "play the lyre and pipe," which relates to entertainment. Tubal-cain was "the forger of all implements of bronze and iron," which relates to self-defense and conquest. Thus, mankind began a joint venture with Satan along these three lines that still enslaves people today (Gal. 4:3; Eph. 2:2). The world is centered upon making a living, entertainment, and attacking others to gain something or defending what has been already acquired. Every invention of the world has one of these three things in view.

## The Material World

Satan uses the world to shape people's hearts and lives so that they end up far from God and His intention. Right now Satan is looking at all the little children and planning a further development of the world to match them. We should not consider this a light matter. People created by God, bright with promise, become captured by professions and careers, a part of the material world. These bend them, taking them far from God's intended goal. They do not develop according to all that is possible for them in God's plan, but rather the potential of their human lives is funneled away by something vain.

The material world also diverts Christians from following the Lord. Do not think that the world only uses sinful things to draw people away. When a high-paying, prestigious, and rewarding career presents itself, many Christians compromise their stand, turn from following Christ, and live a vain and empty life. How we need to hate this age! Look how many are ensnared by it. Though many believers initially set their sights on the Lord and His purpose, few are able to live a life that matches this goal. The attractions and comforts of this age prevent them from obtaining the crown of righteousness (2 Tim. 4:7–8).

With the material world comes the boastful pride of life (1 John 2:16). Others may brag about their cars, shoes, or other things, but our boast must be in the Lord. As others prominently display a certain brand name on their clothing, we must bear Christ. With us there should be nothing called success or satisfaction outside of Christ. In our living we should be content as long as we have Christ. Our living should be simple. As long as we are in this world, it will always be tugging at us and seeking a foothold. Something other than Christ will attempt to grow in us to become our boast. If we want to shine as lights, we cannot allow this. When others see us, they must see a shining that comes from another source within. As those who have received Christ, it has been given to us to be His lights.

## The Religious World

The most difficult aspect of the world for us to deal with as believers is the religious aspect. The religious world plays to "the lust of the eyes" (1 John 2:16). The tree of the knowledge of good and evil was "a delight to the eyes" (Gen. 3:6). It was because of its attractiveness that man fell under its spell. The lust of the flesh has to do with satisfying the fallen body, and the lust of the eyes exists for the satisfaction of the soul. Although the religious world includes the lust of the flesh, it focuses mainly upon satisfying the soul with things that involve God's name and appear right and acceptable. In this pleasing world where Christ and God are spoken of, God's desire is actually frustrated. The religious world is as effective as the sinful world in causing people to become crooked and perverse. When people become involved with the lust of the eyes in the religious world, their conscience is darkened and their spirit is made dull.

There is a kind of pleasure involved in sitting and listening to things pertaining to God even when they do not help us come closer to Him. A charismatic preacher may begin a ministry which is honored by others. It seems to be something of value, but it can subtly turn us aside from what God desires. None of us would seek to be recognized as the greatest sinner, for that is shameful and of the flesh. However, we may compete to be recognized as the most spiritual. This is related to the lust of the eyes.

The only way to escape from the religious world is to allow Christ to have first place in all things (Col. 1:18). If Christ truly has the first place in our lives, then we will be able to live as children of God above reproach in this evil and perverse world. All the world "lies in the power of the evil one" (1 John 5:19). All the power in the world is Satan's to give to whomever he wishes (Luke 4:5–7). Everyone around us is making Satan their god, for he promises to provide for them (Jabal), to make them happy (Jubal), and to grant them protection and victory (Tubal-cain). These are the very things the Lord desires to be responsible for in our lives. Therefore, do not love the world, nor the things in the world (1 John 2:15).

## Appearing as Lights in the World

Paul told us that in the midst of this crooked and perverse generation we should "appear as lights in the world" (Phil.

2:15). Inwardly, we have the divine life as children of God; outwardly, we bear the divine testimony, appearing as lights in the world. Because my children possess something of me, they testify of me in many ways. The Lord is blameless and pure, and we, as His children, shine as lights in the midst of this crooked and perverse generation. In other words, those in the dark world around us can see us living a marvelous life enjoying God's full salvation. While others grasp at things and complain about their situations, we are able to see and experience Christ in all things.

Although we are lights, we are not the source of the light. In a sense, we are nothing, yet we are the means Christ has chosen to shine out to those around us. We have been lit as lamps by the Lord, and He did not light us to be under a basket (Matt. 5:15). When we pour ourselves into something of the world, our potential to shine for the Lord becomes covered. The Lord, however, lit us to shine with others as His testimony. We do not belong under any basket; we belong on the lampstand, for we are lamps the Lord has lit to shine out to this generation.

# 20

# Poured Out as a Drink Offering

*Holding fast the word of life, so that in the day of Christ I will have reason to glory because I did not run in vain nor toil in vain. But even if I am being poured out as a drink offering upon the sacrifice and service of your faith, I rejoice and share my joy with you all. You too, I urge you, rejoice in the same way and share your joy with me.*

*—Philippians 2:16–18*

## Holding Fast the Word of Life

Paul told the Philippians to "hold fast the word of life" (Phil. 2:16). They needed to hold fast to Christ as the living Word (John 1:1, 14) and not be distracted from Him, caught with grumblings and disputes. If they would turn to Christ in this way, Christ would be manifested through them and the apostle Paul would rejoice in the day of Christ because he had not run nor toiled in vain (Phil. 2:16).

## Our Stand, Attitude, and Living

"Holding fast" implies our stand, attitude, and living. It is active and continuous. In order to hold fast the word of life, our stand must be very clear. We may love the Lord and the church, but to hold fast the word of life we must stand firm for what we have seen (see Acts 26:15–19). We cannot have one foot in and one foot out. A man who sees the woman he desires to marry takes a very clear stand: "I must marry that woman!" He does not go to her and say, "Don't feel pressured; I have four other possibilities lined up if you don't agree." No, his stand is very clear. It should be the same with us. Many who proclaim that they have given their all to Christ and the church have not done so in reality. Therefore, they are not able to present a clear and bright testimony to others. We should be able to say, "I live for this, and I die for this. Whether the church is blessed, or whether things are difficult, I will not be moved. Nothing can tear me away from this stand!" By taking such a stand, we hold fast the word of life.

In order to hold fast the word of life, we must also have a learning attitude. We should be able to receive from others and learn from them. This precious word of life is operating not only in us but also in all other believers. There is so much to receive! When the Thessalonians heard the speaking of the apostle Paul, they welcomed and accepted it as the word of God, and it effectively worked in them (1 Thess. 2:13). In order to hold fast the word of life, we need to be receiving all the time. The word of life within us should not be separate from our living. What we have seen, we need to apply. Then the word of life will work effectively among us.

If we take such a firm stand, have a receiving spirit, and apply what we have seen, we can confidently present the word of life to those in the crooked and perverse generation around us. What we see needs to become an outflow. May the Lord bring us all into this process so that others may behold Christ shining out through us.

## Paul's Boast

In verse 16, the Greek word for "rejoice" is *kauchēma*, which means boast, glory, or rejoice (Strong, no. 2745). The Philippians' holding fast to Christ would become Paul's boast in the day of Christ. Such a boast would not be mere bragging, for the Philippians had gained Christ through Paul's labor. Through Paul's struggling, an organic union had been produced between God and the Philippians resulting in a healthy body life. What a boast!

We may be proud of our accomplishments and tempted to boast in them, but can such bragging compare with Paul's boast on the day of Christ? Paul counted all things according to their divine and eternal value (Phil. 3:4–8). He knew that nothing mattered except the accomplishment of God's purpose. His boasting was based upon this, and for this he ran and toiled.

## Running for the Prize

If two words mark Paul's life, they are "run" and "toil." Paul lived like an athlete pressing "toward the goal for the prize" (Phil. 3:14). As athletes run a race, they forget everything around them and focus only on the goal, for everything is geared to winning. In the Christian race, we cannot allow anything to hinder us. We must avoid distractions, for our desire is to gain the top blessing—Christ Himself. So many live a vain existence, but those who run as Paul did always have the highest goal in view, regardless of what circumstance they are in. This is a healthy Christian life.

Paul's running, however, was not just for himself; it was for the body of Christ. His running brought others onward. As he pursued Christ, others became partakers with him of grace (Phil. 1:7). Through his ministry, others became lights, and in this he would have his boast. We need to see and experience the body of Christ as Paul did. Some people's view of the body is that we all conform to the same practices. When we really see the body, however, we will not emphasize such things. Instead, we will run in such a way that all the other members of the body are blessed. Paul ran at an advanced level, opening the way for others to run as well. The Philippians' holding fast the word of life as Paul did became proof that his running had not been in vain.

The reward for running the race is an imperishable wreath, the crown of righteousness (1 Cor. 9:24–25; 2 Tim. 4:8). When we pursue the Lord and grow in life, all those we serve will also pursue Christ for the growth in life. Paul realized that the Christ he pursued would become the Christ that others would enjoy. He wouldn't meet the Lord just by himself; he would meet the Lord together with all those who had pursued and gained Christ because of him (1 Thess. 2:19–20).

## Laboring for a Reward

Like Paul, we should not only run in a race to receive a crown but also work in such a way that we receive a reward (1 Cor. 3:14). Paul labored to cut the way for others as he preached the gospel and raised up churches. The problem today is that many have not produced anything. Rather, they have inherited what others produced. Often, those who inherit everything do not know how to labor to produce anything themselves. They need to consider how to cut the way for the Lord's testimony to continue on further, opening the door for others to labor also.

Paul compared his labor among the Corinthians to that of a farmer, saying, "I planted, Apollos watered, but God was causing the growth" (1 Cor. 3:6). Whatever farmers gain can easily be lost if they do not maintain it. The thorns and thistles seem to pop up again as soon as they turn their backs. It is not easy. It requires wisdom and much labor. We should not have high expectations when we labor. Instead, we should learn to work with the little that we produce in order to gain even more. We should use every ounce of blessing the Lord gives us as our asset. If the Lord gives us one couple, we should labor with them as our companions to gain a third couple. Paul labored in such a way in Philippi, and his expectation was that he would be able to boast that his labor among them was not in vain.

## Willing to Be Poured Out
## as a Drink Offering

The verses that follow are profound in terms of experience. Paul wrote, "I am being poured out as a drink offering upon the sacrifice and service of your faith" (Phil. 2:17). In the Old Testament, a drink offering was a special portion of wine poured out as a voluntary offering (Num. 15:1–10) upon one of the basic or required offerings (Lev. 1–7) that they might be more acceptable and pleasing to the Lord. Paul knew that his labor had produced a healthy church, for the believers in Philippi sacrificed to the Lord by serving in the gospel and caring for Paul, a servant of the Lord. Now Paul was ready to be poured out further as a drink offering upon their sacrifice.

The basic offering here was not of Paul; it was of the Philippians. Through Paul's ministry, they came to know and experience Christ as the One who had saved them from God's judicial judgment (the trespass offering), who was saving them inwardly from their rebellious sinful nature (the sin offering), who was producing the true harmony between them and God (the peace offering), who was absolute for the carrying out of God's purpose (the burnt offering), and who possessed the humanity that God desires (the meal offering). Day by day, the Philippians walked with Christ and enjoyed Him as these offerings until they were constituted with Him and expressed Him in their living and labor. Once they had become such people, Paul, who had ministered Christ to them, could pour himself out further as an enriching drink offering upon the sacrifice and service of their faith.

Though only Paul labored initially, eventually the whole church in Philippi also served. As they sacrificed, Paul poured himself out further upon their sacrifice. When I see what is contained in these verses, I can hardly believe that we could be as blessed as this. We are blessed as members of the body of Christ, for it is in the body that we run, labor, sacrifice, and serve together. What a wonderful body life!

## Grace Bringing Joy and Rejoicing

Paul said, "I rejoice and share my joy with you all. You too, I urge you, rejoice in the same way and share your joy with me" (Phil. 2:17–18). The Greek word for "rejoice" here is *chairō* (Strong, no. 5463), which is the root word for *charis* (Strong, no. 5485), the Greek word for "grace." This joy and rejoicing issues from the enjoyment of grace. It is not tied to the ups and downs of our environment but to the Lord's constant supply of grace. Paul and the Philippians were enjoying the reality of grace together. Grace descended from the throne in the heavens and came to the apostle Paul and to the church in Philippi. Grace became the source of joy and rejoicing among them.

In spite of the fact that Paul was imprisoned and in a seemingly hopeless situation, he rejoiced and was able to share his joy with the Philippians because of their sacrifice and service of faith. He was now ready to be poured out as a drink offering upon their sacrifice. What caused them to grow to this point? It was the grace they had partaken of together with Paul (Phil. 1:7).

Paul had told the Philippians that they appeared as lights in the midst of a crooked and perverse generation (Phil. 2:15). Because they held fast the word of life, Paul had confidence that his running and toiling had not been in vain. The Philippians had become mutual partakers of grace with Paul, and this constituted them with all that Christ is and has accomplished. This picture of Paul and the Philippians running, toiling, serving, sacrificing, and being poured out as a drink offering is a rich expression of grace being lived out in the body life. When we see this picture, we realize that no one could ever manufacture such a thing. Only grace could accomplish this.

# 21

# The Approvedness
# of Paul

*But I hope in the Lord Jesus to send Timothy to you shortly, so that I also may be encouraged when I learn of your condition. For I have no one else of kindred spirit who will genuinely be concerned for your welfare. For they all seek after their own interests, not those of Christ Jesus. But you know of his proven worth, that he served with me in the furtherance of the gospel like a child serving his father.*

*—Philippians 2:19–22*

## Approvedness

According to Paul, the Philippians knew of Timothy's proven worth (Phil. 2:22). This implies that they approved of Timothy. Paul also approved of him, highly recommending him to the Philippians. The Greek word for "proven worth" here is *dokimē*, which means "approvedness, tried character" (Thayer, p. 154). Approvedness only comes after being tried and tested. If, after being tried, we are found approved by both God and the believers, we can become a source of blessing to the churches, for God only entrusts His work to those who are approved.

Concerning his own approvedness, Paul told the Thessalonians, "Just as we have been approved by God to be entrusted with the gospel, so we speak, not as pleasing men, but God who examines our hearts" (1 Thess. 2:4). Because of his approvedness, Paul's ministry and service were of great and lasting value.

There are eight factors that fostered approvedness in Paul: (1) his sincerity and desperation; (2) his clarity of vision; (3) his pursuit of the truth; (4) his desire for fellowship; (5) his living unto the Lord alone; (6) his submission to God's sovereignty; (7) his fruitfulness and effectiveness; and (8) his ability to teach.

## 1. Sincerity and Desperation

The first factor for Paul's approvedness was his sincerity, in that he was unwavering in doing what he believed to be of God. His vision became his burden, and he was desperate to carry it out. Anyone who sincerely loves the church will also be desperate and burdened for whatever profits it. In order to be approved, it is not sufficient for us merely to say, "I love the Lord." Our living must exhibit an absoluteness that proves our sincerity.

Even before his salvation, Paul was marked by sincerity. He was so sincere in his zeal toward God that he tracked down the followers of Jesus and dragged them off to prison, even to their deaths. The zeal with which he served God as a Pharisee was absolute (Phil. 3:5–6, Acts 9:1–2; 22:3–4).

Paul's sincerity also manifested itself immediately after his salvation. He was so burdened to preach about Jesus that the Jews sought to kill him. The disciples had to lower him in a basket so he could escape (Acts 9:24–25). He then went to Jerusalem and disputed with the Hellenists until they also wanted to kill him (9:29). Wherever Paul went, there was a strong reaction. The Jews in Thessalonica said that Paul and those with him "have upset the world" (17:6). Before Felix, the governor, Paul was charged with being "a real pest and a fellow who stirs up dissension" (24:5). Paul's absoluteness was irrepressible. Of course, he was also very rich in truth, experience, and vision, but what primarily characterized Paul was his sincerity and burden.

If we want approvedness, we must first be sincere and

desperate, driven by our burden. It is very easy to take spiritual things for granted and handle them in a common way. We may love the Lord; we may be respectable and faithful in our serving life; we may be rich in truth and experience. However, if we are not desperate and burdened, we will not possess approvedness. When we are desperate and burdened, the things we do will bear a particular fragrance. Our preaching of the gospel will have impact, for others will respond to our approvedness.

## 2. Clarity of Vision

The second factor that produced Paul's approvedness was his clarity of vision, which he received from the Lord at the time of his conversion (Acts 26:16–19). Paul wasted no time. Immediately after his baptism, he began proclaiming Jesus in the synagogues (Acts 9:20). Paul's speaking caused others to seek his death, for he was bold in declaring the clear vision committed to him.

Paul testified that as a minister of Christ, he was "in far more labors, in far more imprisonments, beaten times without number, often in danger of death. Five times I received from the Jews thirty-nine lashes. Three times I was beaten with rods, once I was stoned, three times I was shipwrecked, a night and a day I have spent in the deep" (2 Cor. 11:23–25). Paul's living testified to others that he was charged with a clear vision for which he was willing to live and die.

We must have a very clear vision that drives us. Others should be able to see that we are giving our whole person and life to carry out our vision. If we are driven by a clear vision, we will desire to see the Lord accomplish His work and see others receive the greatest benefit. Like Paul, we will live and die for those around us (2 Cor. 12:15). Our use of time and our manner of life will always have them in view. If others oppose what we are doing, we will not be deterred, for our vision will drive us. In order to be approved, our living and person should match our clear vision.

## 3. Pursuit of the Truth

The third factor related to Paul's approvedness was his pursuit of the truth. Three years passed between Paul's salvation and his visit to Jerusalem (Gal. 1:15–18). During this time, he went to Arabia. Many Bible scholars believe that Paul devoted himself to study the Word during this time. Afterward, the Old Testament was no longer the same book Paul had come to know at the feet of Gamaliel (Acts 5:34; 22:3). It had instead become a book full of visions and revelations of Christ. Paul's understanding of the Old Testament now surpassed even that of the original twelve apostles. He understood the Old Testament according to the New Testament revelation. This took place because Paul sought the truth in the Bible immediately after his salvation.

Approvedness cannot be manifested in us if we handle the Bible with indifference. We must pursue the truth with our whole being. Otherwise, when we begin to minister the truth to others, what we know will quickly be exhausted. Young believers should equip themselves with the truth of the Bible rather than focus mainly on service. How much they can do for the Lord should be secondary to becoming equipped and constituted with the riches of the divine truth. In twenty or thirty years, how many will be sufficiently equipped? If none are pursuing the truth today, the Lord's work tomorrow will be limited. Who will be able to minister the truth? Will there be anyone with an abundance of riches to feed the Lord's children?

We must know the divine revelation found in the Word, and we must know the riches given to us through the Lord's servants who have gone before. Spiritual truths are not obtained cheaply. Work out a plan to memorize a certain number of verses every year. Develop a schedule to read the Bible. Devise a plan for reading spiritual books. Always consider how to be further equipped with divine truth.

To be approved as servants of the Lord, we must pursue the truth diligently. If we know both the Lord and the Word, others will honor us. Our approvedness will be based on how much we have labored in the truth before the Lord.

## 4. Desire for Fellowship

The fourth factor for Paul's approvedness was his desire to maintain fellowship with fellow believers. There is nothing more difficult for Christians than learning to fellowship with their fellow believers, because fellowship limits, confines, and terminates us. We like to be free and left alone. We feel entitled to our own way and opinion. Whether it is politics, the national economy, or the best way to grow grass, everyone has an opinion. In our culture, we are even encouraged to express our opinions. However, spiritually speaking, we experience the greatest blessing when we fellowship.

### Paul's Initial Fellowship
### with Jerusalem

After Paul spent three years in Arabia, he sought fellowship with the disciples in Jerusalem (Gal. 1:17–18; Acts 9:26). At first, however, no one there wanted fellowship with him because they feared him as one who had persecuted the churches. Only Barnabas was willing to receive Paul and introduce him to the apostles, who then extended to him "the right hand of fellowship" (Gal. 2:9).

Without Barnabas, Paul's Christian life would have been very different. Barnabas initiated the fellowship between Paul and Peter. When Paul met Peter, no doubt he shared all the enlightenment he had received while in Arabia. Peter probably did not understand much of what Paul tried to communicate. Even thirty years later, Peter wrote that Paul's letters were hard to understand, yet he still referred to them as Scripture (2 Pet. 3:15–16).

Regardless of Peter's inability to apprehend what Paul had

seen, Paul still sought fellowship in humility. Peter also had an understanding concerning many things. They were two servants of the Lord who had received revelation from God, so their fellowship together would have been a mutual help.

In fellowship, no one should insist on or impose anything, and no one should be subdued by anyone. Our focus should be on Christ alone. We fellowship to bring in a flow of life and a mutual dispensing of the riches of Christ. Whatever we have should become a blessing to others, and what others have should become a blessing to us. Paul always took this way. His life was a life of fellowship.

## Paul's Fellowship with Barnabas

When the Jews in Jerusalem sought to kill Paul, the church "brought him down to Caesarea and sent him away to Tarsus" (Acts 9:30). Eventually Barnabas came again to Paul and brought him to Antioch (11:25–26), where different races and social classes were represented. The church life there brought Paul into a healthier and broader fellowship, and his leadership began to develop.

Then one day while they were fellowshipping and praying together, Barnabas and Paul were sent out under the direction of the Holy Spirit (13:2–4) and raised up a number of churches. Later they decided to go back to visit the churches they had raised up (15:36). Unfortunately, Paul and Barnabas disagreed over whether or not to take Mark with them. Ultimately Paul took Silas and headed north through Syria and Cilicia, while Barnabas took Mark and went to Cyprus (15:37–41).

Barnabas is not mentioned again in Acts and seemingly was no longer in fellowship with Paul. At this point it, would be very easy to judge Barnabas as a failure. However, even if Barnabas' departure was a mistake, that did not mean he was no longer of any use to the Lord. We are prone to think that those with defects should be tossed aside, but the secret of fellowship is to not toss anyone aside. Those who know how to fellowship would never write off any believer. We should never have the attitude, "Either you are for me or against me" (see Mark 9:40). In Paul's case, I am so thankful that he did not exclude Barnabas but rather continued to recognize him as a fellow apostle among the churches (1 Cor. 9:6).

## Fellowship Is Inclusive

Due to our preferences we are naturally selective, but we all must realize that fellowship should be inclusive. A life of fellowship enables us to realize how great and grand the one body of Christ is. Therefore, we must be careful as we contact other believers, for if we are selective, we will forfeit our approvedness.

Although the Corinthians tried to divide Paul from Apollos, saying, "I am of Paul" and "I am of Apollos" (1 Cor. 3:4), Paul wrote, "I planted, Apollos watered" (1 Cor. 3:6), for he knew what fellowship is. Because he valued others, he was able to speak about Apollos in such a positive way.

Whoever practices fellowship and has the reality of the life of fellowship is very inclusive. This is absolutely in opposition to religion. Religious people must decide what side someone is on before they will fellowship with them. They seek a so-called unity based on conformity in practice and terminology. Instead, we should seek after the enjoyment of the divine life in the sweetness of fellowship.

The history of the Plymouth Brethren should be instructive to us. After a dispute on some truth, John Nelson Darby would no longer fellowship with Benjamin Newton. Darby then took issue with George Mueller, for Mueller's church received some who had been in fellowship with Newton. Eventually, the Brethren movement splintered into hundreds of divisions. They all said that they were for Christ, but approvedness does not issue from this alone. It also requires a willingness to fellowship.

If we meet believers from a different background, are we able to fellowship with them, or do we disregard them, assuming

they are somehow inferior? Is it not likely that they are for
Christ? The principle of fellowship requires us to be inclusive
rather than exclusive.

## Paul's Continued Fellowship
## with Jerusalem

Fellowship is the flowing of life. In fellowship we establish
a life-relationship with one another. Fellowship does not
necessarily mean that some direction will be set. Many times
we say we want fellowship, but what we really want is a
decision. We may reach a decision, but that is not the main
objective of fellowship.

Paul's life was a life of seeking fellowship, yet the Bible rarely
indicates that he sought some decision during fellowship. He
made a determined effort to fellowship with the church in
Jerusalem (Acts 9:26; 15:2; 21:15; Gal. 1:18; 2:1; Rom. 15:25–
27). Only one of these times involved seeking a decision. Some
from Judea were trying to force circumcision upon the Gentile
believers in Antioch (Acts 15:1), so Paul and Barnabas went to
Jerusalem to clear up this matter, and a positive decision was
reached (Acts 15:2–29). However, it does not seem that this
conclusion had any effect on those causing the trouble. Men
from James (Gal. 2:12), the very James who settled the issue
of circumcision at the conference in Jerusalem, still went from
church to church to undo Paul's work of the gospel, insisting
that Gentile believers be circumcised. Even though the decision
seems to have been somewhat of a failure, Paul still continued
to seek fellowship with James and those in Jerusalem (Acts
21:17–18). Regardless of whether or not decisions made during
fellowship are honored, fellowship is still to be valued, for it
brings in a relatedness through the divine life we all share.

Do not enter into arguments. Do not make issues. Do not try
to correct matters. When these things are emphasized, fellowship
ceases. Trust that fellowship is able to heal all wounds. Always
seek after fellowship.

## 5. Living unto the Lord Alone

A fifth factor for Paul's approvedness was his living unto the Lord alone. Paul testified to the Philippians, "Whatever things were gain to me, those things I have counted as loss for the sake of Christ. More than that, I count all things to be loss in view of the surpassing value of knowing Christ Jesus my Lord, for whom I have suffered the loss of all things, and count them but rubbish so that I may gain Christ" (Phil. 3:7–8). For Paul, only Christ had value, and only He was the unique goal worth pursuing.

Before we can bear the mark of approvedness, we must be tested as to whether or not we live unto Christ alone. We sing songs about how much we are for the Lord, but then some lose heart and fall away. This may be because they are for some ministry, work, or teaching rather than the Lord Himself, or they may be for a certain feeling they experience when the church comes together. If we are not living unto the Lord alone, one day we will find that things have changed, and we will be stumbled. Many things may be very good and even spiritual, but they are not the Lord Himself. They will not take us through the real testing when it comes. We can only be approved when our stand is unto the Lord alone.

When we begin to live solely unto the Lord, we rise above outward circumstances. Few experienced more tribulations than the apostle Paul (2 Cor. 11:23–28). He could have complained, saying that things were too hard, but since he lived unto Christ, such hardships became the means of his strength (2 Cor. 12:9–10). What price is too unreasonable? If it is for Christ and for Christ alone, the result will be something of the highest value.

Madame Guyon (1648–1717) was imprisoned many years for her faith. While in prison, she wrote,

> A little bird I am,
> Shut from the fields of air,
> And in my cage I sit and sing
> To Him who placed me there. (Martin, no. 281)

She had learned to live unto Christ alone.

Living unto the Lord goes beyond just living for the Lord. It means that Christ Himself is our goal, the center and focus of everything we do. Every day Christ needs to be our aim. Let us live unto Christ!

## 6. Submission to God's Sovereignty

A sixth factor for Paul's approvedness was his submission to God's sovereignty. He realized that all the hardships he suffered were arranged by God on his behalf. He wrote, "Are they servants of Christ?—I speak as if insane—I more so; in far more labors, in far more imprisonments, beaten times without number, often in danger of death. Five times I received from the Jews thirty-nine lashes. Three times I was beaten with rods, once I was stoned, three times I was shipwrecked, a night and a day I have spent in the deep. I have been on frequent journeys, in dangers from rivers, dangers from robbers, dangers from my countrymen, dangers from the Gentiles, dangers in the city, dangers in the wilderness, dangers on the sea, dangers among false brethren; I have been in labor and hardship, through many sleepless nights, in hunger and thirst, often without food, in cold and exposure. Apart from such external things, there is the daily pressure on me of concern for all the churches" (2 Cor. 11:23–28).

Paul did not become bitter due to such things but instead experienced Christ in them. He recognized God's sovereign arrangement as he passed through hardship after hardship, believing that the Lord was with him.

One key to our being approved is our ability to receive everything as from the Lord's hand. Often events and circumstances do not seem fair and have no logical explanation, yet they are according to the Lord's sovereignty. We must submit to the Lord in all the situations He has arranged for us if we wish to serve Him. To be approved, we must be able to discover and experience Christ in the circumstances God arranges for us.

## Tested by Our Environment
## and the Truth

Every truth we see becomes our test. While in Joppa, Peter saw a vision concerning the oneness of the Jewish and Gentile believers. He acted on this vision at the house of Cornelius but later failed the same test at Antioch when he separated himself from the Gentile believers (Acts 10; Gal. 2:11–13). Once we see the oneness of the body, we will be tested. Once we see that we are crucified with Christ, we will again be tested. Every truth we think we know will become a test in our experience. The Lord is in control at all times and in all situations.

If we have coworkers who are impossible, we should praise the Lord. When people seem to waste our time, we should praise the Lord. We are surrounded by people the Lord uses to test us. Achieving approvedness is not easy. In every situation, the Lord is there, especially in our hardships and failures.

God will raise up all kinds of situations in our environment to test us. We typically complain about these things. We complain that our house is not big enough, that our bed is not soft enough, and that the temperature is too cold or too hot. If we desire to be approved, however, we must be able to receive all the sovereign arrangements God has prepared for us.

## 7. Fruitfulness and Effectiveness

A seventh factor for Paul's approvedness was his fruitfulness and effectiveness. Paul testified that a deep concern for all the churches pressed upon him daily (2 Cor. 11:28). He lived to shepherd the churches and to labor according to the vision the Lord committed to him. He cried out, "Who is weak without my being weak? Who is led into sin without my intense concern?" (11:29). Even though it is common for a believer to stumble, Paul was full of feeling at every instance. He burned with indignation.

Paul cared for those who really needed care. Everyone loves to care for those who are doing well and who have obvious potential. When Paul spoke of his deep concern for the churches, however, he first referred to those who were weak. When they were weak, he was weak. He shared the sensation of their weaknesses and their limitations. Typically we try to ignore those who are needy. Paul was different. He was weak when others were weak.

This characteristic of Paul is what made him so fruitful and effective in raising up churches. He reminded the elders of the church in Ephesus that "for a period of three years I did not cease to admonish each one with tears" (Acts 20:31). He described how he shepherded the new believers in Thessalonica, saying, "We proved to be gentle among you, as a nursing mother tenderly cares for her own children. Having so fond an affection for you, we were well-pleased to impart to you not only the gospel of God but also our own lives, because you had become very dear to us" (1 Thess. 2:7–8).

## Fruitful and Effective Labor

Fruitfulness is valuable, but fruitfulness does not necessarily prove that a person is spiritual. A large work may be produced through natural means. However, we cannot say, "Hallelujah! I am spiritual because I never led even one person to Christ!" Nor can we claim to be spiritual if we have never shepherded anyone.

For our service to be fruitful and effective, we need to shepherd and labor with burden. When others are with us, they should be comforted and feel hopeful; they should be helped to grow and develop. They should be inspired by us. Because of us, they should feel that the church life is worthwhile and that a life of serving the Lord is very meaningful. Their level of life must become so strong that their understanding and manner of life begin to change. If lives are being changed due to our service, this is an indication of our approvedness.

Something is seriously wrong if after a year we have neither borne fruit nor helped others to grow and develop in the Lord. I would refuse to live a life like that! Regardless of whether I am tired, beat up, or having difficulties, I must be effective in my labor.

Even the Lord Jesus considered the fruit He bore. He passed through so much suffering, but He did not boast in that. Rather, He boasted in that which His sufferings produced. The Lord boasted of those begotten out of His crucifixion and resurrection: "Behold, I and the children whom God has given Me" (Heb. 2:13). He did not go through a process just for the sake of experiencing the process. He endured that process in order to bear fruit (John 12:24). Consider how many believers have been regenerated through the centuries, all produced through the labor of the Lord Jesus.

If we desire to be approved by testing, we must pay attention to our ability to shepherd. We must consider our labor. Whether or not we are approved by the Lord is seen in the fruit we produce and the effectiveness of our labor. We must be desperate about our effectiveness, for it proves who we are and where we are with the Lord. It is abnormal to labor for one or two years and have no fruit to show for it. We should be fruitful. Our approvedness is declared by the fruit of our labor.

## "Who Is Weak without My Being Weak?"

When we labor or when we shepherd others, our realization should be that we, like them, are in weakness. When we desire that some would love the Lord more, we ourselves must struggle to love the Lord more. When we desire that they consecrate themselves to Christ, we must struggle to consecrate ourselves to Him. When we desire that our church would become prevailing, we must realize that we ourselves are just as weak as the weakest member.

As we shepherd others, our deep sensation should be that we are impotent. This is why Paul said, "Who is weak without my being weak?" (2 Cor. 11:29). This does not mean that we join others in their weakness, but we should have the sensation of weakness. Our feeling should be, "Lord, only You can build the church. Only You can cause people to love You and consecrate themselves to You. Only You can draw people to pursue You. In spiritual things, I can only be Your co-laborer. I cannot generate a love for You in anyone." To have this understanding is not a small thing.

Once, when I was a young Christian, I saw a church elder smoking. I thought someone who had been with the Lord for such long time should be strong and prevailing. I prayed for him, and in that prayer I shared a little in the feeling of his weakness. Two or three weeks later, he gave a testimony, saying, "Do you realize we have no ability to overcome even the three inches of a cigarette?" Soon afterward, he stopped smoking. It would have been easy to judge this brother and even expose him, but how much better to share the feeling of his weakness in prayer.

As we have this sense of weakness, we will become more burdened for those around us. We will become more desperate and spend ourselves more on others. This is what it means to serve the Lord. We will no longer live according to ourselves but according to Christ and according to the need of those we are caring for. What a glorious life! This is a life that is approved by God.

## 8. Having the Ability to Teach

An eighth factor for Paul's approvedness was his ability to teach, as indicated in his word to the elders of the church in Ephesus: "How I did not shrink from declaring to you anything that was profitable, and teaching you publicly and from house to house" (Acts 20:20).

Teaching is an art. It is very difficult to find a good teacher. Throughout my whole life, from grade one until I graduated from college, I only remember having two or three outstanding teachers. Many teachers have a lot to teach, but that does not mean that they are able to teach.

The skill of teaching is more than just having eloquence. We must be able to teach what the Lord has given us and constituted into us. If we are unable to do so, then we are merely lecturers parroting a textbook. True teachers teach that which has been constituted into them through life experiences over many years. Spiritually it is very much the same. In order to be approved, we must have the ability to teach what has been constituted into us.

## Teaching according to People's Need

True teachers are able to teach on the college level, as well as on the grade school level. Their content may be the same for both, but they realize that the students will only understand according to the level they have reached.

When we teach, we should present Christ in a way that fits the need of whomever we are with. The Lord talked about high things with the educated Nicodemus (John 3:1–21), whereas He talked about simple things with the uneducated Samaritan woman (John 4:1–42). In order to be approved, we also must be able to teach according to people's need.

## Teaching by the Anointing

True teachers also teach according to the anointing (1 John 2:20). Without the anointing, our teaching will not be effective. At one time you may have shared something that was so anointed and prevailing. However, when you tried to repeat the same thing in another setting, you may have found that it did not work as before. The Lord's presence was no longer with you. In order to be approved, we must be able to teach by Christ's anointing and not rely merely on the content.

## Teaching with a Goal

True teachers should never teach for the teaching itself. Our teaching must have the goal of leading people to Christ. As we teach, we dispense Christ into them as life. Our teaching should help others advance in their practical living by ushering them into a higher spiritual sphere.

## A Charge and a Burden

True teachers should always present a charge that results in a burden. I am not satisfied when, after speaking to a congregation, no charge is received and no burden is generated. I do not like it when people tell me how good my message was, yet it has no effect on their living. A good message should give everyone the feeling that something has just begun.

Our teaching should be based on what we have received from the Lord, the spiritual need of the hearers, and how the Lord is leading with His anointing. It should bring people to the Lord and elevate them to a higher level in their spiritual life. Our teaching should present a charge that results in a burden, causing people to live another kind of life. If this is the case, then our teaching is effective and we are true teachers. To be approved as Paul was, we must be such teachers.

# 22

# The Approvedness of Timothy

*But I hope in the Lord Jesus to send Timothy to you shortly, so that I also may be encouraged when I learn of your condition. For I have no one else of kindred spirit who will genuinely be concerned for your welfare. For they all seek after their own interests, not those of Christ Jesus. But you know of his proven worth, that he served with me in the furtherance of the gospel like a child serving his father. Therefore I hope to send him immediately, as soon as I see how things go with me; and I trust in the Lord that I myself also will be coming shortly.*

*—Philippians 2:19–24*

## Timothy: A Coworker's Approvedness

God had approved not only Paul but also Timothy. Even the Philippians knew of Timothy's proven worth (Phil. 2:22). Because Timothy was approved, Paul had the confidence to send him to the Philippians. Paul had many coworkers, but it seems that Timothy was the only one who was fully approved. The others sought after their own interests rather than those of Christ Jesus (vv. 20–21). Paul had no confidence that they would genuinely be concerned for the welfare of the Philippians.

Eight factors qualified Timothy to be approved: 1) he became an encouragement to Paul; 2) he was of kindred spirit with the apostle Paul; 3) he was recommended by the churches;

4) he showed his genuineness in tears; 5) he knew the organic order in the body; 6) he pursued with healthy companions; 7) he knew the Scriptures; and 8) he served like a child serving his father in the gospel.

## 1. Becoming an Encouragement to Paul

Paul expected to be encouraged by Timothy's good report concerning the Philippians. In verse 19, the Greek word for "encouraged" is *eupsucheō* (Strong, no. 2174), a compound of two Greek words (*eu* and *psuchē*) literally meaning "good soul." Timothy's report would encourage Paul and give him a good state of soul. It was not only Timothy's report but also his ability to work with Paul that would be such an encouragement to the apostle. Paul was encouraged because Timothy would be able to help the Philippians, for he sincerely cared for their state.

For young Christians to be approved, they must learn to become an encouragement to their church leaders. This is one of the hardest lessons to learn because we are so quick to criticize. We have to learn to stand with those who serve us and be their encouragement, whether we agree with them or not. Blessed is the church whose leaders are in a good state of soul!

One church that I visited regularly was in a troubled state. As I visited them, I was concerned that my own soul would also become troubled and distracted. After a few years, I began to see encouraging things there. They were growing well, and that encouraged me.

Timothy's ability to become an encouragement to the apostle Paul qualified him to be to be an approved coworker with Paul.

## 2. Being Like-souled with Paul

Furthermore, in Philippians 2:20, Paul said that Timothy was of kindred spirit with him. This was the second factor for

Timothy's approvedness. The Greek word for "kindred spirit" here is *isopsuchos* (Strong, no. 2473), a compound of two Greek words (*isos* and *psuchē*) literally meaning "like soul." Whatever occupied Paul's soul also occupied Timothy's soul. The burden of one became the burden of the other. Since Timothy was like-souled with him, Paul was confident that Timothy would genuinely be concerned for the welfare of the Philippians.

At times we may argue and complain with those leading us, saying, "Must I listen to you? This is a free country. I should have my vote!" However, if we insist on having our vote, we might vote ourselves out of the church life. Our church will never become prevailing if we do not know how to be like-souled with those leading us and they do not know how to be like-souled with one another. We must do our best to carry out the burden of our local church.

### 3. Being Recommended by the Churches

The third factor for Timothy's approvedness was his recommendation to Paul by the churches he served. Paul first met Timothy while traveling through Asia Minor preaching the gospel and raising up churches. Two local churches, Lystra and Iconium, spoke well of Timothy (Acts 16:1–2). He probably traveled between these churches and served them. Based on this, these two churches spoke well of him, recommending him to Paul.

Approvedness begins in our local church and with the churches nearby. This was the case with Timothy. Two churches appreciated and respected him. He was from Lystra, but the churches in both Lystra and Iconium recommended him. It is not a small thing to have a good name in our local church. If we have a bad name in our own local church, whatever recommendation we receive from other places means little. It is of no use to be well-accepted by those who live many miles away from us but not by those in our own church.

We should not give those around us the feeling that we are

useless. Instead, they should feel we are full of zeal to the Lord and full of love to His people. To be approved by our own church is crucial. Because they are the ones who really see us, they are the ones who know us best.

We must show love in our church. We must labor in humility and simplicity. As we serve those in our own church diligently, we will gain their appreciation. Without this appreciation there is no approvedness. No mere church-goer can gain approvedness. Only those who know how to give themselves for the church life can be approved. As we live for the church life and serve according to our God-given portion, we will obtain approvedness before God and His people.

## 4. Showing Genuineness in Tears

When the apostle Paul wrote to Timothy, he said, "I recall your tears" (2 Tim. 1:4). When people shed tears, usually they are being very genuine. To have tears is another factor for being approved. Watchman Nee wrote, "Physically speaking, only a tear can wash a man's eyes. The world has so much dust and dirt constantly intruding upon them that, fortunately, with the incessant washing of tears a person may have clearer sight....In the physical realm, a few more tears will cause you to see more clearly. Similarly, without a few tears your spiritual eyes would soon lose their function" (Nee, pp. 4–5).

## Genuine Participation

If we are so touched by a verse from the Bible that we are brought to tears, it shows we are participating in that passage. Tears can also indicate that we are active participants in the lives of others. If we have been Christians for many years and have never shed tears, we must be very lonely and isolated. When we see fellow believers suffering, we shed tears because we partake of their sufferings, and when they experience joy, we shed tears of joy with them (Rom. 12:15). Our tears indicate our genuine participation.

## A Tender Heart

Tears reveal that our hearts are tender, and tender hearts become a source of good works. Many people seem to have no heart. I once read a novel in which one person was so hardened that he shed no tears even after taking advantage of another and causing him to go bankrupt. Some people have this kind of hardened heart. They only care about themselves and have no room in their heart for others. Tears only flow from those whose hearts are very tender. If our hearts are tender, we will have room for others and for the things of the Lord.

Paul surely committed a heavy burden to Timothy when he urged him to "remain on at Ephesus so that you may instruct certain men not to teach strange doctrines" (1 Tim. 1:3). The situation in Ephesus must have been difficult. Though Timothy may have felt that such a commitment was beyond him, he did not give up. However, it did cause him to cry. This is why Paul said, "I recall your tears" (2 Tim. 1:4). Timothy's tears show his approvedness.

Do not look down at people's tears, because in following the Lord, to have tears is healthy. I am not speaking of emotional tears but of tears that show we are one with the Lord, concerned for the church, and participating in others' difficulties. Such tears show our tenderness and allow the Lord to lead us further. To be approved as Timothy was, we must know how to cry before the Lord.

## 5. Knowing the Organic Order in the Body

Timothy was also approved because he knew the organic order in the body of Christ. Paul told the Philippians, "I hope in the Lord Jesus to send Timothy to you shortly" (Phil. 2:19). Paul trusted Timothy because Timothy served together with him "like a child serving his father" (v. 22). Timothy would not have felt he was being ordered to go to Philippi because he honored Paul as he would his father. Paul had confidence that he would not encounter resistance from Timothy, for they had a common view and heart.

Throughout our whole life, this will be a test to us. In our church life, we will receive directions and suggestions about how and where to serve. This should always be carried out in fellowship. We are not living under a dictatorship but are in an organic body which has an order.

When Watchman Nee decided that the work in Taiwan should be developed, he contacted three coworkers, telling them to move to Taiwan immediately. One of the three was a doctor who gave up his practice to answer this call to go to Taiwan. He honored the organic order in the body. As a result, the church life established in Taiwan was healthy and strong. To know the organic order in the body is crucial to gaining approvedness.

## 6. Pursuing with
## Healthy Companions

Our companions are another factor for our approvedness. Paul wrote to Timothy that in a large house there are vessels both to honor and to dishonor (2 Tim. 2:20). The church is a large house, and its members are the many vessels. Paul went on to charge Timothy to "flee from youthful lusts and pursue righteousness, faith, love and peace, with those who call on the Lord from a pure heart" (v. 22).

We must learn to be with those who call on the Lord out of a pure heart. Our companionships reveal something about us. To be approved, we should be with those who are vessels to honor, who follow the Lord, seek only Christ, and genuinely care for the interest of the church. Those we choose to be with will influence us and determine our approvedness (Prov. 12:26).

## 7. Knowing the Scriptures

Another factor for Timothy's approvedness was his familiarity with the Scriptures. Concerning Timothy, Paul wrote, "From childhood you have known the sacred writings" (2 Tim. 3:15). He also charged him to "be diligent to present yourself approved to God as a workman who does not need to be ashamed, accurately handling the word of truth" (2 Tim. 2:15).

How much do we know the Bible? Knowing the Bible does not necessarily mean we can recall every verse perfectly, but at least we should know there is such a verse. Although we may not have thoroughly studied every part of the Bible, we should at least have a general familiarity with the thought of each book. If we want to be approved as servants of the Lord, we have to know the Bible.

## 8. Serving Like a Child with a Father in the Gospel

There is yet another crucial factor concerning Timothy's approvedness. This may even be the most important. Paul wrote that Timothy "served with me in the furtherance of the gospel like a child serving his father" (Phil. 2:22). There are three crucial items we can draw from this verse. First, when we follow the Lord, we should be spiritual children with spiritual fathers. Second, we should serve with our spiritual fathers. Third, our service should be in the gospel.

## A Life Relationship

How did the father-child relationship between Paul and Timothy develop? Paul never traveled around with a banner that said, "I am an apostle looking for a child to raise up and then send to different churches." When Paul passed through Lystra and Iconium, Timothy was recommended to him, and he agreed to take him. A mutual life relationship developed as they spent time together.

This relationship is very crucial to the growth of every young Christian. The relationship between a father and his child is extremely sweet because it is a relationship of life and love. A true father would even lay down his life for his child. Whoever has this kind of father is very blessed.

This father-child relationship is not a matter of formal position but a relationship in life. As children, we should credit our fathers for our growth, spiritual understanding, equipping, and the development of our ability to serve in the church life.

We should desire this father-child relationship, yet there is no need for us to shop around for a father or child. The Lord has set each of us in the right place to develop (1 Cor. 12:18). He has arranged our circumstances.

## A Good Pattern

In a father-child relationship, the father wants his child to grow well, so he endeavors to become a healthy pattern. This pattern is not just in outward behavior but in inward character. It is not just in his living and service, but in his decency, sobriety, and buoyancy. He displays a high understanding and apprehension of spiritual things.

A good father must always be a good pattern to his children. If the father is a drunkard or a gambler, this is very hard on the children and hurts their growth. It is difficult to grow properly without a healthy pattern.

If a spiritual father's conduct is hypocritical, his spiritual child will become a hypocrite. His unhealthy pattern will teach his child that it is okay to tell small lies to smooth over an uncomfortable situation. A father's improper behavior, even in very minor things, can become very damaging to a young Christian's growth. This is why spiritual fathers must guard themselves and be healthy patterns.

## Spiritual Apprenticeship

This father-child relationship is also an apprenticeship. During New Testament times, a son generally continued in his father's footsteps, learning his trade and skills. Joseph was a carpenter, so Jesus was also a carpenter (Matt. 13:55; Mark 6:3). This same principle is also true spiritually. Young believers learn from their spiritual fathers how to read the Bible, pray, share the gospel, shepherd others, serve the church, and handle difficult situations. We learn spiritual things as apprentices from our spiritual fathers.

## Fellow Bond-servants
## of Jesus Christ

The book of Philippians begins with this introduction: "Paul and Timothy, bond-servants of Christ Jesus" (Phil. 1:1). Timothy served with Paul not only as a child with a father but also as a fellow bond-servant of Christ Jesus. This service was an important part of their relationship. They both took the stand of absolute surrender to the Lord.

The father-child relationship can lead to an over-appreciation of a spiritual father, which can lead to the development of factions, divisions, or sects among the believers (1 Cor. 1:12–13). However, taking the same stand together as bond-servants of Jesus Christ can save us from this. We must learn to say, "I am not for my father, and he is not for me. We are both for the Lord." (1 Cor. 3:21–23).

This life relationship is spiritual. It is not common, worldly, or merely human. We may love other believers for many years, invest ourselves in them, and watch them grow and develop with great expectation, but if one day they refuse to take a stand as bond-servants of Christ, that will be the end of the spiritual relationship. We may still be friends, but the father-child relationship will end. It is not because mistakes were made but because the stand as a bond-servant of Christ Jesus was lost.

## Serving with a Commitment

Serving as bond-servants requires a commitment that goes beyond how we spend our time; it demands our whole person. Without this, we are merely employees performing a job. Those who are committed invest themselves to the point of being completely overwhelmed. Sometimes well-intentioned people tell me to take a vacation. Yet, how can I rest? I am driven by my commitment.

A father's commitment does not come and go. He will never say to his child, "So, you finally graduated from a university. Now get out of here! My responsibility is over!" A father's responsibility for his children continues until they have sufficiently developed. This is a commitment. He cannot take a vacation from being a father.

## Our Stand, Commitment, and Labor

Serving as bond-servants requires three things: a stand, a commitment, and a proper labor. Our stand produces our commitment, and our commitment produces our labor.

Suppose we visit a family four or five times with the hope of sharing the gospel with them. They may be happy to see us, but show no interest in the Lord. If our reaction is to conclude, "I've tried and tried. There isn't any hope for these people," then it is not the family that is hopeless but our labor, because we are not laboring with a commitment.

Many times we do not really labor. We merely carry out a duty with no real commitment, like an employee doing out a job. The church leadership may decide that everyone should visit two families every week. We follow the order only because we respect the leaders. Such visitation has very little value. True service has a stand, a commitment, and a labor.

To labor with commitment is very meaningful and enjoyable. It is like a young man and woman getting married. Normally, marriage is preceded by a time of courtship. Suppose a couple skips this time and simply announces one day that they are getting married. This is not nearly as romantic, meaningful, and enjoyable as the young man wooing the young woman's heart until she loves him. In the same way, when we are shepherding younger believers or sharing the gospel with our friends, we should do it in a way that wins their hearts.

When the Lord finally sees the result of all His labor, He will be satisfied. The church is not produced miraculously overnight but through a maturing process that takes a long period of time. The Lord works with each of His children and causes them to grow one by one. He enjoys them and causes them to love Him one by one. He joyfully declares, "Behold, I and the children whom God has given Me" (Heb. 2:13). That is a labor with commitment.

Timothy served with Paul as a child with a father in a sweet relationship that was founded on Christ and grew in Him. However, this relationship was not an end in itself. As a father and child, Paul and Timothy served together in the gospel, laboring together for the fulfillment of God's purpose. They shared the same stand, commitment, and labor, serving together in the gospel. Because of this, Timothy's proven character was evident to the Philippians.

23

# The Approvedness
# of Epaphroditus

*But I thought it necessary to send to you Epaphroditus, my
brother and fellow worker and fellow soldier, who is also your
messenger and minister to my need; because he was longing for
you all and was distressed because you had heard that he was
sick. For indeed he was sick to the point of death, but God had
mercy on him, and not on him only but also on me, so that I
would not have sorrow upon sorrow. Therefore I have sent him all
the more eagerly so that when you see him again you may rejoice
and I may be less concerned about you. Receive him then in the
Lord with all joy, and hold men like him in high regard; because
he came close to death for the work of Christ, risking his life to
complete what was deficient in your service to me.*
*—Philippians 2:25–30*

Paul was a prisoner in Rome living in a rented house while
awaiting his trial before Caesar (Acts 28:16, 30). In addition to
paying rent, he had to pay the expense of the guards constantly
watching him. Although he had such expenses, he could not
get a job, because he was a prisoner. In spite of the fact that
Paul had collected money for those in need in Jerusalem (Rom.
15:25–26; 1 Cor. 16:1–3; 2 Cor. 8:1–5; 9:1–5), there is no
indication that the church in Jerusalem took care of him while
he was imprisoned in Rome.

Paul was in a very difficult situation. Probably many gossiped
about him, saying, "He does not keep the law, even though the

Lord Jesus kept it. He does not keep the Sabbath or administer circumcision." Paul was strongly disliked, even hated, by the Judaizers. No doubt all the churches raised up by Paul were wondering what they should do, especially those in Asia Minor, since they were geographically closer to Jerusalem. Though Paul was in real need financially, he did not receive any care from the churches in Asia Minor, nor from any other church except Philippi (Phil. 4:14–18), which sent Epaphroditus to him with a gift. Epaphroditus remained in Rome to minister to Paul's need.

## Paul's High Appraisal

Paul didn't mention that Epaphroditus had any exceptional talents or abilities, but he appraised him highly, referring to him as his brother, fellow worker, and fellow soldier (2:25). I do not believe there is another person in the entire Bible referred to in such an impressive manner. Epaphroditus had been chosen by the church in Philippi and sent as their messenger to Paul to minister to his needs on their behalf. Now Paul was sending him back to them.

Although we may never become another apostle Paul, we can become an Epaphroditus, an outstandingly common brother. Even though he was not particularly talented, he, along with Paul and Timothy, had become approved. This was shown by Paul's high appraisal of him and by his local church's willingness to send him.

## Distress over the Church's Concern

Paul told the Philippians that Epaphroditus "was longing for you all" (Phil. 2:26). After arriving in Rome, Epaphroditus longed for the fellowship he had with the Philippian believers. Furthermore, Paul wrote that Epaphroditus "was distressed because you had heard that he was sick." This may not seem to make much sense. If Epaphroditus were sick, shouldn't others be distressed about him? And couldn't Paul have rebuked the church in Philippi, saying, "You sent a sick person to minister to me! Rather than helping me, he has become a hindrance. Don't you know what you are doing?"

This case seems unique. The church sent someone to minister to Paul's need, but this one became sick after he arrived, even to the point of drawing near to death. Both Paul and the Philippians must have been anxious for him, but the one who was most sorrowful was Epaphroditus. He became extremely distressed when he heard that the church was worried about him. Rarely have I seen such a sweet relationship between a laboring one and a church, but such mutual concern should be our experience in the church life.

Epaphroditus did not lie on his sick bed hoping the Philippians would send him flowers or words of comfort. It would have been very easy for him to feel he deserved some sympathy, yet he would have preferred to hide his sickness from the church. This is why he longed for them—so he could relieve them, comfort them, and strengthen them. What a manner of life this is! Such an example should affect our care for one another.

## Paul's Sorrow

Concerning Epaphroditus, Paul wrote, "He was sick to the point of death, but God had mercy on him, and not on him only but also on me, so that I would not have sorrow upon sorrow" (Phil. 2:27). Why would Paul have sorrow upon sorrow? In Philippians 1, Paul was so buoyant, joyful, and heavenly. He knew Christ and knew how to stand in oneness with Him. Why would he be brought down because of one sick brother? Paul greatly appreciated Epaphroditus and his service. Even though Epaphroditus may not have seemed particularly striking, Paul referred to him as his brother, fellow worker, and fellow soldier, and as the Philippians' messenger and minister to Paul's needs. There may have been many whom Paul could have spoken of in this manner and who could have cared for his need, but Epaphroditus was one of very few who actually did care for Paul in his situation.

## The Exercise of the Humanity of Jesus

There is no indication that Paul was confident God would heal Epaphroditus, nor did Paul himself try to affect such a healing. We may think that Paul should have just stretched out his hand and said, "In the name of Jesus Christ, rise up and walk!" but that did not happen. Nonetheless, the secret of the church life can be seen in Paul's conduct toward Epaphroditus, which is that we must exercise the humanity of Jesus more than the power of God.

Paul had healed people (Acts 14:8–10; 19:11–12; 28:8) and even raised at least one person from the dead (20:7–12), but at that moment, in that particular place, there was no leading from the Lord to heal Epaphroditus, nor did Paul have the assurance he would get better. Therefore his concern was heavy. As he saw his brother suffering, he also suffered. It caused him sorrow, and if Epaphroditus died at this point, it would have brought sorrow upon sorrow. But God had mercy on both Epaphroditus and Paul, and Epaphroditus recovered. Paul was a great apostle, but the humanity of Jesus he displayed is more precious than any outward exercise of power.

Isn't the Lord's work more crucial than any sick individual? Based on this, we might think Paul should have written to Philippi, "Don't you know who I am in the Lord's work? The one you sent to me is not fitting for the magnitude of the task. Send me a replacement soon." This very way of thinking damages the Lord's work. Many seem to have lost the element of the humanity of Jesus. To them, how the individual believers are doing is no longer important when compared to the overall situation of the Lord's work. However, the believers themselves are the key. The well-being of each believer is the most important element in the church life.

## Paul Becoming Only
## Less Sorrowful

Paul wanted to send Timothy to the Philippians, but even more, he wanted to send Epaphroditus to them. He knew that when they saw that Epaphroditus was healthy, they could rejoice. For this reason he "sent him all the more eagerly" (Phil. 2:28) and charged them to "receive him then in the Lord with all joy" (v. 29). Today one phone call would have settled the matter, but things were different then. Epaphroditus had to travel the entire distance from Rome to Philippi and present himself to the church. Seeing him, the church would be able to rejoice.

Paul wrote, "Therefore I have sent him all the more eagerly so that when you see him again you may rejoice and I may be less concerned about you" (Phil. 2:28). It is easy to understand why the Philippians would rejoice at the return of Epaphroditus in good health, but it is more difficult to understand why Paul would only be less concerned. Why would he not rejoice as well? My feeling is that this episode with Epaphroditus gave him such sorrow that he was not able to fully recover.

While Epaphroditus was so sick, sorrow possessed Paul's whole being. Although Paul told the Philippians to "rejoice in the Lord always" (Phil. 4:4), he himself was sorrowful and testified that if God had not been merciful, he would have had sorrow upon sorrow. He had watched as Epaphroditus was consumed with sickness, even drawing near to death. Once he recovered, Paul sent him back to the Philippians so they could rejoice. Paul loved Epaphroditus, and that experience filled his heart with so much grief that he could not quickly recover.

Epaphroditus came to Rome with a gift for Paul from the saints in Philippi (Phil. 4:18). Paul indicated that Epaphroditus's sickness was related to taking care of Paul and his coworkers, for he wrote that Epaphroditus "came close to death for the work of Christ, risking his life to complete what was deficient in your service to me" (2:30). Possibly, when the gift was used up, Epaphroditus took a job—perhaps even more than one job—to support Paul and those with him. Epaphroditus may have overextended himself, living on very little and sacrificing his own needs for Paul's sake. When this caused Epaphroditus to draw near to death, Paul may have deeply regretted that he allowed him to work so hard. By the Lord's mercy, Epaphroditus recovered, but the feeling of grief remained with Paul.

Let me give an example from my own experience. Once I became desperate for a young believer to grow in the Lord. In my zeal to push him along, I offended him. Eventually, he became cold and discouraged, which caused me heartache. Whenever someone mentioned his name, I felt a twinge of sorrow within my spirit. By the Lord's mercy, he was eventually restored and began to develop again. However, the sense of sorrow over that situation has never totally left me.

Although we need to know the truth, the reality of the church life is in these human interactions. It is precious when others become sealed in our hearts and their growth and well-being fully occupy us. This was the case between Epaphroditus and Paul. We should not simply say to someone who is in suffering, "Trust in the Lord. He will take care of you." We cannot practice the church life like this. Our hearts should be occupied with others' well-being.

## Paul's High Regard for Epaphroditus

Regarding Epaphroditus, Paul charged the Philippians to "receive him then in the Lord with all joy, and hold men like him in high regard" (Phil. 2:29). The Greek word for "high regard" here is *entimos* (Strong, no. 1784), which means "dear, more honourable, precious, in reputation." Having made himself more dear and precious by passing through such a hard situation, Epaphroditus had earned Paul's commendation. I believe he went through the whole experience in a sober, godly, and Christ-like manner, just as the Lord passed through His own suffering. Therefore, Paul encouraged the Philippians to hold Epaphroditus in high regard. Paul himself highly esteemed

Epaphroditus not because of some status or position but because his person had achieved a certain stature.

Once a highly respected political leader had a son. The people of that country held the son in high regard because of his position as the son of this leader. Eventually, however, they came to regard him because of his own integrity and stature. This son himself became a great man, and then had several sons of his own, one of whom enlisted in the military. This son told everyone, including his superior officers, "My grandfather is the Commander-in-chief." None of the officers knew how to handle him. He had high status, but his person was of low quality. When his father found out about his son's conduct, he drove directly to the base and reprimanded him for his behavior. He knew that high regard should be based on the quality of our person, not on our status or position.

The Philippians desired to care for Paul, who had raised up that church, but for some reason there was a lack in their care (Phil. 2:30). They were concerned enough, however, to send Epaphroditus. Upon his arrival, Epaphroditus saw the need and set about working to fill up the Philippians' lack of service toward Paul. I really like this portion of the Bible because it portrays the reality and practicality of the church life. We are not for the work. We are for the organic body of Christ. In this organic body, our relationship should be like the relationship between the apostle Paul, the church in Philippi, Timothy, and Epaphroditus. Praise the Lord for this wonderful organic body!

## A Minister to the
## Apostle's Need

Although Epaphroditus was a common brother, the apostle Paul regarded him very highly. Paul referred to him as his brother, his fellow worker, his fellow soldier, and the Philippians' messenger and minister to his need (Phil. 2:25). This simple brother became a minister to the needs of a great apostle.

There is a long road down which we must travel before we can become such ministers. As soon as some are saved, they want to take a shortcut and immediately become ministers. However, we should consider the sequence of Paul's description of Epaphroditus. He was a brother first, before he could become a fellow worker. Then, as a fellow worker he became a fellow soldier. It was as a fellow soldier that he became the messenger of a local church. It was only because he was a brother, fellow worker, fellow soldier, and messenger that he was able to become a minister. This route is the way for those who are not necessarily that gifted or manifested to eventually become ministers like Epaphroditus.

## Carrying out Practical Matters Spiritually

God's work and speaking and the churches' development came through the apostle Paul (Eph. 3:2; 1 Cor. 3:10). As Paul's need was met, God was able to move and speak freely on the earth. Meeting the apostle's need was not merely something material. Yes, ministry Epaphroditus provided was practical, but he carried out this practical ministry spiritually.

Paul wrote that Epaphroditus "came close to death for the work of Christ, risking his life to complete what was deficient in your service to me" (Phil. 2:30). In reading this, it is possible to take the apostle Paul as the center of Epaphroditus's ministry. In this case the verse would mean that Epaphroditus, a minister, drew near to death to fill up the lack of service toward Paul. Paul himself, however, was not the center. This ministry was a practical service, but it was carried out spiritually. Epaphroditus's calling was not merely to care for Paul's need but to care for God's need through Paul. Paul's well-being was not the center; God and His work were the center.

By the Lord's mercy, some have been able to raise up very large congregations. Others might be impressed by this and seek to copy their success, making the large congregation their focus and center. Our center, however, must be God and His work, and we must carry out our work spiritually, not merely by copying others' methods.

Carrying out practical things spiritually is very precious to God. For example, we may come together with others to plan a gospel meeting. We consider matters such as who should be invited, who should speak, which songs should be used, how the seating should be arranged, and so on. These are practical matters, not spiritual. We must, however, carry out these practical matters spiritually.

The first thing to do in preparing for this gospel meeting is to pray, "O Lord, have mercy on our unsaved friends. Have mercy on us as we carry out this event." We need a lot of prayer, fasting, and fellowship in order to carry out all the details spiritually. Before the meeting, everyone should learn to pray and enjoy the gospel verses. We should train others to pray and give testimonies during the meeting. We should encourage some to spend time with the newly saved ones after the meeting. Eventually, everyone is brought into a spiritual exercise. The highest value of the gospel meeting is not the success of the meeting itself but that the entire church becomes revitalized and bears more spiritual weight.

We could have many good gospel meetings in which people get saved, but if the gospel is not carried out spiritually, eventually the church will tire of such events. If, however, the center is Christ, the result will be the increase of Christ among both the new ones and the church, and the church itself will be enlivened. For this reason, practical things must be carried out spiritually.

## Becoming Ministers

Because Epaphroditus carried out practical things spiritually, he was able to be a minister to Paul's need. Each of us should aspire to this. We may not be noticeably talented or gifted, but eventually we should each become ministers like Epaphroditus.

We may not become ministers to some great apostle's need, but we should be able to meet the church's need. If we are ushers, we can become ministers to meet the church's need by caring for those whom we usher. If we are in charge of parking, we should carry out our service spiritually.

In the Old Testament, there were two types of service to God in the tabernacle—the practical service of the Levites (Num. 1:50–51), and the more spiritual service of the priests (Exo. 28:41, 43). In the New Testament age, however, every believer is a priest (1 Pet. 2:9). Even if we are handling what seems to be Levitical work, we must carry it out in a priestly way. We must carry out practical things spiritually.

Although Epaphroditus was commissioned by the church in Philippi to carry out a practical service, he handled it in a priestly way. He had grown from being only a common brother to being a minister. As such, he became much more than Paul's "ATM"—he ministered to Paul's spiritual need. What an experience of growth! To attain a ministry like this, we must pass through a process of growth.

Because Epaphroditus was able to carry out his practical service spiritually, his maturity was manifested. This is why Paul exhorted the Philippians to hold him in high regard. We don't all have the same capacity. For example, if I asked someone who drives a truck for a living to give a three-day conference, he may feel scared to death. However, whether or not we can give wonderful messages, we can still carry out our service as New Testament ministers. The value of our service will be in how spiritual we become in the process of our learning to serve, how much Christ we gain in that process, and how much our spiritual exercise becomes a help to others.

## A Brother, Fellow Worker, and Fellow Soldier

Because Paul and Epaphroditus shared the same divine life, Paul spoke of him as his brother (Phil. 2:25). Paul went on to call him his fellow worker, not because he could get many people saved or was so capable, but because they had the same vision and commitment. Epaphroditus was also Paul's fellow soldier, for he struggled and fought alongside Paul for the kingdom of the Lord.

Being a fellow soldier is not related to the scale of what we do. We do not have to be one of David's mighty men (2 Sam. 23:8–39). We do not have to get thirty people saved with one gospel message or heal a dying man. We simply have to be faithful to carry out the practical commitment the Lord has given to us in a spiritual way. In this way, we will become fellow soldiers struggling and fighting for the same goal—the Lord's testimony.

There are many who, like Epaphroditus, are not that talented, manifested, or gifted, yet Paul called Epaphroditus his brother, fellow worker, and fellow soldier. Today we also can share this same life, commitment, and struggle for the Lord's testimony together.

## A Local Church's Apostle

If we want to be approved as Epaphroditus was, we must be ready to be sent out by our local church as he was. Because the church in Philippi sent Epaphroditus, Paul referred to him as "your messenger" (Phil. 2:25). The Greek word for "messenger" here is *apostolos* (Strong, no. 652), which can also be translated "apostle" or "he that is sent." When we talk about apostles, our feeling is that they are great, spiritual men who have raised up many churches. It is true that many apostles do raise up churches, but apostles can also be sent out by local churches. Apostles are those sent out with a commitment. In the case of Epaphroditus, that commitment was to bring a gift from Philippi to the apostle Paul in Rome.

Can our local church send us out with a commitment? If we are not approved, we will not be sent out. Our local church is where the reality of our growth in life, commitment, and service are tested. Everything is tested in our local church.

Only those prepared to be apostles of their own local church are qualified to be real ministers of Christ. Most Christians do not reach this point. They make their local church into a nest from which they refuse to fly. Even if the Lord chooses to keep us where we are, in our heart we must be willing to be sent out. We should not build nests in our own church. If we are brothers, fellow workers, and fellow soldiers, we can be apostles sent out by our local church. In this way, we can become ministers who are able to carry out practical things spiritually as Epaphroditus did. He is a pattern to us all.

# 24

# Seven Mountains in Our Pursuit of Christ (1)

*Finally, my brethren, rejoice in the Lord. To write the same things again is no trouble to me, and it is a safeguard for you. Beware of the dogs, beware of the evil workers, beware of the false circumcision; for we are the true circumcision, who worship in the Spirit of God and glory in Christ Jesus and put no confidence in the flesh, although I myself might have confidence even in the flesh. If anyone else has a mind to put confidence in the flesh, I far more: circumcised the eighth day, of the nation of Israel, of the tribe of Benjamin, a Hebrew of Hebrews; as to the Law, a Pharisee; as to zeal, a persecutor of the church; as to the righteousness which is in the Law, found blameless. But whatever things were gain to me, those things I have counted as loss for the sake of Christ.*

*—Philippians 3:1–7*

At the end of chapter 2 of his letter to the Philippians, Paul spoke of sending Timothy and Epaphroditus to them. It seems he was concluding his epistle, yet he did not end there. Instead, Paul said, "Finally, my brethren...." The word "finally" here is not a conclusion, but rather a continuation that opens the door to one of the most profound chapters in the Bible.

## Paul's Goal: Oneness with Christ

Paul wanted to show the Philippians the goal of his living

and service. Though he was imprisoned in Rome, he was able to rejoice as he pursued Christ. His was a life of entering into complete oneness with Christ. This is what a Christian life should be. We are one with Christ in life, we are being mingled with Him in nature, and even more, we must experience being incorporated with Him in person. To be healthy Christians, we must live a life of becoming one with Christ. His person must become our person.

The highlight of chapter 3 is verse 12: "Not that I have already obtained it, or have already become perfect, but I press on so that I may lay hold of that for which also I was laid hold of by Christ Jesus." Christ has laid hold of us; now we must lay hold of Christ. He lives in us, and now we must live Him out.

## Rejoice in the Lord

This living of laying hold of Christ is manifested in our rejoicing. This is why Paul began this chapter with a charge to rejoice. Rejoicing should be our hallmark as Christians. However, rejoicing is not in our nature. If it were, we would never have felt the need to be saved. As Christians, we should rejoice in spite of our awareness of our own failure and the fallen situation around us. We rejoice because Christ is so real to us.

How is this possible? If we know Jesus as Paul knew Jesus, we would surely be a rejoicing people. Paul writes this word to us to let us know that if we are not experiencing such joy, then we have not yet laid hold of that for which Christ Jesus has also laid hold of us. If we are rejoicing in the living person of Christ, we are healthy and ready to advance along the route Paul portrayed in this chapter.

If we are pursuing something other than Christ, even though it may be related to Him, we need to be brought back to Christ Himself. If we do not have the joy of Christ in a particular matter, then regardless how good or spiritual it may be, something is wrong.

The Philippian believers were very dear to Paul. Though

they were faithful and healthy, he wanted to take them another step forward. He wanted to bring them into a life of rejoicing in oneness with Christ. What hindered them from rejoicing, laying hold of Christ, and becoming one with Him? Paul presented seven mountains they would encounter as they pursued such a life.

## The First Mountain: Overcoming Religion

The first mountain is to overcome religion, clearly implied in verse 2: "Beware of the dogs, beware of the evil workers, beware of the false circumcision."

There is something in our blood that seeks assurance that we are right. When we feel we are doing what we should for God, we feel at rest. The problem is that in religion, there is only "I am right and you are wrong." In politics, people are balanced by the opposing party. Ideologically, conservatives and liberals are a balance to each other. For those caught in religion, however, there is no such balance. Once we identify ourselves with a religious ideology, no one can touch us. There is very little room for argument.

Once religious ideology takes over, there is no longer any freedom. Instead, something in addition to the common faith, such as a certain practice or teaching, becomes a measuring stick for fellowship. This prevents people from pursuing Christ.

## Beware of the Dogs, the Evil Workers, and the False Circumcision

Paul used three terms to describe the religious people who were troubling the Philippians: "dogs" has to do with their person; "evil workers" or "workers of evil" has to do with their actions; and "false circumcision" has to do with their practice. These three terms—dogs, evil workers, and false circumcision—all refer to the same people.

The dogs Paul referred to were the Judaizers, the Jewish religionists. However, when it comes to religion, we all have some dog element in our nature. Therefore, we should not be quick to point our finger at others. Rather, we must first apply this word to ourselves. Religion is in everyone's blood. Religious people attract us because we ourselves are religious. We want someone to tell us what to do, thinking that by listening to what they say and doing it, the religious need in us will be satisfied, and we will find rest. This is why we respond to religion. When we hear someone who wants to give us a way, we think, "Now I have found it!" What we haven't realized is that when we receive such teachings, we are finished as far as entering into oneness with Christ is concerned.

In the Bible, dogs are unclean animals that are said to vomit up their food and then return to eat it again (Prov. 26:11, 2 Pet. 2:22). They do not digest things properly. Instead, the same thing passes in and out again and again, but little of it becomes theirs. This is a harsh word. We would probably rather have written, "Beware of false teachers." Paul was bold to simply say, "Beware of the dogs." He was telling the Philippians that some in the church life have a dog nature. These vomit out the things they have taken in. They are always in the process of taking in the Word, but it never becomes a part of them. What is holy, after they are finished with it, is transformed into something unclean.

Those whom Paul called dogs he also called evil workers. The Greek word for "evil" here is *kakos*, which can also be translated "worthless" (Strong, no. 2556). These evil workers were not committing obviously sinful or rebellious deeds. Such actions would not have caused as much damage to those in the church because everyone would have recognized them as evil. Instead, they presented essentially worthless things to the believers in a way that cheated them. Paul had seen the effect of such evil workers on other churches. After these religious dogs arrived, the believers became preoccupied with what they should eat and whether or not believers should be circumcised. Deception was involved. What they presented as having high value in fact took people away from what had true value. Their work defrauded others of Christ, which is extremely evil. Thus, they are not only unclean dogs but also evil workers.

Lastly, Paul referred to these dogs and evil workers as the false circumcision. The Greek word used here is *katatomē* (Strong, no. 2699), which is a derisive term meaning "mutilation." In Paul's mind, the physical circumcision the Judaizers promoted was now nothing but mutilation.

## Distraction from Christ

In order to enter into complete oneness with Christ, the Philippians had to overcome the distraction of religion, which was promoted by these evil workers. They had to realize that although these workers seemed to be good, they actually were doing an evil work, damaging others. It is possible to do something in the Lord's name that damages people by drawing them away from Christ. If we are not aware of the work of such religious people and are drawn away by them, we may not even realize it when we stop following Christ.

Such teachers do not come with anything obviously evil. Instead they come with an open Bible. What they say is according to the Bible, yet their focus is not Christ, so as we listen we are taken away from the living person of Christ Himself. This is such a serious matter!

I first came to the U.S. to attend theological school. Forgive me for saying this, but when I was there, I met many religious dogs. They were nice and even pious men, but though they seemingly were such great students of the Bible, they had little reality of its content. One day, in a chapel service, we were told to bow our heads to pray. Something seemed strange about the prayer, so I looked up and saw that the prayer was being read. There was no life; that was a "doggish" activity. If we are not careful, however, we could do the same thing. We are here to gain Christ. Yet sometimes when we hear others speak about Christ, we pass that speaking along to others without allowing that portion of Christ to become our own. We are distracted from Christ by a teaching concerning Him. What we hear of Christ must become ours! Christ Himself must be our focus, our center, and the One we give ourselves to.

## Teachings and Practices

No teaching or practice should bring us to that teaching or practice itself. All our teaching and practice must bring us to Christ. When the result of everything that happens in the church life is that we are brought to Christ, the situation in the church is healthy. However, when the focus is something other than Christ Himself, we become sectarian.

More than two hundred fifty years ago, a group of believers took this motto as their guide: In essentials—unity; in nonessentials—liberty; and in all things—love. This is why these believers, who came to be called Moravians, were able to prevail for so long. Regarding the nonessential things—things not a part of the common faith—we should allow others to follow the Lord. Religious teachers, however, make nonessential things seem essential and then demand unity on these things. For example, we should consider Christ and His work essential. However, we should never allow practices or nonessential teachings to become an issue that would take away the love from among us. When no one insists that their teaching concerning nonessentials be accepted, but instead, we all focus on Christ alone, we will have brotherly love.

Throughout two thousand years of church history, no group has been able to overcome religion. This is what Paul was confronting. His struggle was with the Judaizers, who were very powerful religious dogs. Though they used the Scriptures, through their teaching they brought people away from Christ. They did this by mixing nonessentials with essentials. They might have said, "Yes, we need Christ, but we also need the Sabbath. Jesus is the Lord, but we also need to be circumcised." Christ became of no benefit to those who received such teachings and practices (cf. Rom. 4:14; Gal. 5:2–4). Any practice we carry out apart from Christ is a mutilation dividing us from Christ. One of Satan's strategies is to offer us teachings and practices as a substitute for seeking and following Christ (John 5:39–40).

Many know how to speak the right language, but they do not know how to follow Christ. How many can honestly say, "I am where I am and I am doing what I am doing because the Lord has led me this way"? Religion hides our true condition. This is why it is so difficult for the Lord to have the preeminence among us. It is much easier to follow a practice or teaching than to come to the Lord Jesus, yet it is His desire that we would know Him. We should learn from Paul that our goal as Christians is to live in oneness with Christ.

We must strive to follow the living Christ. As we are before the Lord, it is normal that He would lead us. It is better to make mistakes as we try to follow the Lord than to do things without Him. He is able to teach us even in our errors. This is the way to healthiness.

## The Second Mountain:
## Having No Confidence in the Flesh

Paul gave three aspects of those who are the true circumcision: They "worship in the Spirit of God," they "glory in Christ Jesus," and they "put no confidence in the flesh" (Phil. 3:3). These three are in direct contrast to the three things mentioned in verse 2: the dogs, the evil workers, and the false circumcision.

Putting "no confidence in the flesh" is the second mountain we will encounter as we pursue a life of oneness with Christ. In verses 4–6, Paul said he might have had confidence in the flesh and gave us seven points to consider: (1) he was circumcised on the eighth day; (2) of the nation of Israel—Paul was not a convert; he was born a Jew; (3) of the tribe of Benjamin; (4) a Hebrew of Hebrews; (5) as to the Law, a Pharisee, which was the strictest sect among the Jews; (6) as to zeal, a persecutor of the church—he was so zealous that he even took it upon himself to stamp out the Christian faith; (7) as to the righteousness which is in the Law, he was found blameless. Each one of these points is impressive. No one surpassed him.

Paul, however, said, "Whatever things were gain to me, those things I have counted as loss for the sake of Christ" (v. 7). We must come to the point that we have no confidence or pride in the flesh. Inwardly, Paul put no stock in such things. He placed no confidence in them.

Young people may secretly think, "Young as I am, I already love Jesus so much. Surely the Lord will greatly use me!" They may feel assured of themselves, thinking they know which way to take, what they are doing, and having confidence that they can do it. Once, when I was in high school, a number of my peers were invited to go away for a week of special fellowship. I, however, was not asked to go, since I was not regarded as one of the promising ones. Sometimes it is a blessing to have nothing. Perhaps if I had been chosen, I would not have developed in a healthy way. Instead, I may have boasted of my self-importance.

Even if we are able to pass the first mountain, overcoming religion, we may still easily be trapped by the second, self-confidence. Until, like Paul, we have no confidence in the flesh, we will not be able to go beyond this second mountain. Oh, how we need to beware of the flesh!

## 25

# Seven Mountains in Our Pursuit of Christ (2)

*More than that, I count all things to be loss in view of the surpassing value of knowing Christ Jesus my Lord, for whom I have suffered the loss of all things, and count them but rubbish so that I may gain Christ, and may be found in Him, not having a righteousness of my own derived from the Law, but that which is through faith in Christ, the righteousness which comes from God on the basis of faith.*

*—Philippians 3:8–9*

### The Third Mountain:
### Counting All Things as Rubbish

For the surpassing value of knowing Christ, Paul suffered the loss of all things (Phil. 3:8). He counted not only the things others admired but all things as rubbish so that he might gain Christ. Counting all things as rubbish is the third mountain we will encounter in our pursuit of Christ.

"All things" here refers primarily to any and all things that might become our calling other than Christ Himself. For example, some people are ambitious to pursue a career, some are ambitious to excel in sin, and some are ambitious in serving their church. Paul, however, counted nothing else in his life to be of any real value except Christ. Therefore, nothing else ever replaced Christ as his unique calling.

What things are gains to you? Your career? A fortune?

A name? Success in Christian service? As long as you have something other than Christ as your gain, you will not be able to know Christ in full. Paul counted all things as rubbish that he might gain Christ. The secret of gaining Christ fully is letting go of everything else and counting all other things as rubbish, garbage, something fit only for dogs.

## Valuing Christ

In verse 7 Paul said, "Whatever things were gain to me, those things I have counted as loss for the sake of Christ." If Christ is to be truly present, everything else must disappear.

Paul continued, "I count all things to be loss in view of the surpassing value of knowing Christ Jesus my Lord" (v. 8). The Greek word for "knowing" here is *gnōsis*. This can refer to knowledge which is subjective and inward as well as an objective revelation (Vine, 2:301). Therefore, when Paul said he was counting all things loss for the surpassing value of knowing Christ, it meant he was pursuing Christ so that he might know Him in all aspects: who He is; what He has accomplished; what He is doing; our eternal status in Christ; our subjective experience in Him; our stand in Him, etc. All such things can be said to be the surpassing value of knowing Christ Jesus our Lord.

Verse 8 concludes, "For whom I have suffered the loss of all things, and count them but rubbish so that I may gain Christ." It was for Christ Himself that Paul was willing to suffer the loss of all things and count them but rubbish. He saw the surpassing value of knowing Christ and desired to gain Him.

## Suffering the Loss of All Things

Naturally speaking, it is not an easy thing to hear the phrase "for whom I have suffered the loss of all things" (v. 8). This goes against what we feel is valuable according to our human nature. Generally, if we didn't value something, we wouldn't have gained it in the first place. That is why it is not easy to give it up. We must be willing to suffer the loss of all things. All things include both the good and the bad, the important and the unimportant, the spiritual and the natural. We find it hard to let certain things go, however, which is why Paul used the word "suffer."

It can be hard to give up even small things. If you have a garage, think about what is in it right now. Many garages are so cluttered with things that they cannot hold the cars for which they were built. That is just how people are. Many homes are also filled with things because of this mentality. Things are cheap, and there are always sales. People purchase things they don't really need, yet they feel they cannot throw them out after they get them home.

Suppose, after investing ourselves in a career and attaining a respectable position, the Lord would lead us to move. Would we be able to count our position as loss? How hard that struggle would be! Would we be able to give up our house and uproot our family? Yet the reward is so wonderful—gaining Christ and being found in Him.

Our hearts have limited capacity. If we cannot give that capacity to Christ, we will not gain Him. If we want to gain Christ, other things will have to go. Our belongings, our interests, our hobbies, our manner of life, etc. will all have to be counted loss so that eventually the only thing occupying our hearts is Christ. This is what it means to say, "For whom I have suffered the loss of all things."

## A Continual Exercise

I am happy when I see people make the decision to drop everything to follow the Lord. This decision may cost them their degree, their profession, and their fortune, but they have made more room for Christ. However, this is only the first of many steps. At every step they will have to declare, "For Christ I have suffered the loss of all things!" It never gets easier to say this. Many who have determined to drop everything to follow the Lord still get caught by something else along the way.

These things that occupy us can be even the most precious things. Through more than fifty years of loving the Lord, I have acquired some amount of spiritual riches. However, the day I begin to consider that I have something—Bible knowledge, all the people I have raised up, or rich revelation—I would have to say goodbye to the further gaining of Christ. Instead of Christ, I would be filled with my fifty years of Bible riches, ministering ability, and fruitfulness. If I value anything in my life more than Christ, He is pushed out.

This applies to churches as well as individuals. The day a church declares, "We have it; we see it; now we have the way!" is the day Christ's presence disappears. So many Christian groups began with fresh revelation from the Lord out of the Scripture. The problem comes, however, as they hold onto this revelation instead of clinging to Christ Himself. They have a wonderful heritage but not much to show for it today. What frustrated their pursuit of Christ was not worldly things but the revelation the Lord had given them. Because they valued this more than Christ Himself, they departed from Him, and He had to pass them by (see Rev. 3:14–22). How serious this is!

This is why Paul counted all things loss and even suffered the loss of all things. When Paul told Timothy that the time of his departure had come (2 Tim 4:6), it seems he was peaceful to go. He had finished his course and had fought the good fight. He didn't say, "I still need more time! I have seen so much. I can still be a help to the churches." Paul did not hold onto the ministry God had given him. What he valued was the gaining of Christ.

## The Consequences of Collecting Rubbish

Some antique collectors fill their houses with so much antique furniture they have very little living space. We may collect spiritual things like this, not realizing how much they occupy us, even to the point that Christ is pushed out. Paul, however, determined never to let such a thing happen. This is why he not only counted all things loss but even counted all things as rubbish.

Some rubbish only occupies; some both occupies and contaminates. I have to be careful or else preoccupation with my furniture will contaminate my heart and affect my spiritual health. Because of this, I must learn to simply reckon such things as loss and count them as rubbish.

We must be careful about what occupies us. We only have a certain amount of room in our heart. If we do not know how to count things loss, we will have less room for Christ. Things that occupy us will contaminate us and our church life. Even the best teaching, when exalted too highly, can replace Christ and become a source of contamination. It is possible for a church to be occupied with a teaching or practice to the exclusion of Christ. We should never consider that any particular Christian teaching or practice is our focus. Only Christ Himself is our focus!

When rubbish is present, our spiritual health and church life will deteriorate. Although we know Christ alone is pure, it is so easy to accumulate things and not quickly let them go. In the Old Testament, the children of Israel were warned not to hold onto the manna from God, otherwise it would breed worms and become foul (Exo. 16:19–20). Anything that was once fresh from the Lord can frustrate the possibility of having a fresh Christ today. This is why Paul was so strong here. He wanted only to gain Christ. Therefore he suffered the loss of all things and counted them as rubbish.

## The Example of Paul

Paul, though so joined to Christ, still had to say, "I have suffered the loss of all things, and count them but rubbish so that I may gain Christ, and may be found in Him." He determined that nothing would contaminate his heart and crowd Christ out. This is why when the Corinthians were disputing about whether or not they should eat meat offered to idols, Paul could simply respond, "Whether, then, you eat or drink or whatever you do, do all to the glory of God" (1 Cor 10:31). When we grow to this extent, issues such as this will not concern us. What did concern Paul, however, were the things that affected the oneness of the body of Christ. To those who began claiming they were of one apostle or another, he was very strong (1 Cor. 3:3–4). Concerning minor issues, however, he honored everyone's conscience as to how they felt to follow Christ, for his goal in the church life was to gain Christ and Him alone.

Anything that replaces or crowds out Christ will damage our church life. If the focus among us is some doctrine or practice rather than Christ, our church life has become contaminated. We need to be before the Lord and pray, "Lord, be merciful to us so that in our church life there is no contaminating rubbish. We want to be occupied only with You."

## The Fourth Mountain: Being Found in Christ

Paul continued, "And may be found in Him, not having a righteousness of my own derived from the Law, but that which is through faith in Christ, the righteousness which comes from God on the basis of faith" (Phil. 3:9). Being found in Christ is the fourth mountain we will encounter as we pursue Christ.

We need to consider what being found in Christ means, because it is very different from our natural concept. Because we want to be found in Christ, we avoid being found in the material world, the religious world, or the sinful world. Instead, we seek to be filled with our own righteousness according to the law, thinking that then we will be found in Christ. However, Paul doesn't say that to be found in Christ means not to be found in the material, religious, or sinful world. According to Paul, we can be found in Christ even though we are terrible. He says his aim was to be found in Him, not having any righteousness of his own.

According to Paul, if we have our own righteousness, we cannot be found in Christ. This simply is not our thought. Our thought is if we lack righteousness, we need to spend time to mourn our poor situation. However, Paul indicated that even though there is nothing good in us, we can be found in Christ by means of the righteousness which is based on faith. It is not our own righteousness but our faith in Christ that causes us to be found in Him. Because we have faith in Christ's redemptive work, we have the righteousness of God. Thus, we are found in Christ.

It is not for anyone but God to say whether or not we are found in Christ. This righteousness that enables us to be found in Christ is not something before men but before God. It is not even we ourselves who determine it; God is the One who determines it. How much better it is if God declares we are found in Christ than if we claim we are found in Christ! The way He determines this is by whether or not we have faith in Christ.

## Righteousness by Faith

Those who truly follow the Lord count all things as rubbish so that they might gain Christ and be found in Him. They no longer cling to their own personal righteousness which is derived from the law. Theirs is the righteousness that is out of faith in Christ, the righteousness which is from God based on faith (Phil. 3:9). In other words, they are found in Christ having a righteousness based upon Christ's accomplished work.

There is no possibility of our being found in Christ based on our own righteousness. It would be a miracle if we could even have our little toe in Christ at any moment. Because of our faith, however, we may be found entirely in Christ. It is good that being found in Christ is not determined by our ability. Instead, it is by our faith, and even that faith is a gift from God (Eph. 2:8).

Are we in spirit all the time? Do we constantly read the Bible? Are we overcoming every hour? Are we continually considering the profit of others and praying for them? To all this, we would have to say, "No." Then how can we say we are found in Christ? We can because, even as we are defeated, we still believe in what Christ has accomplished for us. We believe Christ is our Savior. We believe that we are being carried by Him. This is the faith on which our righteousness is based, and it is because of this righteousness that we are found in Him. When God sees us, He sees us in Christ because of our faith in Christ.

### Three Stages of Being Found in Christ

Our being found in Christ is actually in three stages. Firstly, as we have noted, we are found in His completed and accomplished work. Our being found in Him is based on our faith in what He has done, not on our works. From the moment we took Christ as our Savior, God declared us righteous, and we have been continually found in Christ. Since this is the case, why would Paul still seek to be found in Christ? It is because there are further stages of being found in Christ.

Secondly, this faith enables us to be found in Christ's present work. We may be found in Christ according to His completed work, but are we found in what the Lord is doing now? When the Lord is advancing, we should advance with Him. When the Lord is working, we should work with Him. This is a further stage—we are found in Christ because we live according to Him. For this, we need to know the flow of the Spirit and how to be in it. This flow brings in life. If we are truly found in Christ by being in this divine flow, wherever we go, people will be made alive (cf. Ezek. 47:9).

Thirdly, we are found in Christ by being found in His person. When we reach this stage, we become truly spiritual and even heavenly. We are above issues involving who or what is right or wrong. We are one with Christ and completely trusting in Him.

It is worthwhile to consider how and why Paul wrote these verses. May the Lord have mercy on us. May we have a strong cry within, "Lord, I want to be found in You! I want to be found in Your accomplished work, Your present work, and in You Yourself." May we all find rest in Him and yet be absolute for His desire!

# 26

# Seven Mountains in Our Pursuit of Christ (3)

*That I may know Him and the power of His resurrection and the fellowship of His sufferings, being conformed to His death.*
*—Philippians 3:10*

## The Fifth Mountain:
## Knowing Christ and Being
## Conformed to His Death

If we are gaining Christ and found in Him, we have arrived at a very marvelous stage of Christian experience and are ready to face the fifth mountain: "That I may know Him and the power of His resurrection, and the fellowship of His sufferings, being conformed to His death" (v. 10). This is very much a matter of subjective experience. To really know Christ, we must experientially know the power of His resurrection, the fellowship of His sufferings, and what it is to be conformed to His death.

### Resurrection as Our Starting Point

We may think that suffering should come first, then death, and finally resurrection, but that is not the order presented here for our experience. Our view is that we are on earth trying to reach the heavens. According to Ephesians 2:6, however, we are already in the heavenly places with Christ! God's view is that we begin our Christian life in the heavenly places and grow to maturity by learning to be with the Lord in our situations on earth, becoming conformed to His death in our living.

The more we are conformed to Christ's death, the more we will know His resurrection power, but in order to go through the sufferings of Christ and in order for us to become conformed to His death, we need resurrection as our starting point.

Suffering brings us into death, so suffering and death are companions. However, in order to pass through suffering and death, we must first know Christ's resurrection. As we shall see, resurrection, suffering, and death correspond to our being united with Christ in life, mingled with Him in nature, and eventually incorporated with Him in person.

## The Power of His Resurrection
## Being Ours

Every Christian wants to know Christ, and here Paul indicated the way for us to know Him. He was very practical. First, we must participate in, know, and enjoy the power of resurrection. In experience, resurrection involves strengthening power, enlivening power, ascending power, and even governing power. This same power seated Christ on the throne in the heavenly places (Eph. 1:19–21). By this power, every need of our Christian lives can be fulfilled. This power became ours the day we believed and received Jesus as our Savior. Christ brought us all into His resurrection. Thus, we are in the heavenly places with Him already and have access to this power for whatever is needed in our Christian lives. We will face thousands of challenges and experience continuous needs as believers, but this unfailing power is always present with us to uphold and supply us.

## Rescued by Resurrection Power

One great challenge that requires resurrection power to

overcome is our natural mind. Every culture has its own logic. Americans think one way, Chinese think another. The French think one way and the Germans think another. In spiritual matters, we also have our kind of logic. Each of us has our own view of what it means to follow the Lord. This becomes a great frustration to Him. What seems very reasonable to us can frustrate what Christ wants to do. Our single object must be to gain and obtain Christ. We must let go of all other things. Resurrection power can rescue us from the limitation of our logic.

Our manner of life is another great challenge for which we need resurrection power. As people grow older, they become increasingly inflexible and set in their ways. If it were not for the continuous operation of the power of resurrection in our lives, we all would become peculiar and confined. More importantly, we may not be able to receive what the Lord has arranged for us because our manner of life hinders us.

Some may think of resurrection power as something that is extraordinary or supernatural. However, the normal operation of resurrection is applied to us in our daily life, including to our logic, our manner of life, and even the way we pursue the Lord. For instance, if the Lord leads us to speak something for Him, this resurrection power enables us to do so whether we feel we can or not. We are able to obey and follow the Lord because we all have this resurrection power. In all these things, resurrection power keeps bringing us back to Christ.

## The Power of Resurrection in Our Spirit

One of the things Paul prayed for in Ephesians 1:16–20 was that we would know the power that raised Christ from the dead. According to Paul, the way to know this power is to have a spirit of wisdom and revelation (v. 17). If we truly want to know the power of the Lord's resurrection in our daily life, we must know and exercise our spirit. This is why as we pray over the Bible with our spirit the power of the Lord's resurrection becomes real to us.

Whenever our spirit is made alive, spontaneously all our problems no longer overwhelm us. Sometimes we have issues with each other in the church life. We may feel the church should go one way, while others feel it should go another way. Eventually we must realize that direction is not as crucial as the Spirit. When the Spirit is present in our church life, the power of resurrection is present, granting us the ability to lay hold of Christ in our situation. This is to know Christ and the power of His resurrection. When we are in spirit, we experience this power, and when we each experience this power of resurrection, Christ becomes the center of the church life.

As Paul taught in Romans 14, we should not insist on practices and observances. All should be allowed to live unto the Lord as they feel led. Such a church life is only possible through the power of resurrection. Apart from this power, we all become opinionated and insistent on what we think should be done. There can never be any revival among us if this is our case, for revival can only take place when we have love for one another and give liberty in nonessentials. In fact, when we are experiencing the power of resurrection, we find it possible to love even our enemies (Matt. 5:44). Through such love, many nonbelievers can be brought to Christ. May the Lord grant every church to be saturated with the Spirit to know His resurrection power.

## The Fellowship of His Sufferings

It is through the power of resurrection that we are strengthened to be brought into a deeper relationship with Christ, which is experienced in the fellowship of His sufferings. One aspect of this fellowship is the loss of our rights. Our personal rights are no longer ours to claim.

To give an illustration, the loss of liberty happens spontaneously to a couple when they have a baby. When their baby cries in the middle of the night, they don't say, "I'm not getting up at this hour to feed you. Wait until morning. You're infringing on my right to eight hours of sleep." Parents automatically forfeit their right to certain things. Their child means more to them than their own freedom.

This is also true spiritually. In the process of bringing a person to Christ, spontaneously we surrender our personal rights. Sometimes we may feel we have the right to relax at home after a long day at work instead of rushing off to care for a young believer. Yet if we desire to know the Lord, we must be willing to participate in His sufferings, for Christ forfeited His rights to save us. In order to raise up new believers, we must be willing to give up our rights.

## The Suffering of Christ
## for Our Sake

Christ, being in the form of God, gave up His rights in becoming a man and emptying Himself (Phil. 2:6–7). He did not count His preexistence in the heavenly places as an inalienable right. He did not even insist upon a comfortable human life. He was born in a stable, a place of strong smells and noise. Instead of growing up in a palace, He grew up in a carpenter's home. What caused Him to go through all this? He gave up all for our sakes. "He became poor, so that you through His poverty might become rich" (2 Cor. 8:9).

We have no way to conceive of all He gave up to become our Savior, yet He came. In fact, He was prepared to come from the foundation of the world (1 Pet. 1:20; Rev. 13:8). It was in His heart. He was willing to give up His rights.

Instead of seeking to know the Lord in the fellowship of His sufferings, we usually act as though we have inalienable rights, such as the right to raise issues in the church life or to argue about whether or not a certain thing should be done. Those who know the fellowship of the Lord's sufferings will speak out for the sake of the truth, but they do not claim any special place for themselves or their opinions. For the body's sake, they have renounced their rights.

## The Suffering of Loneliness

In entering into the fellowship of the Lord's sufferings, we also experience what it is to be lonely. The Lord's loneliness is expressed in the following hymn:

> *He held the highest place above,*
> *Adored by all the sons of flame,*
> *Yet such His self-denying love,*
> *He laid aside His crown and came*
> *To seek the lost,*
> *And at the cost*
> *Of heav'nly rank and earthly fame,*
> *He sought me—Blessed be His name!*
>
> *It was a lonely path He trod,*
> *From every human soul apart;*
> *Known only to Himself and God*
> *Was all the grief that filled His heart,*
> *Yet from the track*
> *He turned not back,*
> *Till where I lay in want and shame,*
> *He found me—Blessed be His name!*
>
> *Then dawned at last that day of dread,*
> *When desolate, yet undismayed,*
> *With wearied frame and thorn-crowned head,*
> *He, God-forsaken, man-betrayed,*
> *Was then made sin*
> *On Calvary,*
> *And, dying there in grief and shame,*
> *He saved me—Blessed be His name!* (Martin, no. 50)

The Lord was truly lonely. As a child, He was misunderstood even by His parents (Luke 2:41–51). They did not understand what He was going through—how lonely and misunderstood the Lord was! His disciples could not understand Him either (Mark

9:31–32). Only His heavenly Father understood. Eventually His disciples forsook Him and fled the garden. Peter, His staunchest disciple, denied Him three times that night, as the Lord had foretold. John alone followed Him all the way to the cross.

If we desire to know the Lord, we must know the fellowship of His sufferings. We should not expect to have others' applause, approval, or even understanding regarding this path we have chosen in following Christ. If we try to explain it to them, they will not be able to comprehend.

## Betrayed and Abandoned

Once, after Jesus spoke some particularly hard words, not only the crowds but even many of His disciples left Him. At this point, He asked the twelve, "You do not want to go away also, do you?" (John 6:67). He had just been celebrated as the One who fed the five thousand. That reception turned cold so quickly! Those who had enjoyed His miracles and His teaching were fast deserting Him. Peter responded by saying, "Lord, to whom shall we go? You have words of eternal life" (v. 68). Later, Peter too deserted the Lord on that night of all nights, yet the Lord was prepared for this.

Some whom I raised up and who were close to me later turned against me. The fellowship of Christ's sufferings includes being forsaken. When we are young we may proclaim, "We are for the Lord!" This is our enjoyment of resurrection power. Eventually that same power will bring us into His sufferings, which includes losing our rights and being misunderstood as He was. Yes, we will have many Christian companions, but we must be prepared to walk a lonely path. Eventually, we will be forsaken.

In the meantime, we should not look at others as future betrayers. We should assume everyone loves us, but at the same time we should tell the Lord, "I forfeit my rights. I am willing to live a lonely life. Even if it means being misunderstood and forsaken by all others, I want to know You and be one with You."

## Conformed to His Death

Next Paul wrote, "Being conformed to His death" (Phil. 3:10). Perhaps in our thought, Paul should have written, "Being conformed to His glory." However, this was not the case. Our destination is the tomb. We must be willing to be conformed to Christ's death if we truly desire to enter into oneness with Him.

How great is the need in the church life for those who have experienced being conformed to Christ's death! To be conformed to His death means we no longer have any feeling toward what we were once alive to; we have died to those things. The problem in so many places is that too many believers are very much alive to tell one another what they feel is right or wrong. This kind of being alive damages the church life.

## Becoming Selfless

One indication that we are being conformed to the death of Jesus is that we are becoming selfless. We are no longer as quick to respond to things, or to defend our honor or name. Throughout His entire earthly life, Jesus lived in the reality of death. He didn't speak His own words but spoke the words of the Father. He didn't do His own works but those of the Father (John 14:9–11). To do everything in oneness with another is death to the independent self. The life Christ lived was absolutely one with the Father. When we are one with God and Christ, everything we do will be in the principle of death. This means that as we serve others, we respond to the Lord, not to men (Eph. 6:6). In a sense, we become dead to the reactions of others, for we are alive to the Lord and serve only Him.

In theory, we may agree with the idea of being conformed to the Lord's death, but in practice, we usually do whatever we think is proper and a blessing to the church. How many are actually conformed to His death? This is not something we can pick up as a teaching. It is doubtful that young believers will know much of the fellowship of His sufferings, but they can still partake of His death. It may not be something fully formed in their lives, but being one with the Lord's leading brings them into the process of being conformed to His death.

It is good to tell the Lord that we are willing to follow Him however He leads—to speak whatever He gives us to speak, do whatever He would have us do, and go wherever He would have us go. Our self-life is gone. This was the principle of Jesus' life. He never lived independently from His Father.

The Lord desires that we would follow Him. If He leads us to do something that seems unreasonable or foolish in the eyes of men, we must still do it. Many have given up high positions and moved from desirable locations simply because the Lord led them to do so. In the eyes of the world, it is folly to give up our career and financial security. As we follow the Lord in such things, however, we can experience what it is to be conformed to His death.

## Becoming a Source of Life

Those who experience being conformed to His death become a source of life to others. They may not be preachers or leaders, but they become a source of supply in the church. We ar blessed when we are with such ones, simply because of who they have become by living a life of following God and being conformed to the death of His Son.

When I was a young Christian, I became very discouraged over my seeming lack of spiritual victory. This discouragement caused me to begin to question everything. I became quite downcast. Therefore, taking my sister, I went to see an older spiritual woman. As the three of us prayed together, I experienced the heavens being opened, and I became a different person. I prayed, "I am crucified with Christ! I died with Christ!" I was filled with the Spirit. After that prayer, I was no longer discouraged. I had been totally opened up. Because the element of Christ's death had so greatly operated in that spiritual woman, life was able to operate in me just by praying with her (2 Cor. 4:12). Those who are conformed to the Lord's death open the way for others to experience life.

To be conformed to Christ's death may seem far too high, but we should still seek to enter into it. Both in crucial things and in small things, may we desire to be so one with the Lord that His death might be applied to us and become our reality. Regardless of how much we have experienced these things, we can never grow out of knowing the power of His resurrection and the fellowship of His sufferings, and being conformed to His death.

## 27

# Seven Mountains in Our Pursuit of Christ (4)

*In order that I may attain to the resurrection from the dead. Not that I have already obtained it or have already become perfect, but I press on so that I may lay hold of that for which also I was laid hold of by Christ Jesus.*

—*Philippians 3:11–12*

### The Sixth Mountain:
### Attaining to the Out-resurrection

The previous chapter ended with our being conformed to the death of Christ. Once we are dead, it would seem everything is over, and that now we only need to await the resurrection. Yet, it is here that Paul said, "In order that I may attain to the resurrection from the dead." "May" implies he possibly may not. Why would resurrection be conditional to a person who has experienced conformation to Christ's death?

The Greek word for resurrection here is *exanastasis*, which literally means out-resurrection (Vine, 3:291). Paul was referring to an outstanding resurrection, a better resurrection (Heb. 11:35; 1 Cor. 15:41–42). All believers in Christ who die will be resurrected (1 Thess. 4:16), but the overcoming believers seek a better resurrection. We must enter this struggle of an overcomer to attain to the outstanding resurrection from among the dead. This is the sixth mountain.

205

## Pressing on

When Paul said, "in order that I may attain," he was saying, "I have paid the price throughout the years. I have done so much. But regardless of what I have accomplished, I must continue to pursue." A young man may be eager to join such a pursuit, but an old man would have a different response. He might say, "I need a rest." However, this is not what a Christian is allowed to say, regardless of how far he has come. He can only say, "I press on!" (Phil. 3:12). Regardless of how far we have come in our Christian life, we must still press on if we desire to attain to the out-resurrection.

I am somewhat old now, being around seventy. Have I labored? Have I loved the Lord? Have I been in the truth? Have I paid a price? Have I been through the experiences of the previous five mountains? To all these I can reply, "Yes." Based on this, can I say I am an overcomer? No. As long as the Lord has not yet returned, none among us can boast in this way. We all must lean on the Lord's mercy that we may continue to attain.

## Attaining to the Out-resurrection

Out-resurrection refers to the outstanding resurrection. This implies that there are different categories of resurrection. When the Lord comes, the Christians that meet Him will be at various levels of growth. Though all believers will be resurrected, those who are more mature will enjoy the most outstanding resurrection. The Lord will eventually bring all Christians into eternal glory, but they will not all shine with the same glory. Paul told the Corinthians, "There is one glory of the sun, and another glory of the moon, and another glory of the stars; for star differs from star in glory. So also is the resurrection of the dead" (1 Cor. 15:41–42). At regeneration, we are all the same in that our spirits are filled with the Lord, but we still have fallen souls and corrupt flesh. The portion of Christ we received at regeneration may seem small, but that small portion qualifies us to enjoy the riches of resurrection. If, however, the Lord returns and all we have is what we possessed at the time of our regeneration, our resurrection will be with minimal glory. As we grow by pursuing Christ, our soul becomes more and more transformed, and the life-element in us increases (2 Cor. 3:18). The resurrection power we experience corresponds to that element of the divine life within us. It is that power that will uplift us and shine forth from us in the day of resurrection (Matt. 13:43). We cannot expect that what is seen outwardly will go beyond what we possess inwardly. It must match.

Suppose a poor girl were to marry a millionaire. For her to match her husband's rich lifestyle might require a long process. Over time, she would acquire his rich tastes. It is the same with us and the Lord. Christ, with His unsearchable riches and resurrection power, has come into us. Now we must grow to match Him. In the beginning of our Christian life, there is very little in us that matches Christ. Yet as we grow in Him, we match Him more and more and are able to love and appreciate Him more. If we continue to grow in this way, surely our spirit, soul, and eventually our body will be able to bear a testimony in glory to the Lord, and our resurrection will be outstanding. Our enjoyment of Christ brings us to such a place that in that day our entire being—spirit, soul, and body—will express such a high degree of the Lord's glory. What we have enjoyed of Christ will be transmitted even into our body for all to see for eternity. This is the out-resurrection Paul spoke of.

Many Christians look to the day of resurrection as the day of relief from their troubles. They do not realize that resurrection is a reward for their struggle to gain Christ in this age. Oh, how we should all desire to attain to the outstanding resurrection! I want my soul to become even more transformed. I want my spirit, soul, and body to match Christ in glory to the fullest possible extent. We should not look at resurrection as merely some final process, but should seek more of its substance today. We must keep the attitude, "In order that I may attain...."

## Outward Experience for
## Inward Perfecting

Paul continued, "Not that I have already obtained it or have already become perfect, but I press on so that I may lay hold of that for which also I was laid hold of by Christ Jesus" (Phil. 3:12). This is the height of Christian growth—the Lord has laid hold of us, and now we also lay hold of Him. We want to make sure that everything in our lives—every word, every deed, every decision, every goal—matches the out-resurrection. Paul did not relax or become loose. He did not allow himself to assume he had attained. He kept himself poised to gain more of Christ.

Paul said, "Not that I have already obtained it or have already become perfect." At this point, Paul had given up everything from his Judaic past and had a wealth of experiences in Christ. He was the last one the Lord appeared to (1 Cor. 15:8). He also testified that he had been caught up to the third heavens and was shown things he could not even utter (2 Cor. 12:1–4). Yet he realized there was still more for him to gain. He did not allow himself to feel that he had already attained or been perfected.

It is through our experiences of Christ that we are being perfected. These outward experiences produce inward substance. As we pay the price to pursue Christ, as we labor on Him, and as we struggle to experience Him, something is being perfected within us. However, since Christ is unlimited, we can never say we have fully attained or been perfected.

## Pursuing and Persecuting

The Greek word for "press on" in verse 12 is *diōkō*, which means "to pursue" or "to persecute" (Strong, no. 1377). In fact, Paul used this same word in verse 6 when he said, "as to zeal, a persecutor of the church." When the Lord Jesus appeared to him, He said, "Saul, Saul, why are you persecuting Me?" (Acts 9:4). This same Greek word is used here. Paul also used this word when he testified to the Galatians that he "used to persecute the church of God beyond measure and tried to destroy it" (Gal. 1:13).

When a young man begins courting the woman he wants to marry, he doesn't give up easily. In her mind, it may even seem that in his pursuit he is persecuting her. At midnight she might get a phone call from him. He doesn't care about what seems like an imposition as long as he can win her heart.

Paul was such an absolute person toward Christ. Before he was converted, he pursued the Christians even to foreign cities in his persecution of them (Acts 26:11). He sought and approved of their deaths (Acts 8:1; 9:1; 26:10). At the time Paul wrote to the Philippians, he was still pursuing or "persecuting" the Lord Jesus—now in a good way—even to the point that he didn't care if the Lord could tolerate it. We shouldn't worry about being too much for the Lord Jesus. We should bother Him to the extent He doesn't know what to do with us. This is true pursuing. I'm afraid that our pursuing comes short of this. We just study the Bible a little, pray a little, and then go do whatever we feel is best. We need to be more aggressive in our pursuit, even to the point of becoming a persecutor of Christ. I'm a persecutor of my Bible, especially Philippians. That is why my Bible is falling to pieces. That is persecution. I give my Bible no peace. Can we pay such a high price in our pursuit of the Lord?

When we pursue others, it is always at a cost to ourselves. The young man courting his future wife does so at the cost of at least his time, money, and energy. Everyone who pursues Christ does so at a personal cost. Sometimes, in order to pursue the Lord, we may lose our jobs and careers. We may lose our good name. We lose our right to expect a comfortable life when we set out to pursue Christ.

No matter how mature we are, we must be on guard every day, keeping ourselves in the living presence of the Lord. No matter how much we have attained, if we relax, we may lose the reward of the out-resurrection. That's why Paul wrote in conditional terms, saying, "In order that I may..." (Phil. 3:11) and, "Not that I have already obtained it or have already become perfect, but

I press on so that I may lay hold..." (v. 12). Learn to persecute Christ. Tell Him, "I want You more! I need You more! I want to enjoy You, gain You, and apply You more! I want You to be more real and alive to me than ever before! Be everything to me. Otherwise, I will not let You go! I am willing to pay any price to attain to the out-resurrection."

## The Seventh Mountain:
### Pressing on to Lay Hold of Christ

In church history, probably no one has been more spiritual than Paul. During his lifetime, he produced so much through his labor, even though he only labored for a comparatively brief number of years. It is hard to imagine that anyone else in church history could have been more deserving of the out-resurrection than Paul. Even so he wrote, "Not that I have already obtained it or have already become perfect, but I press on so that I may lay hold of that for which also I was laid hold of by Christ Jesus" (v. 12). He still struggled to pursue Christ, because the riches of Christ are unsearchable. This pressing on to lay hold of Christ is the seventh mountain. We should never assume we have arrived but must continue to pursue Him our whole life. No matter how much we have gained of Christ, so much more remains!

## The Secret to
### Laying Hold of Christ

The Lord Jesus has laid hold of us. The Greek word for "lay hold of" is *katalambanō*, which means "to lay hold of so as to possess as one's own, to appropriate" (Vine, 1:70). The Lord has laid hold of us. Even if we decide to stop pursuing Him, He will not let us go. We are held securely in His hand (John 10:28). "If we are faithless, He remains faithful, for He cannot deny Himself" (2 Tim. 2:13).

Sadly, many Christians do not know this wonderful person who has laid hold of us. They are like a newlywed woman who has only just begun to know her husband. It takes us all our lives to find out how rich, virtuous, able, and wise this One who has laid hold of us is. The more we know Him, the more we want to press on to lay hold of Him.

The wife's secret to gaining her husband is to gain his stomach. Preparing the dishes her husband likes requires knowledge. The Lord has gained us with a strong desire that we would possess Him. We have given ourselves to Christ, but have we embraced all that this entails? If we really want to give ourselves to Christ, we must come to Him, study Him, experience Him, and enjoy Him so that eventually we might fully realize who He is. This takes place by our pursuing Him in a persecuting manner. Then we will discover what a Christ we have. Through our pursuing we lay hold of that for which we also have been laid hold of by Christ Jesus. This is incorporation. Christ is in us, and we are in Christ. His heart becomes our heart, and His desire becomes our desire. As the Lord moves, we move, because we are coordinated, incorporated into one. This is the highest plane of Christian existence.

These seven mountains are our life. By the Lord's mercy, we can pass through them all. For this we need to grow—to grow out of religion, out of everything we might boast in, and out of the world. We also need to grow into the truth so that we know the Lord according to the truth and can be found in Him. We need to grow into the surpassing value of the knowledge of Christ Himself. We need to grow so that every moment we may attain to the out-resurrection. Finally, we need to press on to lay hold of Christ who has laid hold of us. Then He and we become totally matched and behave as one person. How glorious this is! How we need to advance in our experience of Him! What a hope has been placed before us!

# 28

# Pursuing Christ
# as Our Goal

*Brethren, I do not regard myself as having laid hold of it yet; but one thing I do: forgetting what lies behind and reaching forward to what lies ahead, I press on toward the goal for the prize of the upward call of God in Christ Jesus.*

*—Philippians 3:13–14*

In Philippians 3:12, the apostle Paul arrived at a high point in his experience of Christ: "That I may lay hold of that for which also I was laid hold of by Christ Jesus." It is surprising that he then wrote, "Brethren, I do not regard myself as having laid hold of it yet; but one thing I do: forgetting what lies behind and reaching forward to what lies ahead" (3:13). Such a strong statement has a surprising logic. After Paul arrived at what seemed to be a peak in verse 12, he discovered it was a plateau instead of a peak. Once we arrive at such a high experience of Christ, we find unsearchable riches for us to abide in. It is not a peak that we must climb down from. No, it is an immense plateau for us to walk upon! Paul acknowledged that there is more of Christ to experience when he wrote, "I do not regard myself as having laid hold of it yet." No matter how spiritual or mature he was or how much he had gained of Christ, he realized that his pursuit was not over and that he had not yet arrived at his final goal.

Verse 13 is a crucial verse for all who desire to pursue Christ their entire life. In the Christian life, we continue to go higher and higher. At every stage, we think we have so much, but when we arrive at the experience Paul spoke of in verse 13, we discover that Christ is truly unsearchable!

Some Christians, after reading through the Bible many times, feel they have mastered it. They feel they know what every verse is talking about and have received its totality. Yet Paul never felt this way. To him, Christ was an unlimited expanse to be explored. Christ had laid hold of Paul. Now Paul wanted to lay hold of Christ. He realized that he had not yet attained or been perfected. What a wide open plain of the unsearchable riches of Christ lay before him!

Those with limited experience of Christ declare they have attained. Only those who have passed through all the stages of pursuing and gaining Christ can say, "Not that I have already obtained it" (v. 12). Once we arrive at the seeming peak of enjoying Christ, we will declare, "The riches of Christ are unsearchable!" Throughout eternity, we will continue to discover and enjoy further riches of Christ. The Lord's riches are beyond telling!

## Forgetting What Lies Behind

Paul continued, "One thing I do: forgetting what lies behind and reaching forward to what lies ahead" (Phil. 3:13). Forgetting the things behind is seemingly impossible. First, once we have experienced something, it becomes part of our constitution. Second, we cherish many of our experiences and don't want to forget them. Even our negative and troublesome experiences seem impossible to leave behind.

Things that have become our constitution are a part of us. I came to the United States weighing just ninety-five pounds! I have considerably "broadened" since then. I may wish to lose the weight I have gained, but my wishing doesn't change my present constitution. Spiritually, it is the same. All the things we have enjoyed spiritually have become a part of us. We have had many wonderful times of enjoying the Spirit. After our spirit was made alive, we became Jesus-lovers, and our constitution changed. Because of this, we began to see other believers as our dear brothers and sisters. We also remember times of ministry and enjoyment. What wonderful times! Yet according to this verse, we must let go of all such things.

I recall the sweetness I experienced the first time I repented before the Lord. I remember the many times the Lord has touched me since then, often bringing me to tears. All these wonderful things have contributed to the spiritual constitution I now possess. The problem is that holding on to such things prevents me from going on to new experiences of Christ. I carry forward my spiritual constitution, but if I wish to go on further, I must learn to let go of all the things that brought me to this point.

## Five Categories of Things
## to Be Left Behind

The things we must learn to leave behind are of five categories: 1) religious experiences, 2) revelations, 3) experiences of growth, 4) teachings, and 5) our Christian works.

### Religious Experiences

The first thing we must learn to leave behind is our religious experiences. Paul described his own religious experiences, saying that he was "circumcised the eighth day, of the nation of Israel, of the tribe of Benjamin, a Hebrew of Hebrews; as to the Law, a Pharisee; as to zeal, a persecutor of the church; as to the righteousness which is in the Law, found blameless" (Phil. 3:5–6). In order to gain Christ, he counted all these things as rubbish (v. 8).

### Revelations

Revelations are the second category of items to be left behind.

Concerning his own experience of receiving revelations, Paul wrote, "I know a man in Christ who fourteen years ago—whether in the body I do not know, or out of the body I do not know, God knows—such a man was caught up to the third heaven. And I know how such a man—whether in the body or apart from the body I do not know, God knows—was caught up into Paradise and heard inexpressible words, which a man is not permitted to speak" (2 Cor. 12:2–4). Paul himself never boasted in his revelations. He spoke of his encounter with the Lord on the road to Damascus on at least two occasions (Acts 22:6–21; 26:1–19), but never disclosed the content of the other revelations in which he heard "inexpressible words." The reality of the revelations could never leave him, for they became part of his constitution. However, he never held onto the event itself. He preferred to boast in his weaknesses (2 Cor. 12:7–10). He didn't want praise from men because to entertain such a thing is to forfeit further growth.

Many might consider such revelations as grounds to be exalted. Wouldn't it seem reasonable for Paul to open a "Third Heavens Training Center"? As far as we can tell, the Lord never told Paul "No" regarding such an endeavor. However, for Paul, doing such a thing would jeopardize his further pursuit of Christ. Even the very event in which revelation is received can become a frustration when it comes to pursuing Christ. Revelation itself may bring about some growth of life, but the event of receiving it must be left behind.

## Spiritual Growth

Third, we must learn to forget about how much we may have grown spiritually. We should not abide in our own growth. If we start to feel that others are spiritual infants when compared to us, we are finished. Instead of celebrating ourselves, we should sing ourselves a dirge. Though we may have grown, abiding in such a realization can frustrate our further growth.

## Teachings

Fourth, the teachings we have received may also prevent us from going on with the Lord. When we receive teaching regarding a portion of Scripture, it can become formed in us. We may feel, "That's it!" However, the Bible is a divine speaking and is always fresh. If we are only able to accept one interpretation of a Bible verse, then we are not "forgetting what lies behind." Often, we lay hold of teachings instead of the present Christ. It is true that there are certain principles we must abide by in studying the Bible, but too many feel they know exactly what a verse means, and thus cannot receive additional light from the Lord regarding that verse. This realization is well expressed in the following nineteenth century hymn:

*We limit not the truth of God*
*To our poor reach of mind,*
*By notions of our day and sect,*
*Crude, partial, and confined.*
*Now let a new and better hope*
*Within our hearts be stirred:*
*The Lord has yet more light and truth*
*To break forth from His Word.*

*Who dares to bind by his dull sense*
*The oracles of heav'n,*
*For all the nations, tongues and climes*
*And all the ages given!*
*The universe how much unknown!*
*That ocean unexplored!*
*The Lord has yet more light and truth*
*To break forth from His Word.* (Martin, no. 378)

## Christian Work

The last thing that can easily stumble us in our pursuit of

Christ is our Christian work. For instance, years ago in Cleveland we had a glorious meeting once we completed the building of our meeting hall. Can we forget such things? We take forward what has been constituted into us, but we must learn to let go of the "good old days." Someone recently reminded me of a conference I spoke at. He felt at that time he was flowing with divine water, and everyone there was overflowing. Since I gave this conference, I enjoyed hearing his testimony even more than he enjoyed giving it. Such times are so difficult to forget, but when we dwell in them, we are unable to find Christ today.

## The Self's Need for Capital

Our self is always seeking for something to boast in. Before we were saved, it may have boasted in the material world or the psychological world. After we are saved, the self begins to boast in the religious world. When it comes to pursuing Christ, the most troublesome aspect of the world is the religious aspect. It becomes the closest comrade to our self-life. Though it seems supportive of the idea of being for Christ, it is actually taking us away from Christ even as it speaks of Him. The sinful world, makes no such claims. As it leads us into sin, the conscience reacts, and this usually leads us to repentance. However, few see involvement in the religious world as something to repent of, for their conscience seems to remain peaceful.

Our self needs some capital to boast in, and the capital it tries to use is our religious practice, the desire for revelation, the appearance of spiritual growth, knowledge of truth, and accomplishment in our labor. If we dwell in these things, we are in trouble. If we feel, "Ha! Look what I am able to do! Look at what I have seen and how far I have come! Look at what I now know and have accomplished!" then our pursuit of the Lord will be frustrated.

We must realize the danger of the religious world. Even if we give up our pursuit of things in the material or psychological worlds, we may still be caught up in pursuing the things of the religious world, seeking to become someone in the church life. We have no right to become anything. The apostle Paul counted all as rubbish in order to gain Christ. The Lord told us we must deny ourselves if we wish to follow Him (Matt. 16:24). Watchman Nee wrote:

> Let me love and not be respected;
> Let me serve and not be rewarded;
> Let me labor and not be remembered;
> Let me suffer and not be regarded....
> Let me learn, O Lord, You are my reward,
> Let me be others' blessing all my days. (Martin, no. 424)

Our self is comforted by religious practice. It boasts in the fact that we have received revelation. It basks in any stature we have arrived at spiritually. It takes pride in the truth we know. It draws a sense of accomplishment from our work for the Lord. During my past fifty years of following the Lord, I have learned and experienced much. I could write books on each of these five topics, yet I am saved by Paul's word: "Brethren, I do not regard myself as having laid hold of it yet; but one thing I do..." (Phil. 3:13).

## Forgetting and Reaching Forward

Paul continued, "Forgetting what lies behind and reaching forward to what lies ahead, I press on toward the goal" (Phil. 3:13–14). Here Paul portrayed his intensity in pursuing Christ. The Greek words he used for "forgetting" and "reaching" both use the prefix *epi*, indicating intensity (Vine, 2:121 and 4:82). This is not a normal forgetting or reaching forward but one of determination.

The picture is that of a runner straining toward the finish line. His whole being is geared toward running the race. He does not look around to see who may be watching. He does not wave to anyone in the stands. Even if people try to distract him, he gives them no heed. He is totally focused on the goal that is set before him. We should be like such runners, pressing toward a goal. What is our goal? It is Christ! Our one focus is to obtain Christ. Our whole life is only for gaining Christ, and the only danger is that we might miss Him. Nothing else matters. In such a pursuit there is no such thing as retirement. There is simply intense forgetting and continual reaching forward to what still lies ahead in the unsearchable riches of Christ.

Pressing toward the goal now becomes our living. How do we pursue in this way? It is by a stand and by a practice. Our stand is to forget the things that are behind, and our practice is to reach forward to the things that are before. Our living is now a life of pursuing.

### The Goal for the Prize of the Upward Call

Paul continued, "I press on toward the goal for the prize of the upward call of God in Christ Jesus" (Phil. 3:14). The Greek word for "goal" here is *skopos*, which "has the two senses of 'overseer' and 'mark' at which one shoots" (Kittel, p. 1047). The mark at which we aim is Christ, and the One who is overseeing our pursuit toward that goal is also Christ.

Commenting on the phrase, "the upward call," A. T. Robertson wrote, "The goal continually moves forward as we press on, but yet never out of sight." Christ is not a fixed goal. He keeps just ahead of us, based upon our pursuing. If He allowed Himself to be laid hold of, we would stop pursuing. Because we need to be continually growing and maturing, Christ as our goal always remains just ahead of us, calling us onward to a deeper, richer union with Himself. As He continues to reveal Himself to us, we are drawn to Him and continue to run after Him. This is why even Paul could not say, after all his intense pursuing, that he had attained (Phil. 3:12–13).

The Greek word for "upward" is *anō*, which could indicate

"where the calling comes from, or it could point to the direction in which the calling leads" (Rogers & Rogers, p. 456). We have both a destination and a direction, and the goal before us is always moving onward yet always remaining within our sight. This goal we run toward is Christ, and it is overseen by Christ.

## Always Pursuing

When we first became Christians, perhaps our goal was simply to read the Bible. When we grew a bit more, our goal may have become to enjoy the Lord in our daily life. As we pursued this, we saw something more, and our goal advanced again. There is no such thing as retirement for a Christian, for there is always something further for us to pursue in our experience of Christ. Regardless of our different levels of growth, the goal for each of us always remains just ahead—the distance to the goal is the same for each of us.

In the world, our pursuits have an ending. After students graduate, their formal education is done. At the end of a career, there is a retirement. The Christian life is not like this. No matter how long we pursue Christ, our goal still lies just ahead. In following Christ we can never declare, "I have attained!" There is no graduation. No one can say, "I have achieved the top-level 'black belt' in following Christ." No matter how much we have pursued, Christ remains ahead of us. He is our goal.

# 29

# Healthy Patterns

*Let us therefore, as many as are perfect, have this attitude; and if in anything you have a different attitude, God will reveal that also to you; however, let us keep living by that same standard to which we have attained. Brethren, join in following my example, and observe those who walk according to the pattern you have in us.*

*—Philippians 3:15–17*

### Mature and Having a Mind to Pursue Christ

Paul wrote, "Let us therefore, as many as are perfect, have this attitude" (Phil. 3:15). The Greek work used for "perfect" here is *teleios*, which is used to describe a person who is fully grown or mature (Vine, 3:174). Perfection, or maturity, is not a matter of quantity but of quality. For instance, it is not a matter of how many verses we have memorized or how many Christian conferences we have attended. Being perfect, mature, or full grown is our growing up in all things into Christ (Eph. 4:15). We come to a certain stature based on our growth (Eph. 4:13).

Paul indicated that a number had arrived at a stature that he called perfect. This doesn't mean they had laid hold; it just means they had arrived at a place where they could "have this attitude"—the attitude that seeks to lay hold of Christ by "forgetting what lies behind and reaching forward to what lies ahead" (Phil. 3:13). Those who are perfect have the desire to "press on toward the goal for the prize of the upward call of God in Christ Jesus" (v. 14). Therefore, they "have this attitude" that considers everything with this goal in view. They aim at the best and the highest. They can boldly declare, "My living on this earth is for one thing: to gain Christ!"

## The Mind in Philippians

In every chapter in Philippians, Paul mentioned the mind. In chapter 1 he was encouraged to hear that the Philippians were "standing firm in one spirit, with one mind striving together for the faith of the gospel" (v. 27). Our striving together for the gospel has to do with the mind.

In chapter 2 Paul wrote, "Do nothing from selfishness or empty conceit, but with humility of mind regard one another as more important than yourselves" (v. 3). This is a mind of humbling ourselves for the sake of the body of Christ. We can only do this by having the mind "which was also in Christ Jesus" (v. 5). The Lord Jesus humbled Himself. He had a mind to empty Himself, taking on the form of a bond-servant, even to the point of suffering a shameful death on the cross (vv. 7–8). Therefore, the Father "highly exalted Him, and bestowed on Him the name which is above every name" (v. 9).

In chapter 3, the mind is again emphasized. Paul wrote, "Let us therefore, as many as are perfect, have this attitude" (v. 15). The Greek word for "have this attitude" is *phroneō*, which means "think this, or have this mind" (Vincent, 3:451). As we stand fast with one mind for the gospel (chapter 1) and have a mind to humble ourselves for the sake of the body (chapter 2), Paul exhorts us to have this mind, that is, the mind which pursues Christ as the goal, the prize of our upward call (v. 14). After advancing in our experience of Christ to this point in Philippians, our minds become saturated with one thought: We want to gain Christ! Our goal is Christ alone!

Don't think this is easy. Even our Christian work can become a competing goal. Only the spiritually mature care for Christ alone. Our work must simply become whatever it takes to gain more Christ. If we are mature, we should have this mind.

Then Paul said something very encouraging: "If in anything you have a different attitude, God will reveal that also to you" (v. 15). In other words, God is able to remove whatever is veiling us so that we might be brought back to treasuring and pursuing Christ. How good this is! This is to have the mind to pursue toward the goal for the prize of the upward call of God in Christ Jesus (v. 14).

## A Walk according to Our Measure of Christ

Paul continued, "However, let us keep living by that same standard to which we have attained" (Phil. 3:16). Many English translations use the word "rule" instead of "standard" in this verse. When we have a mind such as Paul described, we pursue Christ to gain Him. What we gain of Christ, the measure of our attainment in Christ, becomes the standard, rule, or boundary by which we should walk.

When we overstep the boundary of our attainment in Christ, we may damage others. In the business world, there is a commonly recognized phenomenon called the Peter Principle: successful employees keep getting promoted until they reach a position beyond their level of competence. At this point they may cause more damage than good to the business. A similar thing can happen in the Christian life: when we try to serve in a way beyond the measure of our attainment in Christ, we can cause damage.

Some people insist on walking beyond their rule instead of simply enjoying Christ and walking according their measure. It is this "beyond" that becomes the problem. I am a grandfather, but that does not mean I have the right to treat everyone else's grandchildren as mine. My boundary is the children and grandchildren of my own household. No matter how mature I am, I cannot freely approach the children of others. We all need to learn to function as members of the body within the measure of our maturity in Christ. The rule or standard to which we have attained should determine our service and regulate our living.

Instead of pursuing Christ, too many Christians today pursue things of the religious world in their self-life. Because of this, they harm those they are trying to help. This is why Paul said we should walk according to the standard to which we have attained. When we are all uniquely focused on simply gaining Christ, there are no problems. Problems arise when we attempt to gain something other than Christ or act beyond our measure of Christ.


## Paul's Broadness

Paul continued, "Brethren, join in following my example, and observe those who walk according to the pattern you have in us" (Phil. 3:17). For such a walk, we have patterns we may imitate. In order to follow such patterns, we need to have a learning spirit. Not only do we need to walk within our boundary of Christ, we also need to continue on as learners for the rest of our lives, taking as our pattern Paul and those who walk as he walks.

What a grand view the apostle Paul possessed! The pattern he told the Philippians to follow was not limited to himself and his coworkers but to all who walked as he walked. Paul did not feel as though any church or work belonged to him. He saw himself as exercising just one part in the Lord's ministry. This is why he told the Philippians to imitate any who walked in the same principle that he walked. Paul realized that the Lord had one work of ministry and that although he was carrying a portion in that work, he was not that work in its entirety.

## Many Workers, One Pattern

The Lord's work is being carried out by many groups of workers. For instance, at the time Paul and his group of coworkers labored in Asia and Europe, another group, including Peter, John, and James, labored in Judea. Today there are likewise many laboring in the Lord's one work. These many workers are formed into groups. All the Lord's workers in their various groups should be laboring toward the same goal: that we may all gain Christ. Anyone who is struggling toward this same goal is a worthy pattern.

Paul was surely a grand person to give us such a sweet verse. Though he was a marvelous pattern, he did not consider himself the exclusive pattern. Even though he may have been the Lord's greatest servant, he acknowledged that no matter how useful he was, and how much revelation he had been granted, he was insufficient in himself. Even his many coworkers were not enough. He recognized that there were many others who were walking and laboring in the same principle. Rather than fearing some might snatch the believers away from him, Paul encouraged the believers in Philippi to take as patterns those who walked as he walked.

## Being a Pattern

Paul never claimed to be perfect. He freely exposed his potential to exalt himself. To keep him from such self-exaltation, he was given a "thorn in the flesh" (2 Cor. 12:7). Even though he had such a weakness, he told people, "Join in following my example."

All those who serve the Lord should be such patterns. The Lord's servants should be those whom we can imitate, but because they are keenly aware of their own shortcomings, not all of them would boldly encourage others to follow them as Paul did. Still, they should be able to say that in their pursuit of Christ, there is a pattern for others to follow.

## Patterns and Their Impact

The Greek word for "pattern" is *tupos*, which denotes "'the impress' of a blow, and then 'form' with such nuances as 'mark,' 'mold,' and 'outline' or 'figure'" (Kittel, p. 1193). It is an outward mark or mold that can be used to shape other objects. Those who follow such a pattern will be impacted: BAM!—they will love the Lord; BAM!—they become consecrated; BAM!—they become rich in the Word; BAM!—the whole church becomes revived. If we have such patterns among us, how blessed the churches will be!

It is a tragedy when there are no patterns for the young people to follow. Without such patterns, they may become wild. Young people need to look up to someone. This is why they declare someone is their hero and imitate that person. It is a sad thing if we find no one we can imitate. I still consider the example of the older ones who were my pattern as a young man—how they handled things and behaved—for they continue to be my pattern today. We need teachers, but even more, we need patterns in pursuing, serving, and consecration. We need those who make an impression upon us as with a spiritual mallet! When we find someone who is a proper pattern, that is a real blessing.

## Becoming a Pattern

The change we are after is not merely outward but inward. It does not come about just by imparting knowledge, nor is it a matter of imitating mannerisms. Such things may be unavoidable, but they are not the important thing. The change we seek comes about when people see something divine and powerful in a pattern that changes the meaning of their lives and remolds their manner of living. They become living copies of those who are living patterns. This relationship is organic.

If we are such patterns, others around us become different. As patterns, we draw others and instill something into them based on what they see in us. Although I am seventy years old and not as active as I once was, I believe there is still something in me that affects others.

I am bothered when I see church leaders who are not attractive in this way. They should affect others. They should not simply teach points; they should present what has affected them deeply, inspiring others to lay hold of what has been revealed to them. Paul admonished Timothy (1 Tim. 4:12) and Titus (Titus 2:7) to be such a pattern, and Peter also told the elders that they should be patterns to the flock (1 Pet. 5:3). When others are around such patterns, they become inspired. People are attracted to them and strengthened by them. A proper serving one should be such a pattern to others, someone whose person is worthy of imitation (1 Thess. 1:6–7). Pray for this!

## Healthy Patterns Produce Healthy Traditions

The patterns in a church affect the health and growth of the members of that church. A church is like a family, and the health of a family is based upon that family's tradition (see 1 Cor. 11:1–2; 2 Thess. 2:15; 3:6). If the tradition in a church allows for gossip and criticism of others, then that church will be unhealthy. Traditions such as this depend upon the patterns, who often decide the growth of other members of the church. If those we are with are not healthy, we should not complain. Rather, we should ask whether others can see a healthy pattern in us. If there are a sufficient number of proper patterns in a church, the situation will improve and growth will take place. Therefore, we must look unto the Lord that we may become the kind of patterns that affect others' growth and usher in a healthy family tradition.

May we walk in this way until the Lord comes back. We should be both imitators of healthy patterns and become healthy patterns to others, particularly in the visions and revelations God has given us.

# 30

# A Twofold Walk to Gain Christ

*However, let us keep living by that same standard to which we have attained. Brethren, join in following my example, and observe those who walk according to the pattern you have in us. For many walk, of whom I often told you, and now tell you even weeping, that they are enemies of the cross of Christ.*

*—Philippians 3:16–18*

Paul wrote, "Let us keep living by that same standard to which we have attained" (Phil. 3:16). By the time he wrote this, his spiritual attainment was comparatively high and rich. He was a spiritually mature person. Looking back through the centuries, it is difficult to find anyone who has approached Paul's level of spiritual attainment. Who else has been caught away to the third heaven and to Paradise (2 Cor. 12:2–4)? That was something specifically measured to Paul. As noted in the previous chapter, his attainment became a boundary or rule restricting his walk.

## The Ruling Element and Sphere of Our Walk

This is also true in our own experience. The degree of maturity we have attained in Christ becomes the ruling element of our walk and determines the sphere in which we are able to walk about freely.

The Christ we have gained becomes the ruling element in our daily life. This rule is a living person, and the more we possess Him, the more He will set Himself as a rule over us. According to our concept if we are under some rule, we cannot act freely, for restriction and freedom seem mutually exclusive. However, this rule is not only a boundary that restricts our walk. It also marks out a sphere in which we can freely walk because what the Lord has measured to us is so grand.

## Differing Measures

Paul continued, "Brethren, join in following my example" (Phil. 3:17). Many times when we follow the example of those with more maturity in Christ, we merely imitate their outward behavior instead of their way of gaining Christ. If we see other believers doing something that the Lord has not measured to us and say, "If they can do that, I can too," we will get ourselves into trouble. We must be careful when we follow the example of others, for what the Lord allows them is not necessarily something measured to us. To truly become followers of others' example, we must be inspired by their person, life, vision, service, and riches. These are the things we should imitate.

Our spiritual attainment produces a restriction as well as a liberty in our walk. On the one hand, in Christ we are totally under discipline, while on the other hand in Christ we are totally free. If we go beyond the rule measured to us, we find ourselves walking in a manner that is out of bounds.

As we grow unto maturity, we will find that we cannot do things that others are able to do or say because of this rule. We will also find we are so free within the boundary the Lord measures to us. There is so much Christ for us to experience and so many things we can do because of the freedom we have within that portion of Christ measured to us.

## Two Kinds of People

In these verses, Paul mentioned two different kinds of people. Those in verse 17 have a walk in which Christ becomes so much to them. They walk according to their spiritual level of maturity and become healthy patterns for the younger ones to follow. Those in verse 18 walk according to their religion and become "enemies of the cross of Christ."

## Two Walks

The Greek word for "living" in verse 16 is *stoicheō*, which means to march in military rank, to keep step, or to walk orderly (Strong, no. 4748). In verse 17, the Greek word for "walk" is *peripateō*, which refers to the walk that is free, "to tread all around, i.e., walk at large" (Strong, no. 4043). These are two kinds of walks. In the Christian life, the *stoicheō* walk is to live and be governed by certain basic principles. Many seem to think that *stoicheō*, with its application to the march of an army in one accord, is the more advanced walk, but this is not the case. *Stoicheō* provides the base for *peripateō*, and it is equated to living by the Spirit in Galatians 5:25.

The degree of our attainment of Christ becomes both the boundary and sphere of our walk. It is the boundary restricting our orderly walk (*stoicheō*) and the sphere in which we walk freely (*peripateō*) within that boundary.

## Our Walk in Oneness to Gain Christ

Our walk should be with a clear goal—to gain Christ as our prize. This is our *stoicheō* walk. It is governed by the goal of pursuing and gaining Christ to the fullest extent so that we might win "the prize of the upward call of God in Christ Jesus" (Phil. 3:14).

Christian oneness is the result of our pursuing this unique

goal. Our oneness does not depend on us all observing the same practices, such as everyone rising at the same time to pray. Whether we get up at five or eight, whether or not we focus on praying, reading the Bible, or preaching the gospel, we all have the goal of gaining Christ. This goal maintains our oneness in spite of our differences. However, the moment someone insists that everyone use a certain Bible translation or read books by a certain author, the *stoicheō* is gone, and the oneness disappears. Such insisting makes issues. We all should simply pursue Christ however we are led. Insisting on any issue, whether for or against, replaces Christ as our goal and destroys our oneness.

If we read something, let us read it unto the Lord. If we attend a Christian conference, let us do so unto the Lord. Everyone has a right to follow the Lord. The secret of marching together (*stoicheō*) is to not insist on things other than Christ. Just stay focused on Christ. To do otherwise is to violate the principle of this common walk, which has the goal of gaining Christ to the fullest extent.

If someone should attempt to raise certain issues that we find troubling, our response should be, "I respect you and honor you as one whom I believe is seeking to follow the Lord. I hope you would honor the fact that I am seeking to follow the Lord too." We have the freedom to live before the Lord according to His personal leading. Even though others may attempt to impose things upon us, we must feel free to follow Christ.

## A Walk to Gain Christ
## in Resurrection

For these two walks, we all should become imitators together of the apostle Paul and all others who walk as Paul walked (Phil. 3:17). For our basic walk (*stoicheō*), we need not all conform to the same outward practices, but we must all walk with the sole aim of gaining Christ and maturing in Him. When we all have such a heart, we spontaneously have the *stoicheō* walk. Our attitude toward other Christians is then, "I don't care if your practices are the same as mine as long as we are able to go on together gaining Christ."

At the same time, our Christian living should be a walk (*peripateō*) in the realm of resurrection, that we may reign in life until we are conformed to the image of Christ. Paul described this walk in Romans: "As Christ was raised from the dead through the glory of the Father, so we too might walk in newness of life" (Rom. 6:4). We should all be free to follow the Lord of life as He desires.

## A Boundary and a Sphere

We all have attained to some measure of Christ according to our level of spiritual maturity. This measure becomes the rule that produces two aspects in our walk: the first restricts us to the boundary of Christ as our unique goal; the second allows us the freedom to walk about within the sphere of this boundary. We experience both of these aspects in our walk as we pursue and gain Christ.

# 31

# Enemies of
# the Cross of Christ

*For many walk, of whom I often told you, and now tell you even
weeping, that they are enemies of the cross of Christ, whose end
is destruction, whose god is their appetite, and whose glory is in
their shame, who set their minds on earthly things.*
*—Philippians 3:18–19*

Paul warned the believers concerning those who walk as
enemies of the cross of Christ (Phil. 3:18). There are many who
walk so as to pursue Christ, but there are also many who walk
in a manner that is in violation of the rule, or boundary, of
their measure of Christ. Instead of making the most of their
opportunity to experience Christ according to the rule to which
they have attained, they damage themselves and others by
walking beyond their measure.

Paul indicated he had previously warned the believers
concerning such men, and now he told them again, even
weeping. These men may have loved the Lord, but they simply
did not care for the matter of boundary.

With today's technology, it is very easy for people to affect
many others. So many phone calls and emails contain "fellowship"
which is out of bounds. Instead of walking properly, many walk
in the way Paul described in verse 18, as "enemies of the cross of
Christ." Paul told us previously in this chapter that he desired to
be conformed to Christ's death (v. 10). Many, however, seem to
have forgotten about this experience of the cross of Christ. We

must remember that the way of the Lord is the way of the cross (Matt. 16:24). If we take a way that allows us to escape the cross, we cannot truly say we are following the Lord.

## Escaping the Cross

Those who are enemies of the cross of Christ do not take the way of the cross. They do not agree with the Lord that they must die. This is why they are so free to walk without any boundary. Instead of bearing their cross, they seek to be exalted. Many who are so energetic and active in recruiting others to their cause show no sign of the cross in their lives. They feel free to act beyond the boundary the Lord has measured to them. They contact people far and wide in the name of being global. To communicate with others is a good thing, but if we are wrong in our person, we will spread our sickness across the globe without even realizing it. Though we ourselves may feel liberated, many around us will become sick.

I hope many develop so that their labor reaches the globe. Many should take up the burden to go to Africa or China or other such places to pioneer for the Lord. Yet we should also remember that if we do so, we must not go beyond the boundary the Lord has measured to us. This measure must regulate our walk and labor.

If we walk outside the boundary of what the Lord has measured to us, we walk as enemies of the cross of Christ. Such people refuse to die. They do not receive what the Lord has arranged for them but rather choose to escape it. Instead of living unto Christ, they live unto whatever they feel they should do.

## Taking the Cross

Many times God would ask of us something that we feel to be unreasonable. Consider how God told Abraham to offer up his son Isaac, Joshua to march around Jericho, and Gideon to send away most of his army. Weren't these demands unreasonable? Even Jesus prayed to the Father that the cup of the cross be taken from Him, but He continued, "Yet not as I will, but as You will" (Matt. 26:39).

Quite often unreasonable things happen to us simply because we need to die. God may use illogical situations or unreasonable people to enable the cross to work in us. We find it reasonable to be disciplined when we have done something that deserves discipline, but when we are treated unfairly, are we able to take the cross, or do we fight against it? We must recognize when the cross is at work in our lives and, rather than rebel, simply cleave to the Lord. If we know how to take such things, we will be blessed and grow. This is the secret of how to avoid becoming an enemy of the cross of Christ.

## Becoming an Enemy of the Cross

People become enemies of the cross of Christ when they begin to reject the cross in their lives. They feel, "How can I allow myself to be terminated when I have given my life for this? I cannot let the cross stop me now!" Thus they get caught with something other than Christ Himself. They are no longer living for Christ alone but for Christ plus something else that has become just as important to them as Christ.

If we try to do something beyond what the Lord has measured to us, we walk as enemies of the cross of Christ. We all need to be uniquely and exclusively caught by Christ, nothing extra.

## Whose End Is Destruction

Paul wrote further of such men: "Whose end is destruction" (Phil. 3:19). We may be believers, as were many of the Judaizers of Paul's day, yet still be in danger of destruction (1 Cor. 3:15; 9:27). To an unbeliever, destruction means to be cast into the lake of fire (Rev. 20:15; 21:8), but to a believer who is an unprofitable servant, "even what he does have shall be taken away" (Matt. 25:29). The type of destruction we experience depends on our relationship to Christ.

## Whose Glory Is in Their Shame

Paul also wrote, "Whose god is their appetite" (Phil. 3:19). Their appetite always needs to be satisfied. Rather than seeking to satisfy Christ and find satisfaction in Him, these men sought to satisfy themselves, making themselves their own god.

Paul continued, "Whose glory is in their shame" (v. 19). The Greek word for "shame" here is *aischunē*, which can also be translated "baseness" or "dishonor" (Young, p. 872). Whenever people try to gain a following to satisfy their bellies, it is a shame to them and to those associated with them. One person's behavior may affect many by causing them to boast in something apart from Christ. Those who walk outside their boundary may think they have done a wonderful job in affecting so many people, but the truth is, their base desire for a following has actually damaged others.

Those seeking a following often focus on who is right and who is wrong, but such things do not help anyone gain Christ. For instance, if some insist on speaking in tongues, they find verses to help them win their argument, but is Christ gained through this? It is the same regarding many teachings. Sadly, too often people care more about winning their argument than about gaining Christ. We must be pure when it comes to discussing matters of truth. We should not be for winning the argument just because it is our side.

## Who Set Their Minds on
## Earthly Things

Paul went on to say, "Who set their minds on earthly things"

(Phil. 3:19). We should not desire to be right for our own sakes. If we are in this realm, our mind is set on earthly things. Remaining pure in defending the truth becomes more difficult when the attacks become personal. I am a human being, so when negative things are said about me, I certainly feel something. I have to ask myself, "Is my desire to respond due to some feeling to vindicate myself, or is it due to the need to defend the truth?" If it is for the sake of the truth, all I can do is have honest fellowship with those in error and then leave them to the Lord and their own consciences.

Many countries have a two-party political system. Matters such as which party wins and which loses are earthly things. Zealots in this realm become obsessed with who is gaining ground and whose cause is prevailing. When we bring such earthly ways into the church life, we bring ourselves into shame. We don't need to win any arguments—we need to dispense life and build up the body of Christ! To do otherwise is to set our mind on earthly things.

We don't want to end up exalting ourselves rather than Christ. Those who do so make their appetite their god, thus becoming enemies of the cross of Christ. They may feel what they are doing is glorious, but what they do takes them and others away from Christ and is shameful. Whenever we lose Christ as our central focus and goal, our labor becomes distorted, and the result is loss instead of gain.

We can easily fall into this trap if we are not careful. These two verses are unpleasant to consider, and we may wish they were not in the Bible, but we must be reminded of what can happen when we take something other than Christ as the unique goal in our lives. Christ must be our center, content, reality, inner substance, and circumference. Christ must be everything!

# 32

# Citizens of a
# Heavenly Commonwealth

*For our citizenship is in heaven, from which also we eagerly wait
for a Savior, the Lord Jesus Christ.*

— *Philippians 3:20*

## A Citizenship in Heaven

The previous chapter painted a gloomy picture of how some walk by taking their appetite as their god, mistaking shameful things as being glorious, and caring for earthly things (Phil. 3:18–19). This is very sad, and it is even more disturbing to read that Paul said there are many who walk in such a way. Whenever a person strays from the heavenly Christ, all that remains are earthly things.

Paul, however, did not end Philippians 3 on such a depressing note. Following two very sober verses concerning the enemies of the cross of Christ comes a very encouraging verse: "For our citizenship is in heaven, from which also we eagerly wait for a Savior, the Lord Jesus Christ" (v. 20). Isn't this wonderful? He encouraged us by telling us our citizenship is in heaven. Therefore, we are not an earthly people. Paul told us that even though many walk in a manner that leads to degradation, our citizenship exists in heaven. Be encouraged—we are a group of heavenly people! Our life, living, and labor are heavenly. Many may walk in a way that causes us to grieve like Paul, but our citizenship remains in heaven.

## Our Commonwealth

Some translations, such as Darby's New Translation, use the word "commonwealth" instead of "citizenship" in verse 20. The British Empire was a commonwealth with colonies all over the world, but that was an earthly commonwealth. Our citizenship is in a heavenly commonwealth.

Regardless how different we are from one another—such as in culture, age, or political view—in this heavenly commonwealth, we all share an association in the divine life. I am from China, and you may be from the U.S., but in this commonwealth there is no difference between us. This is not merely because we share common rights as citizens in a political commonwealth. The kingdom of the heavens is very different from earthly kingdoms. It is a kingdom of life, and within this kingdom all the citizens are related through God's life. As citizens of this kingdom, our responsibility is to enjoy this divine life.

When we meet other Christians, we should not make any issues, but should simply enjoy our common heavenly life. To do otherwise frustrates the life relationship that makes us fellow citizens in this commonwealth. All believers are members of Christ's organic body. In this body, we all share in a sweet life relationship. In the divine life, I am related to you and you are related to me. Nothing can break this life relationship. Nothing can separate us, for our relationship is heavenly, divine, and according to the eternal life of God. This organic body encompasses all the life relationships between the members of the body and Christ. We may be of very different temperaments, but we each share the same Christ as our divine life. This is why, though we may be very different from one another, we are able to live a church life together.

## The Constitution of
## Our Commonwealth

Christ is the constitution of our heavenly commonwealth. In the heavens, Christ is the unique center. He is the totality of all that God is and the reality of heaven. Therefore, in this commonwealth we have nothing but Christ Himself. Heaven is heavenly only because Christ is there. He is the essence, the element, and the substance of our heavenly commonwealth. To illustrate, the fiber of an orange is its substance, and yet the fiber itself is made up of the essence of the orange. Essence produces the element which becomes the substance which becomes our enjoyment. An orange is sweet and juicy because of its essence, element, and substance. In the same way, the commonwealth of the heavens is wonderful because Christ is its essence, element, and substance.

In the church life, we are not interested in anything other than Christ Himself. We may do things together, but the purpose of these activities must be to experience our common Christ. If we end up with only the experience of the activity, something is wrong. Every activity should bring us to Christ. That is the criteria for judging the value of any activity. For over fifty years I have been enjoying a church life in which I have grown in this heavenly commonwealth, being brought to Christ by all my fellow citizens. Even in times of weaknesses, I have been helped by my fellow citizens to turn again and again to experience Christ as the inward content of this commonwealth.

In this heavenly commonwealth, Christ is our power and energy (Eph. 1:19–23). He is our *dynamo*. In the church life, we can never truly be dead because Christ is the energizing One. Whenever we are in Him, we become dynamic because Christ is the *dynamo* in this commonwealth. He declared, "I am the resurrection and the life" (John 11:25)! He is full of resurrection power and divine energy. While we may at times experience discouragement and frustration, we must remember that our commonwealth exists in the heavens. Its power is ours to experience continuously.

This commonwealth manifests and testifies only Christ. When others see the church gathering, they shouldn't see merely a group of good people, or even a group of godly people. Instead, they should say, "Christ is here!" (1 Cor. 14:23–25), for this commonwealth is a testimony of Christ alone. Who is the unique center and focus of our church life? It should be only Christ. On that day when Christ brings the kingdom of the heavens to earth, knowledge will disappear, and only Christ Himself will be seen (1 Cor. 13:8). In our church life today, we should experience Christ as the testimony of the kingdom of the heavens on earth.

What a commonwealth is ours! Christ is its essence, element, and substance. Christ is its inward content. Christ is its power and energy. Here Christ is manifested and testified. He is the constitution of our heavenly commonwealth.

## Our Continual Pursuit

Our commonwealth which exists in the heavens is also our upward call. Paul wrote, "Brethren, I do not regard myself as having laid hold of it yet; but one thing I do: forgetting what lies behind and reaching forward to what lies ahead, I press on toward the goal for the prize of the upward call of God in Christ Jesus" (Phil. 3:13–14). We may think that we will one day arrive at a place where our pursuing will finally be over. However, even if we could reach the level of maturity that Paul reached, we would still need to keep pursuing Christ. We can never rest upon what we have already gained or attained. Paul also told us that those who have arrived at a level of growth in Christ, which he called perfect or mature (v. 15), must have a mind to continually pursue Christ, who is the goal of our upward call.

## Christ as the Leader in
## This Commonwealth

There is a divine administration in this heavenly commonwealth. Here, God in Christ is the government. He is its ruler. Christ is the sole owner and leader. He is taking care of this commonwealth. As citizens in this commonwealth, we follow Christ.

After I moved to the United States, I felt the Lord was calling me to serve Him full time. He confirmed this to me often as I was in His presence, so I wrote about it to someone more experienced in such matters. He wrote back, "If the Lord has called you to serve Him full time, you have no choice but to follow Him." This is the ruling of the Lord in this commonwealth—we follow Christ, enjoy Christ, and never stray from Him.

This heavenly commonwealth is the upward call Paul spoke of: "I press on toward the goal for the prize of the upward call of God in Christ Jesus" (Phil. 3:14). We press on toward Christ because we are called into this commonwealth. As we pay the price to pursue Him, we experience and gain Christ as the reality of this commonwealth. Praise the Lord! We can all be saved from walking as enemies of the cross, saved from the shame of our humble state, and saved from the earthly things, for we are heavenly people in this heavenly commonwealth that has Christ as its everything.

# 33

# Conformation to Christ's Glorious Body

*For our citizenship is in heaven, from which also we eagerly wait for a Savior, the Lord Jesus Christ; who will transform the body of our humble state into conformity with the body of His glory, by the exertion of the power that He has even to subject all things to Himself.*

*—Philippians 3:20-21*

### Eagerly Waiting for the Savior

When Paul wrote Philippians, he was mature in the experience of Christ, yet he still needed a Savior (Phil. 3:20). It seems such a mature brother should have written, "Since our citizenship is in heaven, we can now relax as we await the Lord's coming." Why would Paul, being so mature, eagerly await Christ as his Savior? It is because he realized how much he needed Christ as his Savior. He was desperate and eager for the Lord to rescue him, for he knew how fallen he was.

Our eagerness for our Savior's coming has much to do with our realization of who we are. The more we mature, the more we realize we are degraded and vulnerable to Satan's attack. The more we mature, the more we say, "Lord, save me!" Therefore, we "eagerly wait for a Savior, the Lord Jesus Christ" (v. 20).

Maturity may not be what we think it is. As Paul said, "If anyone supposes that he knows anything, he has not yet known as he ought to know" (1 Cor. 8:2). Those who are spiritually mature may be greatly used by the Lord, yet this does not mean they are free from sinful temptations. We need a Savior. Before the Lord's return, we will not be able to fully apprehend Christ. In fact, we will need eternity to explore and enjoy the unsearchable riches of Christ.

No matter how much we have grown, no matter how rich our enjoyment of Christ has been, no matter how much we are able to live a life in oneness with Christ, we still need Jesus as our Savior. I have loved the Lord for more than fifty years, yet today, more than ever, I realize how much I need Jesus as my Savior.

Young believers focus on whatever they think should be next in their lives. They may anticipate becoming involved in some type of Christian service. Perhaps they also expect to begin studying the Bible in a more excellent way, preaching the gospel in a more prevailing manner, and fulfilling their ministry, however they envision it. There are so many things they think they are going to do! The more we mature, however, the more we realize that the Savior's coming is the most important thing. Until He returns, whatever we can do is relatively limited. The older we get, the more we should sense our limitation and our need for the salvation that only comes with His return.

Only after we become aware of who we are do we truly treasure our salvation. At first, we have little idea of what it means to be a sinner, only recalling some bad things we have done. As we mature, however, we become aware of the power of sin in the flesh. We find ourselves yearning for the Savior's coming, longing to be saved through the transfiguration of our body. Thus Paul concluded this chapter by writing of the Lord as the One "who will transform the body of our humble state into conformity with the body of His glory" (v. 21).

## Our Body of Humiliation

The Greek word for "humble" in this verse is *tapeinōsis*,

which means "humiliation, be made low, low estate, vile" (Strong, no. 5014). "The body of our humble state" is a body of humiliation. Years ago, I could easily run up and down a flight of stairs. Today, I need help climbing stairs, and as I do, I firmly hold the handrail. Furthermore, I experience so many aches and pains. I often cannot sleep through the night. I used to speak vigorously, but today my voice is raspy, no longer as vibrant as it once was. Oh, how our body increasingly manifests itself as a body of humiliation day by day!

Even a young man must know that his body is a body of humiliation, for every human body is a body of flesh, and the flesh can never be fully subject to God. This is why, when referring to the flesh, the Bible also mentions the cross (Gal. 2:20; 5:24). The flesh can never be fully dealt with until the Lord returns. Whenever we are in Christ and enjoying Him, we are not thinking about sin. Apart from Christ, however, we may easily become involved with sinful things. We want to be pleasing to God, but our body of humiliation will always frustrate us (Rom. 7:18–20).

When we see a very aged person walking slowly along, we should realize that this will be our lot. That, however, is just the outward aspect of our body of sin. Its inward aspect is even more humiliating. None of us can afford to expose all that goes on within us. That would simply be too humiliating.

## Transfiguration

Christ will "transform the body of our humble state into conformity with the body of His glory" (v. 21). This is transfiguration, Paul's final point in Philippians 3. This transfiguration not only frees us from our lowly body but conforms it to Christ's glorious body. By this transformation and conformation, we will match the glory of Christ!

As believers, we first experience regeneration in our spirit. Then we begin to experience the renewing and sanctification work of the Spirit in our soul. One day we will experience the transfiguration of our body. These are the three stages the seekers of Christ experience as they pursue Him throughout their lives. We may not consider the amount of Christ we have gained as something so grand, but when we are transfigured, the Christ we have gained throughout our life will be manifested. Just as "star differs from star in glory," so we will all shine, but with varying degrees of glory (1 Cor. 15:41). However, regardless to what degree of glory we have attained, the humiliation of our body will be gone.

## Spiritual Growth

Once we are regenerated, we enter the process of spiritual growth, which includes renewing, sanctification, transformation, and conformation. This growth process is our life-long experience and eventually culminates in our transfiguration at the Lord's return.

These four things—renewing, sanctification, transformation, and conformation—happen simultaneously, beginning from the day we are regenerated. Renewing is the basic experience of all of these (2 Cor. 4:16). The Christian life is a renewing life. How much we are renewed decides how much spiritual reality we have. Sanctification is the inward result of renewing. Transformation is the outward display of renewing. The degree to which we are renewed, sanctified, and transformed is the degree to which we are conformed. Conformation is not something in the future—it is a prize we possess today.

Every time we experience renewing, we have a deeper and higher experience of sanctification inwardly. At the same time, we outwardly experience transformation in our living. The degree of our sanctification and transformation has so much to do with how much we are renewed. Tell the Lord, "Lord, renew me day by day. Renew my spirit, my mind, and my apprehension of spiritual things." Our growth has so much to do with our renewing.

Things that once were so precious to us no longer hold the

same value as we experience the renewing of our mind (Rom. 12:2). As the Lord unveils more of Himself to us, we begin to see things differently and our judgment is changed. What we treasured and boasted in we now count as rubbish so that we may gain Christ (Phil. 3:8). With the renewing of our mind, we have an inward sanctification, a separation unto God from things that do not match Him. Out of this renewing comes a transformed living.

The more we are renewed, the more we are sanctified and transformed. Eventually, we will have a greater and higher degree of conformation to Christ. This very conformation will be our glory in eternity.

## Using Every Day to Gain More of Christ

The Lord's resurrected body in glory is our future. One day our bodies will be transformed into conformity with His glorious body. Today, the Lord gives us time that we may become more conformed to His image (Rom. 8:29). What a blessing it is to live a long life! Every day is given to us that we might use it to be further renewed, sanctified, transformed, and conformed. The degree that we are conformed in time will determine the degree we are glorified in eternity. Therefore, use every day to gain more of Christ.

When we consider what we have accomplished or have experienced in our Christian life, the real issue should be how much we have gained of the Lord. We should not think that the Lord will magically glorify all believers equally. Too many consider Jesus to be such a magician, pulling a rabbit out of a hat where there was no rabbit before. This is not the case. It is true that we will experience the power that raised Christ from the dead and seated Him in the heavenly places (Eph. 1:18–20; 2:6). The difference is this: what Christ experienced was total, whereas what we experience will be proportional to our degree of conformation.

## The Shaping of Conformation

Paul spoke of conformity in verse 21, not glorification or transfiguration. This is because Christ is using our environment to shape us "by the exertion of the power that He has even to subject all things to Himself" (Phil. 3:21). As Paul said elsewhere, "God causes all things to work together for good to those who love God, to those who are called according to His purpose...to become conformed to the image of His Son" (Rom. 8:28–29). Our environment is subject to Christ, and He causes even the minor things for our conformation, which in turn determines our glorification. In that day, the result of all the Lord's work will be manifest. In that day all things will be made clear to us (1 Cor. 13:12).

Today, the Lord is using everything—even the unreasonable things—so that we might grow to the greatest degree of glory. This is the sweet conclusion to Philippians 3. We can restfully take all things from His hand, knowing that what is taking place is for our conformation today and our glorification in that day.

34

# Three Causes
# for Rejoicing

*Therefore, my beloved brethren whom I long to see, my joy and crown, in this way stand firm in the Lord, my beloved. I urge Euodia and I urge Syntyche to live in harmony in the Lord. Indeed, true companion, I ask you also to help these women who have shared my struggle in the cause of the gospel, together with Clement also and the rest of my fellow workers, whose names are in the book of life. Rejoice in the Lord always; again I will say, rejoice!*

*—Philippians 4:1–4*

## Paul's Purity

Paul began this fourth chapter in such a sweet way, referring to the Philippians as "my beloved brethren whom I long to see." This shows that his relationship with the church was not that of a worker with his work over which he exercised control. Rather, he loved them and desired to see them grow properly in the Lord. Paul was an extremely pure coworker. He didn't feel that any church belonged to him.

When I read verse 1, Paul's purity brings tears to my eyes. I pray that the Lord would keep me so pure in all my relationships with the churches I serve. No church is under my control.

## Beloved and Longed-for Brethren

The Philippians were so precious to Paul. In chapter 1 he said, "How I long for you all with the affection of Christ Jesus" (Phil. 1:8). They were beloved and longed for. He did not consider the church as just a field in which to labor. To say, "my beloved brethren whom I long to see" is very much a matter of feeling.

By referring to the Philippians as brethren, Paul indicated that he was related to them organically. They shared the same life. But when he said, "beloved brethren whom I long to see," his emphasis was on his feeling rather than his life relationship.

Paul's relationship with the church is so pure because it was so much in love and in the divine life with the divine economy. Oh this is precious!

## Joy and Crown

Next, Paul referred to the Philippians as "my joy and crown" (Phil. 4:1). This is a great lesson. The condition of a church is proved by its relationship with the apostles who minister to it. A healthy church is an apostle's glory and joy (1 Thess. 2:20). Joy is inward, whereas a crown is outward and visible, something that can become a boast (2 Thess. 1:4). The Philippians were Paul's inward joy and outward crown.

By the Lord's mercy, I have raised up a small number of churches. Do I have Paul's purity? If so, I must not consider these churches as my work to control. They are not my territory. They don't belong to me. I must keep my relationship with them so pure. They are my beloved brothers. I long for them. We have the organic life together in the divine economy. They are my inward joy and my outward crown.

## Stand Firm in the Lord

Paul continued, "Stand firm in the Lord, my beloved" (Phil.

4:1). The way to stand firm is to take the same stand the Lord took in humbling Himself (2:7–8). It is the way Paul took in his pursuing (3:12–14). So in the same way, "stand firm in the Lord, my beloved."

## Corporate Harmony

Paul was concerned for the harmony among the members of the church in Philippi (Phil. 4:2–3). Such harmony is the mark of a healthy church life.

Being peaceful does not necessarily indicate harmony because peacefulness can also be a result of death. Some might feel everything is quite harmonious, but this is only because they avoid one another. What we seek is a harmony of life, not of death. The harmony of life is a sign that a local church is healthy. If, however, there is arguing and infighting, there is reason for concern.

Those who love the Lord, pursue Him, and give themselves to Him know how to keep themselves in harmony with others. The secret to harmony is laying hold of Christ. If other things replace Christ as our focus, our harmony will disappear. We are here only to gain and possess Christ. This is what we must stand for. We must be willing to pay any price to lay hold of Christ. Otherwise, we will not experience true harmony.

The church in Corinth is an example of a church which lacked harmony. They made an issue of which apostle they should follow (1 Cor. 1:11–13; 3:3–4). To follow Paul, Apollos, or Cephas should never have been an issue. No servant of the Lord should ever become an issue among the churches. We should appreciate every member of the body of Christ, but we cannot allow any servant of the Lord to become an issue among us. They are here to serve us and to help us to focus on Christ and gain Him (1 Cor. 3:21–23).

## Be of the Same Mind

Paul addressed a particular situation in Philippi where harmony was lacking. He said, "I urge Euodia and I urge Syntyche to live in harmony in the Lord" (Phil. 4:2). The phrase "live in harmony" can be literally translated as "think the same thing" (Vincent, 3:429). Although in the past these two women were able to labor together with Paul in the gospel (v. 3), they were no longer of the same mind. Therefore, he implored them to think the same thing in the Lord.

It seems Paul was asking for the impossible. In the fifty years that I have served the Lord, I have never seen two people whose minds were the same. Even a husband and wife are different. Some people say that a man and woman should have a long courtship to see if they are compatible. From my observation, however, whether couples have a long or short courtship, once they marry, they always discover how different they are. Euodia and Syntyche may have been opposites—one sweet and the other like thunder. Paul implored them to live in harmony in the Lord. He didn't say to do the same thing but to think the same thing.

Christ's longing for us is that we, like Paul, would have a mind to press on toward the goal of gaining Christ (Phil. 3:14–15). For this we need to think the same thing. When other things become our goal, they become issues which trouble the church. For example, if we make anyone's ministry an issue, our oneness will be gone. The same is true if we insist on a music style, biblical interpretation, or tongue-speaking. These things can become toys to us, and we may care more for these toys than for what is profitable to the church. It is better to drop our insistence than to lose the oneness. We need to labor faithfully without making our teaching an issue. If I make myself, my labor, or my teaching an issue, the oneness will be gone. What brings us together is Christ. The sweetness among believers is that we only care for Christ. Many Christians are very different from me, yet I have no enemy. I can say with a clear conscience, I love them all. Sometimes they upset me, yet I still love them because I appreciate the Lord's work in them.

Harmony doesn't come easily. To think the same thing means to consider only Christ, who humbled Himself by becoming a man, even taking the form of a bond-servant, and dying on the cross for us (Phil. 2:7–8). So today, let us have a mind to gain and possess Christ. May Christ be formed in us until we are occupied with nothing but Christ Himself. If the whole church in Philippi had this focus, then Euodia and Syntyche would be in harmony.

## Together

Paul continued, "Indeed, true companion, I ask you also to help these women who have shared my struggle in the cause of the gospel, together with Clement also and the rest of my fellow workers, whose names are in the book of life" (Phil. 4:3). In this verse, Paul used four very interesting Greek words that are all compounds beginning with the prefix *sun*, meaning "together with" (Parkhurst, p. 644).

The first of these compound words is "companion," which in Greek is *suzugos*. This word is made up of *sun* and *zugos*, which means "a yoke." Together they mean "a yoke-fellow, an associate or companion in labour" (Parkhurst, p. 638).

The second is "help," which in Greek is *sullambanō*. This is made up of *sun* and *lambanō*, and means "to take, receive." Together they mean "to help, assist,...to take a burden, or the like, together with" (Parkhurst, p. 640). Once again, Paul stresses "together."

The third is "struggle," which in Greek is *sunathleō*. This is made up of *sun* and *athleō*, which means "to strive." So together they mean "to strive or labour together with" (Parkhurst, p. 645). Euodia and Syntyche had once struggled together with Paul, striving in the cause of the gospel.

The fourth compound word is "fellow workers," which in Greek is *sunergos*. This is made up of *sun* and *ergon*, which means "a work." Together they mean "a worker with another, a fellow-worker or -labourer" (Parkhurst, p. 650).

In this verse, Paul stressed being together by his use of these four compound words that all begin with the prefix *sun*. In the body of Christ, we bear the yoke together as true companions, help one another together, and struggle together in the gospel, serving as fellow workers together.

For Euodia and Syntyche to work together harmoniously again would require the work of the cross. For Paul's true companion, Clement, and the other fellow workers to assist these two women in working together would also require the work of the cross. When we are alone as individuals, we may be nice and sweet, but once we begin to work together with others, we find the need to deny our self and take up the cross (Matt. 16:24). This is the church life.

## Rejoice in the Lord

Then, "Rejoice in the Lord always; again I will say, rejoice!" (Phil. 4:4). There's not much to say, just rejoice. Rejoicing is the spontaneous result of three things: being pure, caring only for Christ, and laboring together in harmony.

The first item is purity. Our relationships should be so pure. No one should exercise control over the churches or believers whom they serve. If we are pure, we will see one another as beloved brothers (v. 1) in an organic testimony.

The second source of rejoicing is being of the same mind by caring for nothing but Christ. Focusing on anything else divides the body, regardless how good it is. Even the most heavenly revelation, if it becomes an issue, will divide the church. No one had revelation higher than Paul, who was caught up to the third heaven (2 Cor. 12:2), yet he did not preach this revelation. Who can be richer than Paul? Yet all his epistles lead us to Christ.

Euodia and Syntyche once labored with Paul in the gospel. At that time, their goal was the same. Over time, I believe they allowed issues to come in, causing them to argue. We each have to say, "I die." We cannot just care for our Christian work. Christ must have the preeminence in all we do.

The third source of rejoicing is that in the church life there is togetherness. This togetherness crosses out the self. Our self life is the cause of most of the trouble in the church life. Everything we do should be in the principle of the body with togetherness. This is why verse 3 says we are companions together, we help together, we struggle together, and we are fellow workers together. All our relationships and service should be in the principle of togetherness.

Our purity, being of the same mind by focusing on Christ, and togetherness will result in a church life full of rejoicing.

# 35

# Christian Forbearance

*Let your gentle spirit be known to all men. The Lord is near. Be anxious for nothing, but in everything by prayer and supplication with thanksgiving let your requests be made known to God. And the peace of God, which surpasses all comprehension, will guard your hearts and your minds in Christ Jesus.*
*—Philippians 4:5–7*

### Gentleness and Forbearance

Chapter 4 of Philippians is on the practice of the church life. In this portion, Paul told the Philippians, "Let your gentle spirit be known to all men" (Phil. 4:5). Why? Because "the Lord is near."

What is a gentle spirit? The Greek word used here is *epieikēs* which means "a humble, patient steadfastness which is able to submit to injustice, disgrace, and maltreatment without hatred and malice, trusting in God in spite of it all" (Rogers, p. 457). It is sometimes translated "forbearance," as in the American Standard Version. We often find ourselves in seemingly unreasonable situations. What is the secret to forbearance in such situations? It is to give up our rights. In other words, others know they can take advantage of us, because we have given up our legal rights to make any claims for ourselves. We should be able to declare, "If I have any food in my refrigerator, it's yours! If I have a couch you want, feel free to come take it!" Others should know that everything we have is theirs, because we live for them.

In my house there are many vases. One day I discovered two vases were missing. I searched through the house but could not find them. I had told others that they were free to take anything in my house. Someone took me up on that word and took the two vases. Whatever we have belongs to the church.

Paul's word, however, is that our forbearance should be known not just to our close companions but to all men. All who are acquainted with us should know this about us. Who can exercise such gentleness and forbearance? Only those who realize "the Lord is near."

Some may ask, "Is the Lord near in terms of distance or time?" It is true in both senses. He is with us in our spirit, and He is also coming to be with us. These facts are the secret to our practice of the church life by way of forbearance. When things become impossible, there is a strength within that enables us to remain joyful even as others seem to take advantage of us. In this process, we experience and learn that the Lord is near. If we only live for ourselves, He will seem remote to us. However, if we live for the church and for others, we will sense the Lord is near, that He is with us, and that He is coming soon.

## Individual Restfulness

Paul was concerned for the restfulness of the Philippians. The Christian life, in principle, is a restful life. He said, "Be anxious for nothing, but in everything by prayer and supplication with thanksgiving let your requests be made known to God. And the peace of God, which surpasses all comprehension, will guard your hearts and your minds in Christ Jesus" (Phil. 4:6–7).

When we come to a major turn in our lives, often we become nervous, wondering, "What should I do next?" We begin to consider, "If I do this or that, will others be happy with me?"

How quickly we lose our restfulness! Why do we experience anxiety? Because we do not touch the Lord "by prayer and supplication with thanksgiving" (v. 6). Only those who enjoy Christ have real peace.

## Prayer and Supplication

Prayer is largely neglected by Christians. We are much more prone to discuss and consider things than to pray about them. Generally, prayer is not as strong among Christians as teaching, preaching, and mutual encouragement. Daily prayer is not commonly practiced. How many speak to the Lord and have fellowship with Him for half an hour every day? This simple matter is woefully short among us. It is because of this that we lack spiritual strength.

I am thankful that when I was a young believer, I was helped to build up a habit of prayer. Gradually it became a part of my person. Today, while doing other things, I pray. This should be an integral part of every Christian's daily life.

It is one thing to let others see our forbearance; it is another to be a praying person. As we exercise forbearance, we need to pray. Actually, in order to forbear and be free of anxiety, we need to pray. As Paul said, "In everything by prayer and supplication with thanksgiving let your requests be made known to God" (Phil. 4:6).

Prayer stresses fellowship, while supplication refers to intercession for a particular matter. Prayer leads to supplication, and supplication generates prayer. They both end up with thanksgiving.

If we want to carry out the Lord's move and work, we must be in fellowship with Him through prayer. As we spend time in His presence, certain specific matters will come up in our heart, and we will begin to petition the Lord concerning these matters. If we practice this kind of prayer, what the Lord desires will be worked out among us.

I hope that if we are ever asked why we chose a certain way

in our life, we would be able to say, "Because the Lord told me." The Lord must be able to move among us. Thus Paul first told us that we must not be for ourselves. Instead, we should be able to do what others cannot by showing forbearance toward all. Second, he told us to pray. We must speak to Christ and fellowship with Him. Practically, I would suggest everyone pray at least half an hour every day. While praying, it is too easy for our minds to wander. We should use the Lord's name often in our prayer to keep our focus on Him. As we pray in this way, we are brought into a quietness before the Lord. That is a powerful thing. Once we enter into this quietness, we will find it easy to pray for prolonged periods of time.

In addition, I would also suggest that we read a few verses from the Bible out loud as we begin to pray. This also will quiet our soul and make it easier to pray. Singing a spiritual song to the Lord can also help in this way, particularly if we sing some portion over and over. For instance, we can sing:

> Each day let Thy supporting might
> My weakness still embrace;
> My darkness vanish in Thy light,
> Thy life my death efface. (Martin, no. 220)

Then we can pray, "O Lord, each day I worship You for Your supporting might." A few verses or lines from a hymn can bring us into a quieted state before the Lord.

## The Peace of God

Paul's word is that we should come to the Lord in all things and trust Him in all things. If we can do that, "the peace of God, which surpasses all comprehension" will be ours (Phil. 4:7).

As we pray in the midst of all that concerns us, peace comes. This peace is not just any peace. It is the peace of God which is far beyond our understanding. If we were offered a job promotion that would take us far away from the church we have been serving, we may be torn between whether to take the offer for the sake of our family or to turn it down for the sake of the church. This inner conflict causes us to lose our inner peace. As we pray, however, our soul is brought back to a peaceful state, even before we know the Lord's mind in this matter. The peace that goes beyond our comprehension has come.

Whenever we touch the Lord in prayer, everything is fine. If we are anxious, that surely indicates Christ is not involved in what we are doing. We may have our idea of why we should or should not do something, and we may even pray according to those thoughts, but once we touch the Lord, we are touching the One who has a plan that is greater than ours. As we pray and petition the Lord, this One who has the understanding that is higher than ours knows how to work with us. Eventually we become so thankful that everything is in the Lord's hands. This is when we really experience the peace of God.

The Lord may not answer our prayers and petitions in the way we desire because His answer is not according to our thought, but according to our need of transformation. We may have a specific need, and it is proper that we pray for it, but the Lord desires something much higher for us than we realize. Therefore, the Lord may not answer our prayers in the manner we expect, yet we will experience the peace of God which surpasses all comprehension. We may not get what we want, but the peace is there. The peace of God will guard our hearts and minds in Christ Jesus because we have a prayer life.

We may be disappointed when our prayers are not answered in the way we expect, but in eternity we will be very thankful that the Lord did not always give us what we prayed for. In fact, the process itself is precious because it causes us to know the Lord. Eventually, as we go through this process, we find we love the Lord more.

Many Christians do not pray. Instead, they just do what they think needs to be done and never check with the Lord. They may seem to be successful in what they do, but they do not gain Christ in the process. We have to pray and allow Christ to govern everything, from our haircut to our manner of life and our labor. We must let Him know what bothers us and what we desire. We should talk to Him about everything.

I hope all of us would pick up the habit of praying a certain amount of time every day. This will result in genuine forbearance in all our interactions, and the peace of God will guard our hearts and minds in Christ Jesus.

# 36

## Christian
## Growth

*Finally, brethren, whatever is true, whatever is honorable, whatever is right, whatever is pure, whatever is lovely, whatever is of good repute, if there is any excellence and if anything worthy of praise, dwell on these things.*

*—Philippians 4:8*

We can divide the items Paul lists in Philippians 4:8 into three groups. The first group includes things that are true, honorable, and right. The second group includes things that are pure, lovely, and of good repute. The final group consists of any excellence and anything worthy of praise. These three groups relate to our spiritual growth.

### Whatever Is True

One characteristic of new believers is that they are true. Their prayers and testimonies are genuine, never faked or forced. After a little while, however, they learn how to perform. The root of our Christian life must be this virtue of being true. That which is true knows nothing of display or pretense. We shouldn't try to build ourselves up, appearing to be someone we are not. As newborn Christians, nearly everything we do is true, for we do not yet know how to act according to others' expectation. This experience of being true is necessary if we want to know life.

When I first began loving the Lord, I believed everything I was told. I was once told that Christians shouldn't read the newspaper, and I believed it. Then I saw someone in the deacon's office reading a newspaper. This bothered me so much that I told the one who had laid down this rule. He answered, "He was just trying to find gospel material." I took his word as true, whether it was or not. I even believed it when I was told that a Christian I saw looking at a movie poster was actually looking to the heavens!

Throughout our lives, we should never stop being true. We should never allow ourselves to become cynical. The more we grow and progress in our Christian lives, the more we will discover how corrupted things can be. No matter how spiritual we become, our sinful part also develops. Paul said, "Whatever is true...dwell on these things." Remember how you began.

## Whatever Is Honorable

The Greek word for "honorable" here is *semnos*, which carries the idea of "a dignity or majesty which is yet inviting and attractive, and which inspires reverence" (Vincent, 3:458). It thus carries with it the sense of expressing God. Those who are true and genuine pay attention to those things that truly express God. They are touched whenever they hear a prayer or testimony that genuinely expresses Him.

We should respect the things that express God. For instance, we may see someone drop some money into the church offering box. We should respect that, because they are doing a holy thing. Don't say, "The Bible says, 'When you do a charitable deed, do not let your left hand know what your right hand is doing.' Here I am watching you, and you dropped it in anyway!" Such a person lacks the ability to appreciate that which is dignified. There are many holy, divine things happening around us, and they should be respected in light of their dignity. Whatever is truly of God is honorable and dignified.

The wealthier people become, the more they tend to feed

their fleshly desires. They buy items for their own comfort. Such things are a contrast to what is honorable and dignified. Instead of appreciating them, we should appreciate and respect the things that express God. Those who are true pay attention to what is honorable. While some may pay undue attention to those who are of repute, hoping to advance their own stature in the eyes of others, those who are true appreciate the testimony of even the most lowly person, if it expresses God. If we develop this ability to appreciate what is honorable, we will grow.

One time I heard two young Christians talking. One commented on a certain prayer which was particularly filled with the Spirit. The other responded that he too was so helped by that prayer. When I heard this, I was happy, for these two were learning to appreciate that which was dignified. We must broaden our ability to value things and not be narrow in our interest. We all need to appreciate the heavenly things manifested through others for these are the result of the operation of the divine life within them.

What people should see in us is an attractive and inviting dignity. We should not try to impress them with our talent or knowledge of the Bible. We should be approachable and manifest a dignity that issues from God's life within us.

## Whatever Is Righteous

The Greek word for "right" is *dikaios*, which can also be translated "righteous" (Strong, no. 1342). We may say that righteousness is God's nature in action. When God works in us and imparts His nature into us, we begin to live out the righteousness which God has imputed to us by faith.

Righteousness comes from the Lord and is expressed through His desire, move, and work. What people should see in us is not merely proper behavior. Rather, they should see a living that expresses divine righteousness. Being righteous means more than merely doing the right thing or acting according to the moral standard of God. It is a living that spontaneously flows from abiding in God. This is the true righteousness.

I admire my wife's ability to appreciate the work of the Lord in me. She has never discouraged me from following Him, even though it has meant that she has had to bear with much. The reason she has been peaceful is because she recognizes that God has been operating in me. By the Lord's mercy, this operation of God has caused me to live and labor in a righteous way.

How blessed we are to have older ones who encourage us! We are most blessed if we grow spiritually among a group of Christians who appreciate what is righteous. Sometimes, however, our peers discourage us from expressing the Lord's inward work as righteous acts. They may appreciate our love to the Lord and faithfulness to the church, but when we are ready to pay the price to follow the Lord, they will ask, "Are you sure?"

I hope that those who have known me for many years can appreciate how the Lord has grown in me. They should not think that, since I am now seventy years old, I no longer need to grow. The divine operations that produce the righteous acts are still at work within me.

As we serve others, we should appreciate the growth that comes from God's work in them. It is not enough that we open our home to young people and spend time teaching them. We should also watch for their growth in the Lord and appreciate it. If a young brother tells us what he enjoyed during his reading of the Bible, we should appreciate that as something righteous and speak positively about it. We should tell him, "I hope you have more of the Lord's speaking like this to bless the whole church!"

Spiritual growth begins with recognizing what is true. Then we begin to appreciate whatever is of God, that is, the things that are honorable. Whenever something of God is displayed through others' actions, we should appreciate the operation of the Lord in them, which means we appreciate the things that are righteous. Though these are basic matters, we can never outgrow them. Always appreciate what is true, what is honorable, and what is righteous.

## Whatever Is Pure

Paul continued by writing, "Whatever is pure, whatever is lovely, whatever is of good repute." These three form the second group, which takes us to another level. These matters touch our constitution. The more we grow, the more we can become impure. Those who are young and simple are more likely to be pure. Those who have more experience in the church life may look at things from other angles. They may look at others and consider how to gain them as their followers rather than simply appreciate them as lovers of Jesus. How we view others is based upon who we are.

The real test of our growth is our purity. The apostle Paul was very pure. When he looked at the believers or the churches, he saw them as beloved. They were his joy and his crown (Phil. 4:1; 1 Thess. 2:19). His only expectation was that they would become Christ's. Don't think this is such an easy matter. Those who serve the church often have to deal with hidden motives.

For example, Christian workers may desire to see a certain number of people show up for an event they have planned. If fewer people than this show up, they are disappointed because their goal was not met. Sometimes when I ask about such an event I am told, "Our attendance is normally better, but a certain family was sick, another was out of town," and so on. However, I am not an inspector, I am a brother in Christ. I have not come to see how well someone has done his job. It is fine to pray for a thousand to come, but we should be just as thankful if some lesser number shows up. We work with people, not numbers.

The first group begins with "true;" this second group begins with "pure." The beginning of our Christian life is characterized by being true. However, it is difficult to pursue spiritual growth and still remain pure. As we grow, we should be concerned with remaining pure. We should not let things defile us. Nothing should replace Christ.

## Whatever Is Lovely and of Good Repute

Next, Paul said, "Whatever is lovely." In the church, many lovely things happen. The gospel is preached and people get saved. They learn to love Jesus and their fellow believers. They give themselves wholly to the Lord and treasure His Word. Such lovely things are to be appreciated.

What is true has its eventual manifestation in what is pure. What is honorable or dignified has its expression in what is lovely. Whatever is righteous becomes a good report. We should appreciate such things throughout our entire Christian life. We never graduate from these, for they are needed for our growth. Eventually our Christian lives become the testimony of a good report.

## Any Excellence and Anything Worthy of Praise

For the third group Paul wrote, "If there is any excellence and if anything worthy of praise." Excellence refers to the divine attributes, while the things worthy of praise result from living out the divine attributes as our human virtues. When these praiseworthy things are present, we know that something of God has been constituted into us and is being lived out.

## Think on These Things

Paul concluded, "Dwell on these things," or, as most English versions translate it, "Think on these things." Paul listed eight items: "whatever is true, whatever is honorable, whatever is right, whatever is pure, whatever is lovely, whatever is of good repute, if there is any excellence and if anything worthy of praise" (Phil. 4:8). We are to think about these eight items that constitute our Christian growth.

# 37

# The Philippians' Care for Paul

*But I rejoiced in the Lord greatly, that now at last you have revived your concern for me; indeed, you were concerned before, but you lacked opportunity. Not that I speak from want, for I have learned to be content in whatever circumstances I am. I know how to get along with humble means, and I also know how to live in prosperity; in any and every circumstance I have learned the secret of being filled and going hungry, both of having abundance and suffering need. I can do all things through Him who strengthens me. Nevertheless, you have done well to share with me in my affliction.*

*You yourselves also know, Philippians, that at the first preaching of the gospel, after I left Macedonia, no church shared with me in the matter of giving and receiving but you alone; for even in Thessalonica you sent a gift more than once for my needs. Not that I seek the gift itself, but I seek for the profit which increases to your account. But I have received everything in full and have an abundance; I am amply supplied, having received from Epaphroditus what you have sent, a fragrant aroma, an acceptable sacrifice, well-pleasing to God. And my God will supply all your needs according to His riches in glory in Christ Jesus. Now to our God and Father be the glory forever and ever. Amen.*

*Greet every saint in Christ Jesus. The brethren who are with me greet you. All the saints greet you, especially those of Caesar's household.*

*The grace of the Lord Jesus Christ be with your spirit.*
—Philippians 4:10–23

Paul was concerned for the Philippians' handling of money (Phil. 4:10–19). This is one of the most crucial things in our lives, both individually and corporately, because it manifests our spiritual growth. The Lord told us clearly that we cannot serve both God and wealth (Matt. 6:24; Luke 16:13). We cannot serve two masters. Notice that instead of saying "Satan," the Lord said "wealth," or money. Money is a direct means Satan uses to control fallen mankind.

We should not fall into Satan's trap but should instead use our money for the Lord. Paul told the Corinthians, "He who sows bountifully will also reap bountifully. Each one must do just as he has purposed in his heart, not grudgingly or under compulsion; for God loves a cheerful giver" (2 Cor. 9:6–7). When we plant money as a life-seed by offering it to the Lord, we will reap bountifully. Paul encouraged the Philippians to give, not for his own benefit but that they would experience "the profit which increases to your account" (Phil. 4:17). He concluded, "And my God will supply all your needs according to His riches in glory in Christ Jesus" (v. 19).

The way Paul addressed the use of money in this chapter provides us a window through which we can see his struggles, his living and service before the Lord, and his relationship with the churches.

## Flourishing Care

Paul wrote, "I rejoiced in the Lord greatly, that now at last you have revived your concern for me" (Phil. 4:10). The phrase, "now at last," indicates that Paul had been watching and waiting for something. When Epaphroditus arrived bearing the gift from the Philippians, he rejoiced. Paul's rejoicing was not merely for the money that the Philippians sent to him (v. 18) but for their care for him. The Greek word for "revived" is *anathallō* which means, "to sprout again, to shoot up, to blossom again, to put forth new shoots" (Rogers, p. 457). In other words, Paul knew the Philippians had him in their heart, but he longed for an expression of that love.

After a couple has been married for thirty years, their love may not blossom as before. Though they truly love one another, they may not say "I love you" as often. A young couple can't stop saying how much they love each other. After thirty years, however, their love may be deeper but no longer openly flourishing. Though their love may have grown, it is not as manifest. It is very good for a husband to tell his wife often, "Honey, I really love you," and to give her flowers. That tells her his love for her is still flourishing.

Paul continued, "Indeed, you were concerned before, but you lacked opportunity" (v. 10). Paul knew that the church in Philippi loved him, but he suffered because their love had no opportunity to flourish. Now he was able to rejoice because the blossoming of their love had come. Paul knew that the Philippians always considered how to show their love and care for him but lacked opportunity to express that love.

## Being Content

The apostle Paul rejoiced at the Philippians' care for him, but it was not because he had been in need. Paul said he did not speak from need, but that does not mean he had no need. As he was writing to the Philippians, he was in prison. In fact, during his whole life of serving the Lord, he faced dangers and pressures of every kind. He wrote to the Corinthians, "In far more labors, in far more imprisonments, beaten times without number, often in danger of death. Five times I received from the Jews thirty-nine lashes. Three times I was beaten with rods, once I was stoned, three times I was shipwrecked, a night and a day I have spent in the deep. I have been on frequent journeys, in dangers from rivers, dangers from robbers, dangers from my countrymen, dangers from the Gentiles, dangers in the city, dangers in the wilderness, dangers on the sea, dangers among false brethren; I have been in labor and hardship, through many sleepless nights, in hunger and thirst, often without food, in cold and exposure. Apart from such external things, there is the daily pressure on me of concern for all the churches" (2 Cor. 11:23–28). He told the Philippians, "I have learned to be content in whatever circumstances I am" (Phil. 4:11). The phrase "in whatever circumstances" includes all of the circumstances, events, happenings, difficulties, and encouragements in Paul's life. He had learned to be content in all these things.

The Greek word for "content" is *autarkēs*, which means "sufficient for one's self, strong enough or possessing enough to need no aid or support; independent of external circumstances....Subjectively, contented with one's lot, with one's means, though the slenderest" (Thayer, p. 85). Paul was self-sufficient in all circumstances because he was inwardly supplied by Christ, who strengthened him (v. 13). Christ was his unfailing strength.

Sometimes we become discouraged, yet every discouragement leads us to an unfailing strength. At such times we might think, "It's over. I don't think I can love the Lord anymore." Yet for some reason, no matter how discouraged and incompetent we feel, there is an unfailing strength within us. The resurrected Christ restores us and becomes our encouragement. This is what it means to be content.

When we begin to fight for the Lord's interest and testimony, the spiritual combat becomes unspeakably fierce. In the midst of this battle we may feel we should give up. It is like Job's wife who told him to just curse God and die (Job 2:9). Yet, at the same time, there is an unfailing strength. Every time we think it is too much, something rises up within us, causing us to continue. As we abide in Christ as our unfailing strength, we experience contentment and satisfaction.

## Learning to Be Abased and to Abound

Paul continued, "I know how to get along with humble means, and I also know how to live in prosperity" (Phil. 4:12). Paul knew how to live in both lowly and prosperous circumstances. Sometimes we are so limited financially, physically, or even spiritually, that we can only say, "Lord, what should I do now?" Once I was down to my last dollar, and I went to the store to buy a loaf of bread and some milk. I was so happy I was singing hymns and praising the Lord. An old lady asked me, "How can you be so happy when the prices are inflating like this?" I didn't answer her, but within me I said, "I'm so happy because I have only one dollar. I have no idea what I will eat tomorrow, but I know the Lord." Something just rose up, so I knew how to be content in a circumstance of humble means.

Paul testified, "In any and every circumstance I have learned the secret of being filled and going hungry, both of having abundance and suffering need" (v. 12). His learning was not just theoretical but full of application.

Though Paul was mainly speaking of being full or hungry physically, this can be applied to our psychological and spiritual need also. We all go through times of being full. We also go through times of hunger. That is when we are tried. When we are filled, we may become proud. When we are hungry, we may look to things other than Christ. No Christian has the Lord's presence continuously. No one has an open door all the time. When we are very much in need, we shouldn't be bothered, because Christ within us is our unfailing strength to lift us up.

## The Strengthening Christ

Paul wrote further, "I can do all things through Him who strengthens me" (Phil. 4:13). This was the source of Paul's contentment in verse 11. Sometimes I am so tired and my mind is not clear, yet when I begin to minister, life is there. This is because the divine provision is so rich and the divine power is so strong and capable. I am strengthened to do all things. This causes me to be content and very restful.

The Greek word for "strengthen" is *endunamoō*, which means

"infuses strength into me" (Vincent, 3:460). Paul was able to be content no matter what his circumstance because Christ infused Himself into him as strength to meet the need.

## Support in Distress

In verse 14, Paul told the Philippians, "You have done well to share with me in my affliction." The Greek word for "affliction" here is *thlipsis*, which generally means "a pressing together, pressure" (Thayer, p. 291). In its biblical usage, however, it is used metaphorically to mean "oppression, affliction, tribulation, distress, straits" (Thayer, p. 291). This one word sums up Paul's Christian walk and serving life. His labor in the Lord was filled with affliction. His gospel preaching was filled with tribulation. His care for the churches pressed him (2 Cor. 11:23–28). In addition to all this, he was in distress financially. Those who are true servants of the Lord bear the mark of the cross of Christ. Their living is marked by affliction. The apostle Paul was such a person. He was in affliction because he had a charge, a goal, a purpose: to satisfy the Lord's desire.

When Paul was in affliction, Christ was with him to strengthen him (Phil. 4:13), but he also needed coworkers and churches to stand with him. This is why he genuinely appreciated his coworker Epaphroditus and the church in Philippi. Without their care, even Paul, a spiritual and powerful apostle, would have been limited in his service.

This is shown by what Paul wrote in verse 15: "You yourselves also know, Philippians, that at the first preaching of the gospel, after I left Macedonia, no church shared with me in the matter of giving and receiving but you alone." The city of Philippi was in Macedonia. When Paul left that region, only the Philippians cared for him. What a lonely apostle! Paul could have written to all the churches, "Brothers, the Lord's work has a need. Every church must donate." I'm happy that he didn't do that. Paul had already raised up many churches, but it seems that in this matter they had all forgotten him.

Paul testified that his labor in Corinth was directly helped by the offering that came from Philippi. He told the Corinthians, "When I was present with you and was in need, I was not a burden to anyone; for when the brethren came from Macedonia they fully supplied my need, and in everything I kept myself from being a burden to you, and will continue to do so" (2 Cor. 11:9). Without the supply from Philippi, Paul would have been unable to freely present the gospel to the Corinthians.

In fact, the Philippians began to care for Paul even before he left Macedonia. After Paul left Philippi, he passed through Amphipolis and Apollonia and came to Thessalonica (Acts 17:1). These are all cities in Macedonia. He wrote, "For even in Thessalonica you sent a gift more than once for my needs" (Phil. 4:16). Thessalonica is less than one hundred miles from Philippi, but in ancient times that could be a journey of several days. Right away, the newly saved believers in Philippi began to send aid to Paul. This is all the more impressive given that Paul had been with them for only two to five weeks. It seems the Philippians cared for the apostle Paul on an ongoing basis.

## Abounding Fruit

When Paul wrote verse 17—"Not that I seek the gift itself, but I seek for the profit which increases to your account"—he was very bold. The Philippians could have taken it as an excuse to stop supplying him, thinking that he had no need. Although he didn't seek the gift from them, he did seek the fruit for their benefit.

Some say that the profit here is money—since the Philippians gave Paul money, the Lord would give them more money. My conscience has never allowed to me to interpret it this way. Instead, I believe that when the Philippians gave of their material supply, they gained Christ as their spiritual profit. This profit would abound to their heavenly account (Luke 12:33).

## A Fragrant Aroma

Paul testified, "I have received everything in full and have an abundance; I am amply supplied, having received from Epaphroditus what you have sent, a fragrant aroma, an acceptable sacrifice, well-pleasing to God" (Phil. 4:18). The Greek word for "abound" is *perisseuō*, which means "to superabound, to abound richly...to have more than enough, to have superabundance" (Robinson, p. 576). When Paul said, "I have received everything in full and have an abundance," he was speaking of more than money. He had been in hardship and longed to have his coworkers with him and to have the churches stand with him. When his coworker Epaphroditus arrived with the supply from the church in Philippi, he felt full, satisfied, and even overflowing.

Paul's description of the supply the Philippians sent to him through Epaphroditus was with three extremely sweet phrases: "a fragrant aroma, an acceptable sacrifice, well-pleasing to God" (v. 18). Sometimes our offering has no fragrance, but other times it is a sweet smelling aroma. According to Paul's word to the Corinthians, this sweet, aromatic fragrance comes from two things. First, it comes from our knowledge of Christ: "But thanks be to God, who always leads us in triumph in Christ, and manifests through us the sweet aroma of the knowledge of Him in every place" (2 Cor. 2:14). Second, this fragrance is our person: "For we are a fragrance of Christ to God among those who are being saved and among those who are perishing; to the one an aroma from death to death, to the other an aroma from life to life" (vv. 15–16). When we preach the gospel to unbelievers, their response determines their eternity. When they refuse the gospel, we become an aroma of death leading to death. When they receive the gospel, we become an aroma of life leading to life. When we are so much with Christ, we become a fragrant aroma.

Paul described the things he received from the Philippians as a fragrant aroma. Even money can become a savor when it is associated with the right person. Our money will be a test to us our whole life—will it become a fragrant aroma or not? A wealthy person can easily write a check without being touched. Others, like the poor widow whom Jesus observed, give out of their lack (Mark 12:41–44). Even when they are under financial pressure, they are faithful to the Lord. That becomes a sweet-smelling aroma. Offering is the first practical lesson we should learn to become a healthy Christian. Once we are saved, we have to learn to offer of what the Lord has given us according to His leading. Such an offering becomes "a fragrant aroma, an acceptable sacrifice, well-pleasing to God" (v. 18).

## God's Supply

Paul continued, "My God will supply all your needs according to His riches in glory in Christ Jesus" (Phil. 4:19). When we offer our money, God promises to fill our every need—whether spiritual, psychological, or physical. His promise to care for us also includes our financial needs. When a church learns to stand with the Lord's servants in their affliction, its every need will be met according to God's riches—who He is, what He has, all He has accomplished, and how He operates.

I have never met a man who totally gave himself to Christ and eventually regretted it. I am thankful that the Lord has never been stingy with me. I hold nothing. I am afraid of nothing. I never give others the impression that I'm in need, even though I have experienced being down to my last dollar. When we learn to be responsible to Christ, especially in our finances, the Lord will meet our every need according to His riches.

God supplies all our need "according to His riches in glory." What we want may be a little house, a little security, and a comfortable living. However, as believers we shouldn't be limited to such common expectations for our lives. Instead, we should expect God to supply us according to His riches in glory. Though the process of this blessing may mean going through afflictions, in the end nothing can be more glorious! That is why Paul continued, "Now to our God and Father be the glory forever and ever. Amen" (v. 20).

## Final Greetings

Paul began this book addressing "all the saints in Christ Jesus who are in Philippi" (Phil. 1:1) and ended by greeting "every saint in Christ Jesus" (4:21). This shows what Paul cared for. He didn't say, "Greet the church," but, more specifically, "Greet every saint." Every saint is crucial.

"All the saints greet you, especially those of Caesar's household" (v. 22). Those of Caesar's household belonged to the highest class. As such, they were separated from the common people. However, because of Paul's gospel, members of this household were now one with the Philippians. Isn't this sweet? They had become saints, members of the body. Those who once were separated by class distinction now made a special effort to greet the saints in Philippi. The gospel has the effect of bringing separated people together.

Paul concluded this letter to the Philippians with this simple prayer: "The grace of the Lord Jesus Christ be with your spirit" (v. 23).

# Works Cited

Kittel, Gerhard, ed., Gerhard Friedrich, ed., Geoffrey W. Bromiley, trans. and ed. *Theological Dictionary of the New Testament.* Grand Rapids, MI: Wm. B. Eerdmans Publishing Company, 1964.

Kittel, Gerhard, ed., Gerhard Friedrich, ed., Geoffrey W. Bromiley, trans. and ed. *Theological Dictionary of the New Testament, Abridged in One Volume.* Grand Rapids, MI: Wm. B. Eerdmans Publishing Company, 1992.

Martin, Del, ed., Richard Yeh, ed. *Songs and Hymns of Life.* Ann Arbor, MI: Good Land Publishers, 2009.

Nee, Watchman. *Practical Issues of This Life.* New York: Christian Fellowship Publishers, Inc., 1975.

Parkhurst, John. *A Greek and English Lexicon to the New Testament.* London: J. Johnson, et. al., 1809.

Rienecker, Fritz, Cleon L. Rogers, trans. and ed. *A Linguistic Key to the Greek New Testament.* Grand Rapids, MI: Zondervan Publishing House, 1980.

Robertson, A.T. *Word Pictures in the New Testament.* Nashville: Holman Bible Publishers, 2000.

Robinson, Edward. *A Greek and English Lexicon of the New Testament.* London: Longman, Brown, Green, and Longmans, 1850.

Rogers, Cleon L., Jr., Cleon L. Rogers III. *The New Linguistic and Exegetical Key to the Greek New Testament.* Grand Rapids, MI: Zondervan Publishing House, 1998.

Strong, James. *A Concise Dictionary of the Word in the Greek Testament.* Madison, NJ, 1890.

Thayer, Joseph H. *Thayer's Greek-English Lexicon of the New Testament.* Peabody, MA: Hendrickson Publishers, Inc., 2002.

Wuest, Kenneth S. *Wuest's Word Studies in/from the New Testament.* Grand Rapids, MI: Wm. B. Eerdmans Publishing Company, 1973.

Vincent, Marvin R. *Word Studies in the New Testament.* Grand Rapids, MI: Wm. B. Eerdmans Publishing Company, 1980.

Vine, W. E. *An Expository Dictionary of New Testament Words.* Old Tappan, NJ: Fleming H. Revell Company, 1966.

Young, Robert. *Analytical Concordance to the Bible.* Grand Rapids, MI: Wm. B. Eerdmans Publishing Company, 1978.

# Online Ministry by Titus Chu

**MinistryMessages.org** is the online archive for the ministry of Titus Chu. This includes audio messages, articles, and books in PDF format, all of which are available as free downloads.

**FellowshipJournal.org** is an online magazine that features recent sharing by Titus Chu. It also provides brief, daily excerpts from his ministry, as well as news of upcoming events.

**"Daily Words for the Christian Life"** is an e-letter sent out every Thursday. It features selections from the writings of Titus Chu. To subscribe, visit FellowshipJournal.org/subscribe.

# Books by Titus Chu

The books listed below are available in print, Kindle, or iBook format. To purchase them, go to MinistryMessages.org/order. They are also available via Amazon.com and iTunes.

David: After God's Heart

Elijah & Elisha: Living for God's Testimony

Ruth: Growth unto Maturity

Philippians: That I May Gain Christ

A Sketch of Genesis

Two Manners of Life

www.ingramcontent.com/pod-product-compliance
Lightning Source LLC
LaVergne TN
LVHW041314080426
835513LV00008B/457